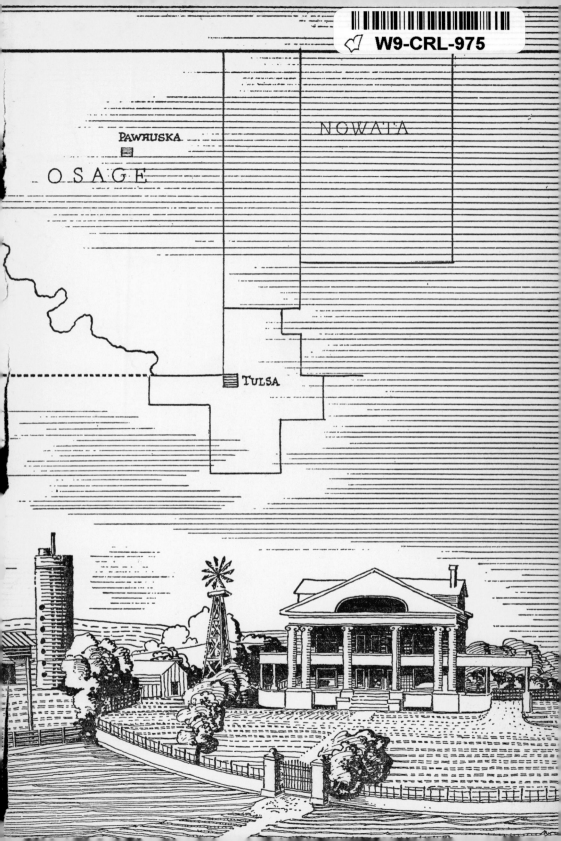

OSAGE

PAWHUSKA

NOWATA

TULSA

THE 101 RANCH

OIL PAINTING BY A. L. EAGLESON, OKLAHOMA CITY

Up the trail with Texas longhorns

The
101 Ranch

BY

ELLSWORTH COLLINGS

IN COLLABORATION WITH

ALMA MILLER ENGLAND

DAUGHTER OF THE FOUNDER OF

THE 101 RANCH

UNIVERSITY OF OKLAHOMA PRESS

NORMAN, 1938

SET UP AND PRINTED AT NORMAN, OKLAHOMA, U.S.A.
BY THE UNIVERSITY OF OKLAHOMA PRESS
PUBLISHING DIVISION OF THE
UNIVERSITY

TO

COLONEL GEORGE W. MILLER

FOUNDER OF THE

1O1 RANCH

Generous to a fault, true to his friends, never forgetful of a kind act, a real cowman of the old school—a gentleman unafraid.

ACKNOWLEDGMENT

I WISH to acknowledge my sincere thanks to those who were a source of help in making possible this story of the 101 Ranch. They are: Colonel Zack T. Miller of the 101 Ranch, and President of the Cherokee Strip Cowpunchers Association; Louise England, daughter of Alma Miller England; W. A. Brooks, assistant manager of the 101 Ranch for a number of years; George W. Miller, son of Colonel Joe Miller; Corb Sarchet, newspaper correspondent, and author of a number of articles on the 101 Ranch; Dr. Edward Everett Dale, Professor of History, University of Oklahoma; Hugo Milde, trail driver, Vice-President, Cherokee Strip Cowpunchers Association, and longtime friend of the Millers; Charles W. Hannah, cowboy on the 101 Ranch during the early nineties; Oscar Brewster, Secretary, Cherokee Strip Cowpunchers Association, trail driver and cowboy on the 101 Ranch during the early eighties; Margaret Tierney, Secretary to Colonel George L. Miller; Louis McDonald, Ponca Indian and lease agent for the 101 Ranch; Charles Orr, trail driver, cowboy on the 101 Ranch during the seventies, and an employee of the Millers for a number of years, John Hiatt, cowboy on 101 Ranch during the late seventies; Frank Harper, President, Watchorn Oil Company; A. L. Eagleson, Western Artist; and Joseph A. Brandt, Editor, University Press, University of Oklahoma. These people have been exceedingly courteous and patient in many long interviews and have contributed valuable first-hand information. Without their help this story of the growth and development of the 101 Ranch would have been impossible.

Indebtedness is also gratefully acknowledged to three printed sources of information. First, the 101 Ranch Records. These records, stored for years in the "White House" of the 101 Ranch and now located at the University of Oklahoma tell the story of the huge enterprises of the 101 Ranch in every detail. I wish to acknowledge with appreciation the courtesy of

Colonel Zack T. Miller for the use of this material. Second, the Phillips Collection, University of Oklahoma; the general library, University of Oklahoma; and the Oklahoma State Historical Society. The collections of newspapers, books, and photographs in these institutions contribute much information on the 101 Ranch from its beginning to the present day. Third, the following newspapers have published a great variety of articles on the 101 Ranch from its early beginning to the present time; *The Daily Oklahoman* and the *Oklahoma City Times, Ponca City Courier, Ponca City Democrat, Ponca City News, Tulsa World, The Tulsa Tribune, Boston Post, New York Times, Kansas City Star, Bristow Record, Oklahoma News, Wichita Eagle, Denver Post, New York Sun, Guthrie Daily Leader, Hastings Tribune* (Nebraska), *Dallas News, Daily Picayune* (New Orleans), *Daily Chronicle* (London), *Daily Mirror* (London), *Daily Citizen* (London), *American Magazine, Chronicles of Oklahoma, Literary Digest, World's Work,* and *Time.* Without these sources of information the complete story of the 101 Ranch would have been impossible.

ELLSWORTH COLLINGS

TABLE OF CONTENTS

LIST OF ILLUSTRATIONS

INTRODUCTION

THE buffalo and longhorn are gone from the prairie of Oklahoma. Modern cities rise where the tepee of the Indian once stood. The West of romance and adventure has passed from the American scene. The early day West has passed but it has not perished. Its spirit lived on in the great 101 Ranch, whose vast expanse of 110,000 acres was devoted to perpetuating the atmosphere of the days when courage and self-reliance were inborn in those who rode the plains.

George W. Miller, the founder of the 101 Ranch, came to Oklahoma when great herds of wild buffalo roamed at will on the great fertile plains. He lived to see these magnificent animals wiped out by the hands of white settlers who came flocking into the territory when the Cherokee lands were thrown open to the white settlers. Mr. Miller had already established his ranch at that time; as a cattleman, he operated on a large scale. He had lived through the days of the old West, and he saw them fast passing under the encroachments of modern civilization. But the old order still persisted on the 101 Ranch.

When Colonel Miller died in 1903, the ranch passed into the hands of his three sons, Joe, Zack, and George, who determined to make it a monument to their father's love for the West of pioneer days. The longhorn cattle, so familiar in the early days, were fast passing out of existence, their place being taken by thoroughbred cattle, which type was favored by the meat packers. The Miller brothers saw to it that a herd of the rangy longhorn steers was carefully preserved on the ranch. And the old time cowboy with his picturesque costumes—all of these were as much a part of the new ranch as the old. The Miller brothers kept the ranch as the only spot in the country where the spirit of the old West lived on in its true atmosphere.

And the new 101 Ranch was not merely a show place. Huge herds of pure bred cattle grazed on its fertile plains where once the longhorns roamed, crops were diversified, oil wells spouted wealth, lights twinkled in a hundred cottages, and the 101 Ranch was noted as the greatest diversified farm in the world. The Miller brothers toiled early and late to bring to fruition this change from the old order of the cattleman to the new order of the diversified farmer. They saw the broad and rolling prairie scarred with farming tools, the cow camp of the plains crumble into decay and the modern home supplant it, the fractious longhorned steer exchanged for the scientifically bred and blue-ribboned type of cattle, the fodder shock replaced by the silo, and the blue stem plowed under that the harvest might be reaped to sustain life in the new order of things. And this transition from a cattle range to the greatest diversified farm in the world is the story of the growth and development of the 101 Ranch. It is the story of how the Miller brothers met, joined, and led in all these changes; how, after turning to the blooded breeds of cattle, they introduced pure bred hogs, horses, and poultry. New and better varieties of wheat, corn, potatoes, alfalfa, and forage crops were harvested. Fruit trees were imported, acclimated, grafted, and re-grafted with scientific methods applied every step of the way. Under the father the 101 Ranch was noted as a vast cattle range, but under the brothers it was famous as a diversified farm.

I have endeavored at all times in this account of the growth and development of the 101 Ranch to present only facts as revealed through careful researches from many sources of information. Fortunately, I have had the assistance of Alma Miller England, only daughter of the founder of the 101 Ranch, in appraising the truthfulness of the great mass of facts collected. Her intimate knowledge of the 101 Ranch from its beginning down to the present day has been a valuable source of help in this undertaking. Her son, George Miller England, has also rendered valuable assistance in this respect.

From my boyhood days, I have known the 101 Ranch on the Oklahoma plains, and during all this time I have continually read, studied, observed, and wondered about its vast enterprises. As in thousands of other boys, it kindled in me an everlasting interest in the romance and adventure of the West of the old days. To me, the 101 Ranch is a "thing of beauty and a joy forever."

THE 101 RANCH

UP THE TRAIL WITH TEXAS LONGHORNS

I

FROM early times, the ox has been the mainstay of man in his struggle for existence. Whether he served as a burnt offering to appease the supposedly wrathful gods of people, or to satisfy the hunger of nations, he has always proved one of the great necessities of life. Even in early biblical times the raising of cattle was considered one of the highest callings of man, and it has maintained this prestige down to the present time. The beginning of this industry on the continent of North America dates from the sixteenth century when the Spanish conquistadors on their voyages of discovery brought livestock into Mexico. Great ranches were established and the surplus stock gradually migrated to the north into southern Texas, California, and the vast range country in between, which is now divided into Arizona and New Mexico. The herds of cattle spread out over Oklahoma, Kansas, Wyoming, Montana, and then into Canada. This northward migration of the cowmen and their herds is one of the historic pastoral movements of the world, and though its duration covered but a brief period of years, romance, comedy, and tragedy were enacted to their fullest measure and left an indelible mark on the country.

These multitudes of cattle roamed at will over great, unfenced areas, fattening throughout the summer on the range grasses that made even better beef than the corn-fed products. Under the influence of the rarefied and moisture-free atmosphere of late summer and early fall, these native grasses cured up and provided hardy and strength-giving feed on which the cattle lived during the long winters. Each outfit chose its home range with a view to securing well distributed water, winter protection from storms, and natural barriers to check the cattle from roaming too far. More drama seems to have centered around this industry than any other business in the world, and in all times it has had a peculiar appeal to those of adventure loving and pioneering natures.

This, no doubt, explains largely the migration of Colonel George W. Miller, father of the Miller brothers, from Crab Orchard, Kentucky, the Millers' ancestral home, to the prairies of the Southwest. As was the custom in that day, the title "Colonel" was attached without official decree to the names of prominent men as a mark of respect and, for that reason, Mr. Miller was known widely as Colonel Miller. He was born February 22, 1841, on his father's plantation in Lincoln County, near Crab Orchard, Kentucky. His father died soon after he was born and his grandfather, John Fish, reared him on his large plantation, also situated near Crab Orchard. John Fish was a typical southern plantation owner, possessing many slaves and operating his hundreds of acres industriously and efficiently. Like most Kentuckians, he was a great lover of livestock, particularly of fine horses. It was in this southern environment that young Miller grew to manhood. With his grandfather he was *de facto* manager of the big plantation and was from the very beginning initiated into doing things in a grand manner, a dominating characteristic in his future years. This background of experience molded the character of young Miller and greatly influenced his life in subsequent years. He, like his grandfather, was a great lover of livestock, and during the Civil War he traded in government mules. With the money thus acquired, at the close of the war he purchased a small portion of his grandfather's plantation.

On January 9, 1866, Mr. Miller married Miss Mary Anne (Molly) Carson in Louisville, Kentucky. She was the daughter of Judge David B. Carson and was born August 26, 1846, on her father's plantation in Rock Castle County, Kentucky. She, too, was reared in the traditions of the Old South, which provided the foundations of hospitality, graciousness, and executive ability she possessed so abundantly in later life. They were perfectly matched. He was a rugged Kentuckian of tall and powerful frame—every inch of him pure American. She was a wholesome motherly woman, handsome, and the perfect complement of such a man. He was good natured but of a volcanic temper while she was genial and jolly.

Soon after their marriage, they assumed complete management of the plantation, since the grandfather desired to retire from active life. Here their first son, Joseph Carson Miller, was born March 12, 1868. Mr. Miller's ambition was to continue operation of the plantation on the same scale as his grandfather before him had so successfully done, but soon he found himself greatly handicapped as a result of the war, due to the fact that the Negro slaves had been freed and severe conditions imposed upon his state immediately following the war, preventing his becoming the sole owner of the big plantation.

Defeated in Kentucky, he began to consider a new location. At the time there was considerable talk of the new western country, particularly California, and the possibilities of new ranch homes and livestock production. Thus lured, Mr. Miller sold his share in his grandfather's plantation and started overland in 1870 with Mrs. Miller and their two-year-old son, Joseph, for California in search of a location where he could realize his ambition—a mammoth livestock ranch. It was late in 1870 that Colonel Miller arrived at St. Louis, Missouri, then the railroad terminus. Here he bought a pair of mules and an "outfit," ferried the Mississippi at St. Louis, and struck out southwestward across the open country for California. After leaving Missouri it was Colonel Miller's intention to follow the Arkansas-Indian Territory border and then take the southern route to the Pacific coast. However, as they progressed westward, he kept scanning the vast prairie lands with a speculative eye. Here at his very feet was opportunity for a great livestock ranch. This was a cattle country, without cattle.

With winter coming on, Colonel Miller pitched camp at the little village of Newtonia, Missouri—then a frontier outfitting point—and was held there by the charm of the prairie. He was a born trader and an opportunist, the kind of man who would go to town on Saturday with a buckboard and a pair of colts and return home with a spring wagon, a mare, and a couple of cows. There were settlers scattered not distant from the little village of Newtonia who had hogs they wished to dispose of, and Colonel Miller soon began to trade various possessions for hogs.[1] That winter he converted the hogs into hams and bacon. When spring came, he set out with twenty thousand pounds of bacon for Texas, for he had learned from the cowboys coming up the trails that cattle were so cheap in Texas that one hundred pounds of bacon could be traded for a full-

[1]Colonel Zack T. Miller to Ellsworth Collings, December 19, 1935.

[5]

grown steer. This was soon after the Civil War when cattle in Texas were almost worthless. Arriving at San Saba County, the heart of the cattle country, he found the plains alive with cattle and the ranchers anxious to trade steers for bacon. With no trouble he exchanged the entire ten wagon loads of bacon for cattle, receiving a steer for every fifty pounds of hog meat. With a small herd of four hundred Texas steers, he struck back over the Eastern Trail, grazing his cattle as he went, through Indian Territory and arrived with his herd at the south line of Kansas, near Baxter Springs. Obtaining permission from the Quapaw Indians to graze his cattle on their reservation, he established in the early part of 1871 his first cattle ranch, a few miles south of Baxter Springs, Kansas, near the present Miami, Oklahoma. This herd was the nucleus of the great 101 Ranch to be, and was so successfully marketed at Baxter Springs that Colonel Miller gave up all thought of California, and plunged into the cattle business on the scale he had dreamed of.

Colonel Miller's first ranch, near Miami, Oklahoma, was known as the "L K" Ranch. Lee Kokernut was a noted Texas rancher with whom Colonel Miller had formed a partnership in the cattle business. The brand K (Lee Kokernut) was on many of the cattle arriving at Baxter Springs from Mr. Kokernut's ranch in Texas, and, for that reason, Colonel Miller adopted this brand for his new ranch. He maintained his family home at Newtonia, Missouri, about twenty miles north of his ranch. Here he built a comfortable dwelling for his family and on June 21, 1875, Alma, his only daughter was born, and Zachary Taylor, his second son, April 26, 1878. Mrs. Miller had several younger brothers, living at Crab Orchard, Kentucky, some of whom joined her at Newtonia for company and protection while Colonel Miller was in Texas on his trips, which usually occupied three months and longer. In order to provide his new cattle ranch with necessary supplies, Colonel Miller established a general merchandise store at the family home at Newtonia, which Mrs. Miller, with the assistance of her brothers, conducted successfully during her residence at Newtonia.

Newtonia was a town of about two hundred people and like many western towns, it was built with great expectations and laid out in magnificent style. The town was settled mainly by

North Carolinians and the social life prevailing was, for the most part, typical of the small towns of the older states. Mrs. Miller was a prominent member of the church, active and zealous in all good things and always a leader "of the quality" in the town. Colonel Miller was a generous man, but on Sunday generally had some cattle to brand and so took the "absent treatment" so far as church services were concerned. However, on Thanksgiving or Christmas or any other special event when there were big feasts, he was always present, since he enjoyed immensely such occasions. As was the practice at that time in most small towns, when the leaders saw the need of some improvement in the community, they called upon the citizens to contribute whatever was needed and found Colonel Miller ever ready to give.

On his first trip to Texas, Colonel Miller learned that the ranchers cared little for any form of paper money, considering only gold as having any value. The Texas soldiers had just returned from the War, and, having been paid off in worthless Confederate currency, looked with disfavor upon any form of money other than metal. On succeeding trips, therefore, Colonel Miller took gold instead of bacon, since steers priced at $6.00 could be purchased for $3.00 in gold. A while before his death, J. D. Rainwater wrote Colonel Zack T. Miller an account of the first cattle drive of his father, George W. Miller. Corb Sarchet reports this account as follows: "Colonel Zack Miller of the 101 Ranch, Hugo Milde, Ike Clubb and other early day cowmen of the Cherokee Strip country believe that the only personal account of a trip to Texas for southern cattle for the Oklahoma ranges is that left by the late J. D. Rainwater, one of the first cowboys to work within the present state of Oklahoma. It was Rainwater's first trip over an early trail that went southward via Fort Smith, Arkansas, and across southeastern Oklahoma, then Indian Territory.

"Jim Rainwater was Oklahoma's oldest cowboy, when he passed away last November [1933] in a soldiers' home at St. Louis. On September 16, just prior to Rainwater's death, Colonel Zack Miller had a letter from him, calling attention to the fact that not only was that date the anniversary of the opening of the Cherokee Strip to settlement in 1893 but also the anniversary of the start on the same date of the 101 Ranch by

[7]

Colonel George W. Miller, father of the Miller brothers. At that time, too, Rainwater sent to Colonel Zack Miller this account of the first trip to Texas for southern cattle.

"Rainwater was head cowboy for Colonel George W. Miller even back to the time when the Millers were living at Newtonia, Missouri, sixty-three years ago. The trail then, over which cattle were brought from Texas overland to southwestern Missouri, according to Rainwater, was via Newtonia to Pierce City, Missouri, and not long afterward it was from San Saba, Texas, to Baxter Springs. Rainwater and the late George Van Hook of the 101 Ranch accompanied Colonel Miller many times. Van Hook had come with Miller to Newtonia from Crab Orchard, Kentucky, the Miller ancestral home. Rainwater was a native of the vicinity of Fayetteville, Arkansas.

"It was a very pretty winter day on February 16, 1871, when this first trip to southern Texas for cattle started overland from Newtonia, Missouri. In the party were Colonel George W. Miller, his brother-in-law, George W. Carson, Frank Kellogg, Luke Hatcher, Perry Britton, a Negro, and Rainwater. The men with the exception of Britton rode horseback. The Negro drove a chuck wagon. Progress was slow, for at noon they had arrived only at Rocky Comfort, Missouri, where they had dinner and at night they camped at Keysville, near the Missouri-Arkansas border.

"Rainwater describes at some length his experiences in passing over the Pea Ridge battleground, the next day, where northern and southern armies had fought in 1862. There were still many broken trees and broken limbs with other still fresh evidences of the battle. He notes that they went across Cross Hollow, where now is located Rogers, Arkansas, and that night they camped at the town of Springdale, then known as Nubbin Ridge.

"Rainwater's diary shows the next day was Sunday and that morning they traveled through his native town of Fayetteville, stopping for dinner just south of town. During the afternoon they forded the west branch of White River ten or twelve times, camping on its bank at night, just a mile from the foot of Boston mountain. It required a tiresome climb of half a day to reach the summit of Boston by the following noon, and he records: 'The world sure looks big when you are on top of a mountain.' That night, after fording Lee's Creek sixteen times while going down the mountain, they spent the night just out of Van Buren, Arkansas. It must have been an unusual sound for he put in writing that 'we heard the frogs holler.'

"The first sight of a ferryboat was in leaving Van Buren the following morning, which was February 20, and crossing the Arkansas River into Fort Smith. Not long afterward they forded Poteau River, and camped on a tributary creek for supper and for the night. Rainwater recalls that Colonel Miller passed around a bottle of liquor, which also must have been unusual, for at no other time does he report such an occurrence. He was the butt of the party during the remainder of the trip because he did not like the liquor 'and spit it out.'

"The Red River was crossed at Colbert's Ferry and soon afterward they were in Sherman, Texas; thence to Fort Worth, and then on to Comanche, where Rainwater records that he saw 'the largest tract of red sandy land' in his memory, then or afterwards, so long as he lived.

"An interesting incident to Rainwater occurred between Comanche and Brownwood, Texas, when they met twenty to thirty men, all armed with Winchester rifles and six-shooters, escorting two men in a wagon, being taken overland to Waco for trial on charges of murder. They were the first men arrested in Brownwood since the close of the Civil War. 'We camped that night on Jim-Ned Creek,' writes Rainwater, 'and then went into Brownwood the next day and camped there that night.'

"The trip from Brownwood into San Saba County and to the county seat of San Saba was uneventful, but there they found the man for whom they were looking, 'Red' Harky, the cattle agent for that county. Harky took a bunch of cowboys, went up the river and rounded up near San Saba all the cattle he and his boys could find. Colonel Miller and Carson looked the bunch over, picked out the individual heads they desired. Immediately these were cut out from the main herd and held together nearby by Rainwater and the other men who were in his party. Those cattle, not selected by Miller, were simply turned loose to wander anywhere they might desire to find grass, of which there was plenty.

"It was necessary, according to Rainwater's account, to go through a considerable amount of red tape, prior to the cattle actually being bought. The livestock that Miller had selected

[9]

were placed in a corral near San Saba, where they were passed single file through a chute. This was done so that the county recorder and county treasurer might make a note of each head, putting down the age and brand. The bill of sale was made to Miller from this record, which became a permanent record of that county, no doubt to this day.

"Rainwater gives an interesting account of the stampede of the Miller herd on Easter Sunday. It was on the return trip with the cattle northward, and they were in the vicinity of Fort Worth. There was a Mr. Sanders then with the party, evidently as foreman. A storm was brewing and as the cattle began to drift eastward Sanders understood they might stampede away from the storm. Accordingly he told each man personally the work cut out for him, in case of a stampede, and declared, 'We are going to have one hell of a storm.' Rainwater, who had celebrated his fifteenth birthday while on the trip, accompanied Colonel Miller during the storm that followed, attempting to hold the cattle. 'That morning Colonel Miller had given me a $5 raise per month in wages, placing me on an equal scale with the rest of the men,' Rainwater writes.

"The herd did stampede in the face of the storm and the most of the horses stampeded with them, carrying their riders away. Colonel Miller, Carson and Rainwater, who was riding a trained pony, held the herd eventually and continued to do so until 11 o'clock that night, when the cattle were finally quieted down. In the morning as the cattle were leaving their beds to graze along the trail, they were counted by Colonel Miller who found not a head missing. For this effectual work during the previous night, Rainwater was presented with a white and black two-year-old steer by Colonel Miller, which meant that whatever the cattle brought finally on the market the money from that steer was his. The next day Colonel Miller gave him also a pair of pants and overcoat which he states 'was the greatest treat of my life up to that time—first time in my life that anyone, who wasn't any kin to me, had given me anything.'

"Rainwater describes the crossing of Trinity River near Fort Worth and a few days later that of Red River near Sherman. It was while in a general store at Sherman, where Colonel Miller was getting sugar, bacon and other supplies, that he bought the pants and overcoat for Rainwater. All the cattle,

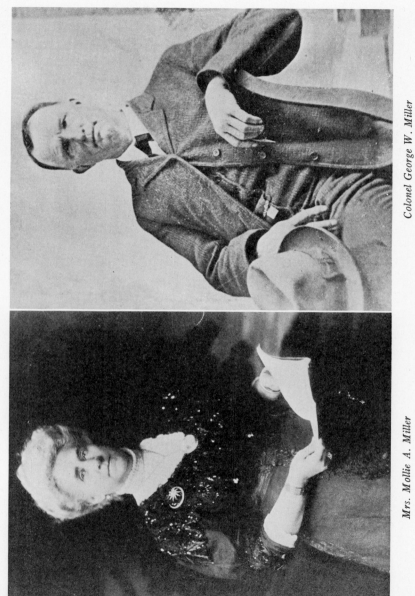

Colonel George W. Miller

Mrs. Mollie A. Miller

excepting one two-year-old, crossed the Red without incident. This one wandered up a canyon, followed by Rainwater, who discovered that he was not going to be able to head it off and return it to the herd. Consequently he shot the steer. Some river men skinned and dressed the carcass, tying a quarter of the beef to his saddle. Arriving in camp on the Indian Territory side of the river with the beef Rainwater was commended for killing the steer rather than permit it to escape.

"An interesting incident, in which Colonel Miller nearly lost his life by drowning, is related. This occurred just after the herd had successfully crossed the North Fork of the Canadian River. A deep tributary creek was encountered, making it necessary for all the cattle and horses to swim across. This was accomplished by all excepting Colonel Miller. 'When the horse, which Miller was riding,' says Rainwater, 'felt its front feet touch ground, the animal quit swimming, although its hind feet drifted into deeper water. It was necessary for Miller to dismount in the water. The horse caught him between its feet and attempted to drown him. But Miller caught finally the horse by the tail and was thus pulled to shore when the horse finally swam out.'

"Rainwater describes the next stop as Okmulgee, Indian Territory, where there were the Indians' 'council house and storehouse and several small homes. There is prairie grass as far as you can see, east, north and south.'

"Within a few more days the herd was crossing the Arkansas River at Childer's Ferry, and within another few days the Neosho, and then Cagin Creek and Rock Creek and into Baxter Springs, Kansas, the end of the railroad and the end of the cattle trail. Rainwater says he was a helper at the tail of the herd and states 'that ever afterward I have thought there should be two men at the tail.'

"Rainwater's diary covers more briefly a second trip to San Saba County for cattle, starting from Baxter Springs on March 6, 1872. They crossed the Arkansas near Muskogee, where they camped, and he describes it as the only railroad station south of the Arkansas in Indian Territory, but there was a stage line in operation between Muskogee and Sherman.

"On this trip Rainwater seems to have overcome his dislike of liquor, for when the cowboys were in camp near Fort Worth and Marion Busby expressed a desire for a drink of whiskey, Rainwater had the only bottle in the party, a half-pint that he admitted buying at the Old Corner saloon in Baxter Springs, prior to starting on the trip. When pressed for an explanation as to why he bought the liquor, Rainwater replied that he had heard of people using it in case of sickness and thought it would be a good medicine to have along.

"Colonel Miller tried to buy cattle near Fort Worth but failed and they went on south to Kimble Bend in Brazos County, where Rainwater remembers they paid $1 a bushel for corn. 'There are no farms west of this point,' he writes. Traveling on into Bosque County, Rainwater 'cannot remember seeing a town or village in the county, and I guess they didn't have any.'

"How Colonel Miller lost $2,000 in gold while the party was in camp in Bosque County is related by Rainwater. 'Miller showed one of the boys that much money in gold,' says Rainwater, 'and also he showed this same man where he hid it. Two days afterward when Miller looked for the money it was gone. We went on to San Saba, got our cattle and on the way back we again camped at the same spot where the money was stolen. The next morning we had a trial, the hats of all the boys were placed on the ground near a sack of shelled corn. All the boys were sent away from camp, each with a grain of corn, and returning he was to place the grain in the hat of the man he thought guilty. The result was that all the corn was put in one man's hat—we all suspected the same fellow. This man picked up his hat, looked at the corn, shook it out, put on his hat, got on his horse and rode away, and I presume he is riding yet.'

"An encounter with Indian horse thieves and how they were punished is related interestingly by Rainwater. They were camped on the south bank of the North Canadian River, waiting for the water to go down, so they could cross with the herd. During the afternoon two young Indians rode into camp and asked Colonel Miller if he desired to buy two ponies. Receiving an affirmative answer the Indians went away but returned the next morning with the two ponies they had described. The deal was made and the Indians rode away again.

"About two hours afterward, Rainwater writes, twenty or thirty light horse police came into camp and asked where we got the two ponies. We told them of the trade with the two Indians, one of whom was about twenty years old, the other twenty-five. The police explained the two ponies were stolen the night before, but told us to keep them and they could get the thieves. About twenty miles distant they caught up with the two boys and brought them back to our camp.

"The trial of the two young Indians was held the next morning within our camp, with our boys called as witnesses. The two were declared guilty. Their hands were tied behind them, their feet roped together and a rail placed between their legs. A rope was thrown over a limb, thus making the bodies of the prisoners stand up straight. The penalty consisted of lashes on their bare backs. One Indian was given fifty lashes, as this was his first offence, and the blood ran down to his heels. It was the other's second offence. He was given 100 lashes and notified that under the Indian law, if he were ever convicted a third time, he would be shot to death. When the whipping was over the police put a handful of salt in a pan of water, washed the backs of the two prisoners and turned them loose.

"Rainwater explains that the first bridge ever put over the North Canadian in Indian Territory was then in place at the point where they were in camp. As soon as the water receded sufficiently, they attempted to drive the herd across the bridge, Only twenty-five or thirty head had crossed when the bridge broke and all cattle, then on the bridge, went down with the structure into the water. All that had crossed or had fallen into the river swam back to the remainder of the herd on the south side. A few days later they passed through Okmulgee, crossed the Arkansas at Childer's Ferry, the Neosho farther along, Cabin and Rock Creeks, and again into Baxter Springs, end of the trail.

"Reminiscing in connection with the anniversary of the opening of Cherokee Strip in 1893, Rainwater says in his diary that Colonel Joe C. Miller, oldest son of Colonel George W. Miller, rode a thoroughbred Kentucky horse and made the run along with thousands of homesteaders on that famous September 16. By that day also Colonel George W. Miller had acquired enough Ponca Indian lands by lease to establish his long-to-be-remembered 101 Ranch, '101' being his cattle brand."[2]

[13]

His cattle business having grown to such extent that he found it necessary to have his family home and headquarters nearer the ranch, Colonel Miller sold his Newtonia home and store and removed his family in the fall of 1880 to Baxter Springs, Kansas, at that time headquarters for many cattlemen operating in the Indian Territory and on the Texas trail. His headquarters at Baxter Springs were approximately five miles north of his cattle ranch near Miami. Here on September 9, 1881, George Lee, his youngest son, was born, the "Lee" being for Lee Kokernut.

As the railroad moved westward, opening up new cattle ranges, Colonel Miller moved with it. His first ranch, the LK Ranch, soon proved inadequate for the great herds of cattle coming up the eastern trail from Texas. The herds ranging from 1,000 to 1,500 were driven up a day's journey apart in order to insure adequate water and grass and to avoid stampedes.[3] He therefore, set about to establish himself on a range providing more abundantly the necessities of an ever expanding outfit through leasing lands in the famous old Cherokee Strip. The Strip was a cattleman's paradise. Indian-owned, in the very pathway of the Texas cattle trails, land could be leased for from two to five cents an acre per annum. The grass was rich and there was abundant water; the winters were mild and the summers long. Not a fence stood in all of the Strip, so that vast herds could roam at will until the round-up. Here Colonel Miller leased in 1879 from the government two large pastures, about equal in size, including a total of 60,000 acres of grazing land.[4] One of the pastures was known as the Deer Creek Ranch, since it was located on Deer Creek about twenty miles south of Hunnewell, Kansas. The headquarters included only a camp for the cowboys herding cattle on this pasture. The other pasture was known as the Salt Fork Ranch, since the headquarters were located on the Salt Fork River near the big sand mound not far from the present site of Lamont, Oklahoma. The headquarters included a three-room log house with dirt roof, a horse corral, a branding pen and chute, a log house

2 The *Daily Oklahoman,* June 17, 1934.

3 Alma Miller England to Ellsworth Collings, January 10, 1936.

4 Senate *Document,* Forty-ninth Congress, first session, p. 309, Phillips Collection, University of Oklahoma, Norman, Oklahoma.

to store corn, and a horse barn with a hay roof.[5] The Salt Fork Ranch was Colonel Miller's main headquarters, since all branding was done at this ranch. When the first barbed wire fence was built in the Cherokee Strip in 1880 to enclose an extensive pasturage on the Deer Creek Ranch, it was Colonel Miller who built it. In the spring of 1881, after Mrs. Miller and the children had made their annual visit to Crab Orchard, Kentucky, Colonel Miller moved his family from Baxter Springs to Winfield, Kansas, to be near the new location. Thus established, he set about to realize his cherished dream—a mammoth cattle ranch.

At Winfield, Kansas, Colonel Miller purchased a large, two story brick dwelling for his family. Servants were employed to do the household work and a new carriage and prancing bays were provided each year for the family, in addition to a surrey and gentle mare for Mrs. Miller's personal use. Miller, when home, always would attend church with his family, dressed in formal clothing, including a silk hat and gold-headed walking stick.

George Miller had at last begun to realize the ambitions he had formed as a boy on a Kentucky plantation. Thousands of cattle roamed over the vast ranges of his ranch across the Kansas-Oklahoma line. In Winfield he and his wife were in the forefront of society and cowboys coming up the trails were charmed with the open southern hospitality of the Miller home. With a generosity typical of him, Miller instructed the Provident Association of Winfield to take care of the poor by giving orders for beef to supply their wants from the meat market he had established.

And for the first time appeared the brand mark which was to become famous throughout the world, the "101" brand. At the time of establishing the Deer Creek and Salt Fork ranches in 1879, Miller had still been in partnership with Kokernut and so continued to use the K brand. The next year he had purchased the holdings of his partner and decided on a new brand.[6]

[5] Charles Orr and John Hiatt, cowboy employees of Colonel Miller at the time the Deer Creek and Salt Fork ranches were established in the Cherokee Strip.

[6] John Hiatt, Hunnewell, Kansas, cowboy employee of Miller at the time of establishing the Deer Creek and Salt Fork ranches, to Ellsworth Collings, September 6, 1936.

[15]

The cowman always considers several factors in the choice of a new brand. It must be simple, easy to read and to describe, and preferably, made up of straight lines. These factors Miller had in mind when he adopted the 101 as the new brand for his ranch in 1881. At first the brand was not burned into the steer's hide, but consisted of a small brand burned in its horns. John Hiatt of Hunnewell, Kansas, reports he helped to build the first fire in 1881 to burn the 101 on the horns of steers. From 1881 to 1887, Colonel Miller branded his cattle with the 101 on the left horn and No on the left side. The K brand was used on the left shoulder of the horses. In 1888, he discontinued burning the 101 on the horns of the cattle and began that year to brand all cattle and horses with the 101 exclusively on the left hip, thus abandoning entirely the use of the K brand on horses and No on left side of the cattle.

The *Brand Book* of the Cherokee Strip Livestock Association, published March, 1882, shows the following registration of brands by Colonel Miller: "NO on left side of cattle and 101 and brass knob on either horn. Also J Y on left side; T cross T left side; I C left loin; connected K lying down on left loin; circle bar on both jaws; X on left side; and K on right side. Horse brand connected K on left shoulder, I I on left side; X left hip and dewlapped."[7]

Why Miller selected the 101 brand is not so definitely known. One of the most popular explanations was that the ranch contained 101,000 acres and was so named accordingly. As a matter of fact, at the time the 101 brand was selected by Colonel Miller in 1881, the ranch included only 60,000 acres of leased lands. The Millers never claimed 101,000 acres for the ranch at any time in its history. The largest acreage it ever attained was about 110,000 acres. There were 17,492.31 acres of deeded land, approximately 10,000 acres of leased land with preferential rights, and the remainder included leased lands varying in amount from year to year.

Another version is that Miller bought the 101 brand from the 101 Ranch Company operating near Kenton, Oklahoma. This company was organized in 1881 from three previously existing Texas brands: The 101 brand owned by Mr. Doss;

[7] *Brand Book*, March 1882, p. 21, Cherokee Strip Live Stock Association, Caldwell, Kansas.

Joe C. Miller, the farmer   Zack T. Miller, the cowman   George L. Miller, the financier

the VI brand owned by Mr. Taylor; and the 88 brand owned by Mr. Horn.[8] The company assumed the 101 brand, and established in 1881 its headquarters four miles east of the present town of Kenton, Oklahoma. The headquarters were moved in 1891 very near to Amarillo, Texas. In 1893, the company began to dispose of its cattle and it is claimed Colonel Miller purchased the remnant of the herd and the 101 brand and adopted the name for his ranch. This explanation seems unlikely since it is definitely established that Colonel Miller selected his 101 brand in 1881 and used it that year in branding cattle on the Deer Creek and Salt Fork Ranches. Even though he purchased the cattle and brand of the 101 Company near Kenton, the fact remains he had been using the 101 brand a number of years previous to that transaction.

Colonel Zack T. Miller gives an entirely different version. He says his father was buying cattle down around San Antonio, Texas, and there was a cabaret in that city named the 101. The cowboys spent so much of their time at this cabaret that his father could hardly get them out on the range to take care of the cattle. So he told them that if they liked "101" so well he'd brand his cattle "101" and they wouldn't have to go to town to find it. And, according to Colonel Miller, that was the way the "101" brand originated on his father's ranch.

Another explanation is that Colonel George W. Miller, in assembling the acreage of the Salt Fork Ranch, bought a small ranch in the vicinity called Bar-O-Bar. The —O— was its livestock brand. Miller liked the brand and the name and retained them for his ranch. The brand as thus written could not be easily seen at a distance when burned on the left horn of cattle. Miller turned the bars upright and made it read 101. It was only natural that the brand in that position should be called "hundred and one." The simplicity of the brand, easy to read and describe, stuck and soon became commonly used. By the time the brand had been changed from the left horn to the left hip, it was in common usage on Colonel Miller's ranch.[9]

An incident occurred during this time that reveals the

[8] Fred Hollister, Springfield, Colorado, cowboy employee of the 101 Ranch operating near Kenton, Oklahoma.

[9] Alma Miller England to Ellsworth Collings, March 10, 1935; and W. A. Brooks, to Ellsworth Collings, April 8, 1935.

shrewdness of Colonel Miller as a cattleman.[10] One fall he turned 5,000 steers into the Cherokee Strip and herded them west. At the time of the spring round-up he found 4,970, showing a loss of thirty steers. That winter the Santa Fe railroad had a big crew working on their road with camp south of the ranch. It occurred to the cow boss, Jim Moore, that the steers might be found and he suggested to Miller that they go down to the railroad camp which had been moved in early spring near Mulhall. He explained that on the day before as he rode by the abandoned railroad camp he found a steer's head with the "101" branded on its horn. The following morning he and Joe, the eldest son, were sent down to the new railroad camp, and upon arriving, Moore said to the boss of the crew, "I've come to collect."

Feigning innocence, the boss replied, "What do you want?"

"You know what I want," snapped Moore grimly.

"Well," inquired the boss meekly, "how much is it?"

"Figure yourself the steers at thirty dollars a head," retorted Moore.

The railroad boss excused himself as he stepped into a tent nearby and, after a short discussion with some one of his crew, came out and gave Moore a check for $900, the price of the thirty missing steers.

Miller was a great lover of horses and was always loath to dispose of them when they became of little use on the ranch.[11] Because of this sentimentality, he accumulated a large number of old horses, in spite of the insistence of his sons to dispose of them at any price. Finally, during the fall of 1888 he selected more than a hundred head of his old horses considered no good for his cow business and advertised a public sale at Winfield, Kansas. On the day of the sale many Kansas farmers attended in the hope of buying some horses at a cheap price. Miller failed, through an oversight, to print the terms of the sale on the bills, although it was customary at such sales to allow convenient terms. Naturally, when the auctioneer opened the sale, a farmer inquired about the terms. The presidential campaign was then on between Grover Cleveland and Benjamin Harrison. Colonel Miller sensed the situation quickly and instructed

[10] Colonel Zack T. Miller to Ellsworth Collings, December 10, 1935.
[11] Colonel Zack T. Miller to Ellsworth Collings, December 10, 1935.

[18]

the auctioneer to explain to the farmers that they could give their notes at 10 per cent interest payable when Grover Cleveland should be elected president. Of course, this brought a yell from the farmers, mostly Republicans, who considered it a splendid opportunity to buy the horses for nothing. They promptly yelled bids at prices far beyond the value of the horses. The auctioneer knocked the horses off to the farmers at prices exceeding $100. The same horses could have been purchased at the time on the open market for about $75. Grover Cleveland was defeated in the election and the farmers, of course, laughed loudly about the sale. Colonel Miller filed the notes away in a large walnut secretary at his home and dismissed them from his mind, until the election of 1892. The same candidates opposed each other for the presidency and this time Grover Cleveland was elected. Colonel Miller took the old notes out of his secretary and secured the services of a Winfield lawyer to collect at 40 per cent accrued interest. The notes were paid, with few exceptions, and Colonel Miller enjoyed immensely many a laugh about the sale.

The region included in Colonel Miller's ranches in the Cherokee Strip was part of a vast Indian country, inhabited by bands of roving Indians, living in tepee villages. Pioneers among the white men grazed their herds of cattle over this Indian reservation and Easterners hunted game over its plains and wooded valleys. It was known as the Cherokee "Strip," or Cherokee "Outlet," because it had been ceded to the Cherokee Indians by the United States government in order to provide them an outlet from their larger reservation farther east to their summer hunting grounds in the Rockies.

Not only in those days of the Indian and cattleman, but for many years to come, the hills of the "Strip" and the hills of the Osage provided outlaw hiding places for three decades. The Dalton boys grew up in this region. Bob Dalton, who was killed in the Coffeyville raid, bought his famous "Red Buck," the white-faced horse with curly coat, from Henry Wilson, a cattleman who worked the range just east of the Arkansas River from where Ponca City now stands. Emmet Dalton not only grew up in this region, but he lived here for many years after his brother was killed in the Kansas hold-up. Henry

[19]

Starr, perhaps the most notorious bank robber the West has seen, likewise ranged over the hills of this same region.

In those earlier days, the dusty trails over which the cattle of the Texas plains were driven to market, passed through this same Strip. The scar of ten million hoofs can still be seen across the country. This was the trail blazed by Chisholm. Great herds of fattened beef were transported over this trail to the nearest railroad point in Kansas, from which they were shipped by train to the slaughter houses of Chicago. That was when the Great Plains of the West made America the largest producer of beef in the world. Stock pens at the time made up a big part of where Ponca City is now located and the round-up and its branding of cattle were the chief industries of that location.

The Cherokee Strip could not remain long in its natural, undeveloped state when the territory to the north of it, in the state of Kansas, was a region of homes, and when the pioneers of north and east were constantly extending the western fringes of civilization. Men who wanted farm lands could not remain contented when there was before them a vast domain, its hills used only as grazing grounds for cattle, its valleys cow camps for the round-ups, its cities nothing but Indian villages, and its homes tepees that might be moved in a night.

Bands of settlers were organized at Caldwell and other Kansas towns to seize the land from the cattlemen, drive out the Indians and build new homes in the Indian country. Captain David L. Payne repeatedly led expeditions into this region, each time to find the United States soldiers destroying his settlements and escorting him and his followers to the Kansas line. These men were called "boomers." They planted one colony at Rock Falls, in the northwestern part of what is now Kay County, in 1884. Payne died that autumn at Wellington, Kansas, but his followers continued the contest. Their fight for homes caught the sympathy of the country and Congress was forced to provide for the opening of a part of the Indian Territory in 1889. Other smaller tracts were opened each year until 1893, when Congress arranged for the "Big" opening of the Cherokee Strip.

Such is the genesis of the present 101 Ranch. On the one hand, there was the spirit of vision, hospitality, of boldness of the Old South transplanted abundantly through Colonel George W. Miller and his wife to the open ranges of the West. It was this spirit, the heritage of old Kentucky, that enabled them to overcome failures that would have crushed men and women less stalwart; it was the force that guided them in building a cattle empire on the broad and rolling prairies of Oklahoma. On the other hand, there was the West of the old days, of vast open ranges where buffalo roved in herds that blackened the prairie. There was rich grass everywhere. There was abundant water in all seasons. The winters were mild and the summers long. To the south in Texas thousands upon thousands of cattle roamed over the ranges. Here was opportunity at the feet of men with vision and the spirit of boldness. This was a cattle country without cattle. And the blending of the Kentucky heritage of the Millers with the opportunities presented in the new country to conduct a cattle business on a big scale, is the story of the development of the 101 Ranch from the open cattle range to the greatest diversified farm in the world.

THE WHITE HOUSE ON
THE PLAINS

II

IT was in Baxter Springs that the long and happy association between the Millers and the Ponca Indians began and it was Colonel Miller and his eldest son Joe who converted what appeared to be a Ponca trail of tears into a happy journey to a new home in the present state of Oklahoma.

The government had removed the Poncas from their northern home with the intention of exchanging that land for new land in the immense holdings of the Cherokee Nation in the Cherokee Strip. Unfortunately, the tribe was moved before arrangements with the Cherokees had been completed and thus it was that Chief White Eagle and his tribe were waiting disconsolately at Baxter Springs, homesick for the north and increasingly uneasy as sickness afflicted many of the tribe, a sickness attributed to the new climate. Colonel Miller and Chief White Eagle had many conferences over the plight of the tribe and from those conferences arose a mutual and lifelong respect.

While inspecting land in the Cherokee Strip with a view to acquiring ranging rights for his cattle, Miller, Joe and a number of cowboys found themselves near the proposed Ponca reservation. They made camp and the father and son thoroughly investigated the new land. From his explanation Miller was satisfied that if White Eagle would visit the country he would accept the offer of the government and that after the natural homesickness of the Indians had been overcome they would find health and happiness in their new home.

Knowing that White Eagle intended to leave soon for Washington to make final refusal of the land and to attempt once more to induce the government to return them to the north, Miller realized that it was imperative to convey what he had discovered to the chief. To send a written message under the circumstances would be worse than useless. Not wanting to abandon his own trip, Miller decided to send Joe as his messenger. Many fathers would have hesitated to send a mere boy on such a trip but Miller knew that his son was fully competent to care for himself under all conditions to be met in the open, as he had observed from the constant companionship of his son, and furthermore, Joe possessed other qualifications for the mission, for not only did he speak the Indian language with considerable fluency, which he had learned from Indian boys at Baxter Springs, but also he was thoroughly familiar with his father's arguments and desires with regard to Ponca settlement in the Cherokee Strip.

If Joe felt any hesitancy in starting upon the long ride to White Eagle's camp at Baxter Springs, it was not evident as he rode away from his father's camp with a boyish smile upon his face and a parting wave of the hand. He rode early and late through the Osage country and through the Cherokee Nation and arrived at the Ponca camp in less time than his father had expected. He was just in time, for White Eagle was planning to leave for Washington the next day.

The chiefs and head men of the Poncas gathered that night in the tepee of White Eagle and for the first time in the memory of the tribe a white boy sat in the center of the council and answered their questions in their own tongue. Little did anyone in that council realize that in the years to come this boy, grown to manhood, would be in the council circle at White Eagle's right hand and the Poncas would call him chief. Far into the night the Indians smoked and talked. The boy, hesitating at times as he searched his memory for the best word to use, answered their questions with a frankness and directness which convinced them of the truthfulness of his answers.

With a stick Joe drew upon the dirt floor of the tepee a rough map of the country. He showed them where the Chicaskia met the Salt Fork and where that river ran into the Arkansas; where the valleys widened and where the high prairie was to be found. He told them of the horse high bluestem grass in the valleys and the heavy vines of wild grape in timbered bends; of the tall pecan trees and the thickets of wild plums; of the prairie chickens which flew from under the pony's feet, and of the deer and turkey which ranged through the timber; of the red bluffs of the Salt Fork River, and the streams of water where a pony could always drink. They wondered when

[23]

he told them how sand bars in summer whitened with salt. To the Poncas, homesick and famished, stricken with fever and with no land to call their own, the picture of the country made in their minds by the report of young Joe was that of the Promised Land.

After this description, the Indians smoked in silence. With a look White Eagle questioned his chiefs; he found his answer in their eyes. Knocking the ashes from his pipe as a sign that the council was ended, the chief spoke to the boy, saying: "We have listened to you because you speak the words of your father. Your message is good and we knew him for our friend. Tomorrow I will ride with you and we will see this country of which you speak. I hope we will find a home for our people. You have ridden far to bring us this word and the Poncas do not forget. Now you shall sleep."[1]

The next day Joe led White Eagle and a group of observers toward the land which he had so vividly described. The Indians found it so much to their liking that they returned to their people and advised that they accept the offer of the government. This was done and the Poncas moved in 1879 to their new home. There they still reside and they have not only found contentment and health but prosperity. White Eagle died February 1, 1914, at the age of ninety-seven years, but he lived to see his statement that the Poncas would not forget proved true.

While Joe was negotiating with the Poncas, Colonel Miller continued his journey up the Salt Fork River and selected in 1879 the location for his second ranch, known as the Salt Fork Ranch, near the big sand mounds where Lamont, Oklahoma, is now located. This was outside the limits of the Ponca country and was leased from the Cherokee Indians. On this ranch the 101 made its home for years until the sale of the Cherokee Strip and the announcement of the government to open it for settlement in 1893.

In the meantime Joe, grown to young manhood, was partner with his father in the operation of the Salt Fork Ranch. Through all the years he kept up his acquaintance with the Poncas who lived on the new reservation south of the ranch. The distance from the ranch to Ponca village being only a few

[1] *101 Magazine*, April, 1925, p. 9.

[24]

miles, visits back and forth were frequent. Foreseeing the opening of the Cherokee Strip to settlement, Colonel Miller directed Joe to open negotiations with the Poncas with a view of leasing their lands for grazing purposes. The Poncas did not forget their previous statement, and when their friend Joe again came to their council circle he had but to state his needs and the Indians extended the use of their lands to him for such time as he might need them. The individuals in charge of the Indians' affairs did not transact business in such offhand manner, but Colonel Miller experienced no difficulty in securing the government's approval of the leases which gave the 101 outfit control of the grazing lands in the Ponca country.

Before the Cherokee Strip country was cleared of cattle and opened to settlement in 1893, the 101 cattle were moved in the fall of 1892 a few miles down the Salt Fork River; a new dugout was made in the side of the bluff; a corral was built and the 101 settled down into its new headquarters.

It was an ideal location that Colonel Miller chose in the fall of 1892 for the headquarters of his third ranch—the present 101 Ranch. There were thousands of acres of rolling prairie for range which he could lease from the Poncas as he pleased, and which he could purchase in time. There were wonderfully fertile bottoms for wheat, corn, alfalfa, vegetables, and fruits of all kinds. The Salt Fork River wound its way through it all to provide during all seasons an abundant supply of water for the big herds. All the natural resources were present for the establishment of a permanent cattle empire on the prairie.

In the vernacular of the West a ranch is known as an "outfit" and whether it happens to be owned by an individual or by a company, it is universally called by the name of the mark with which the cattle are branded. There is, for example, the "Bar C" outfit, the "Spur" outfit, the "Four 6's" outfit, the "XIT" outfit. The brand of a big ranch is an intangible asset of great value. It is the insignia of the cattleman and stands at once for honesty in dealing and for the quality of the cattle he raises. Just as in the science of heraldry the coat of arms stands for noble deeds and accomplishments, so in the code of the cattle country a brand represents years of endeavor to produce a certain quality of cattle. When the cattle of a well-known brand are offered for sale, prospective buyers know at

[25]

once the kind of stock they can expect to see. They know that for years the cattle bearing this particular brand have always conformed to certain standards. Such brands on the side of a steer have the significance of the hall-mark of a piece of silver.

Colonel Miller's cattle brand was "101" and when he moved his "outfit" down from his Salt Fork Ranch, he continued to use the 101 brand on the cattle and from that brand the present 101 Ranch got its name. The first headquarters was a dugout erected in 1892, on the south side of the Salt Fork River opposite the present "White House." The front of the dugout was of lumber, the roof was of sod, and the back of the house was set in the hill. It provided headquarters for the new 101 Ranch from 1892 to 1903, during which time the family home was maintained at Winfield, Kansas, in order that Colonel Miller's wife and younger children might be more comfortable. The delay in building a new headquarters home was due to the uncertainty surrounding purchase of the land from the Ponca Indians. Restrictions required the Poncas to secure patents from the Indian Office at Washington before they could sell their lands, and, for that reason, purchase was delayed for several years. It was not possible to build permanent improvements until title to the land was acquired. Buildings on leased lands belonged to the tribe. When Colonel Miller finally secured satisfactory options on several tracts of land, he selected the present site of the "White House" on the north side of the Salt Fork, and proceeded to formulate plans for his new ranch home.

The plans called for a pretentious building. Colonel Miller's familiarity with the beautiful plantation homes of his native Kentucky no doubt greatly influenced the architecture of this new structure. This influence, coupled with his ambition to own a large estate explains Colonel Miller's plans for palatial splendor on the then open prairie of Oklahoma. The completed building was a three story frame house with basement, furnished with the handsome things from the Winfield home. A complete waterworks plant occupied part of the basement and every comfort and convenience of that time was installed. In its setting it was indeed a palace on the plains. On all sides there were miles upon miles of broad and rolling prairie inhabited only by bands of roving Indians living in tepee villages.

[26]

There were no broad highways—only the dusty trails over which the Texas longhorns had traveled to northern markets. It was new country and it was in such a setting that Colonel Miller visioned his new headquarters on the prairie along the Salt Fork River.

Unfortunately Colonel Miller did not live to see his new home completed. He died of pneumonia at the old dugout headquarters on his ranch, Saturday, April 25, 1903, at the age of 61 years and 20 days.[2] Short funeral services were held at the ranch home on Sunday, conducted by the Methodist missionary at the Ponca Agency, and his body was shipped to Crab Orchard, Kantucky, the old home of the family, for burial. An escort of cowboys rode beside the hearse as it passed alongside the ranch's great wheat fields, across a broad pasture where the cattle grazed in sight of the trail road, and thence to the railroad station at Marland (formerly Bliss). Many Ponca Indians, from whom most of the ranch lands were leased, accompanied the body. Chief White Eagle, together with several of his head men, viewed the body at the ranch house, but refused to go to the railroad station. White Eagle was a proud man and said: "I would not weep where men and women could see me. I must retire alone."[3]

Colonel Miller had always been vigorous in body, but he felt his vitality slipping from him soon after he was stricken and said he would not recover. He called his family to his bedside and made known his final wishes in the management of his 50,000 acre ranch. He left no will, but decreed that the huge ranch should remain intact forever in the Miller family. To his wife, Mrs. Mollie A. Miller, he left $30,000 in life insurance. He said that the approach of death did not alarm him, and he watched its coming without distress. He played with his grandchildren almost to the end, his mind remaining clear and active.

His Kentucky blood was shown in his unusual personality. He made strong friends and bitter enemies; to one he was steadfast, to the other defiant. His hospitality was unbounded, and on his ranch and at his city home in Winfield, he gave guests the best his table and cellar could produce. Three hours

[2] *Ponca City Courier*, April 27, 1903.
[3] *Kansas City Star*, April 27, 1903.

[27]

before his death he insisted that friends who had come to bid him farewell should sit down to dinner, and regretted that his health was not such as to permit him to join them. He gave freely to the poor, and his compassion for their distress was such that on Thanksgiving day he always gave a steer to those in greatest need.

At the time of his death, the 101 Ranch had grown to huge proportions. Mr. Miller paid the Ponca and Otoe Indians $32,500 annual rental for his 50,000 acre ranch; other running expenses amounted to $75,000 annually. The year before his death, 13,000 acres were sown to wheat, 3,000 in corn, and 3,000 in forage crops. The income was from $400,000 to $500,-000 annually. Two hundred men were employed on the ranch and $33,000 worth of tools and machinery were used in the fields and more than 200 ponies were used in herding cattle on the ranges.[4]

For thirty-one years, Colonel Miller had engaged in the cattle business in Oklahoma, and his judgment of the value of cattle on the hoof was remarkable, few persons being better able than he to tell what the worth of a lean steer turned loose on the range in the spring would be at shipping time. He had mastered the economics of farming to such a degree of perfection that the 101 Ranch was noted as the most profitable farming property in the West. He had a system of double planting the corn fields that gave double use of the land. By the time the corn had been harvested, the cow peas had grown high enough to make good pasturage. Also, after the cutting of wheat in June and July the fields were plowed and sowed in kafir corn. This was ready for the pasture in October, but the field was first drilled in wheat and the cattle were allowed to tramp in the wheat and nibble off the blades of kafir corn. During the winter, after the kafir corn had been eaten, the wheat grew up and was pastured until spring. This system of getting two returns from a single field was an idea originated by Mr. Miller. It was his most successful plan for making money out of farming.

Colonel Miller's plans for the new ranch home were carried out immediately after his death by Mrs. Miller and her sons. The new structure, when completed late in 1903, was consid-

[4] *Ponca City Courier,* April 27, 1903.

Upper left, the family home of Colonel Miller at Newtonia, Mo.; upper right, dugout of the first headquarters of the 101 Ranch, 1893; lower left, the family home of Colonel Miller at Winfield, Kansas; lower right, corrals of the first headquarters of the 101 Ranch, 1893

ered one of the finest residences in Oklahoma. The Winfield
(Kansas) home was sold and Mrs. Miller, her three sons, and
daughter ate their first meal in the new residence on Christmas
day, 1903. The first social event to take place in the new home
was the marriage, October 31, 1903, of Alma, Mrs. Miller's
only daughter, to William Henry England, an attorney-at-law
at Winfield. The marriage took place before the building was
fully completed and before the family had moved in, as a result
of the earlier postponement of the marriage due to Colonel
Miller's death. Through mutual agreement, Mrs. England received at the time of her marriage her share in the 101 Ranch
estate.[5]

Mrs. England had received an excellent education. Her
father had been a man of prodigious pride, not content unless
he had supplied his family with every comfort and advantage,
as demonstrated by maintaining for it a comfortable home in
Winfield while he resided in the cruder dwelling at the ranch,
and by his interest in his children's education. Winfield offered
better religious and educational advantages and it was partly
for this reason that he maintained his home there so long. Miller's background forbade his children attending the public
schools of Kansas with Negroes—the practice there. Therefore
he employed private tutors, following the custom of Kentucky.
Later Alma went to Miss Nold's Seminary for Young Ladies in
Louisville, Kentucky, completing her formal education at Vassar College, where she was graduated in June, 1889. The sons
were given actual business training in the affairs of the ranch
when they were very young, for Miller looked to them to carry
on from generation to generation the management of the cattle
empire he was building on the Salt Fork.

At the death of Colonel Miller, following his expressed wish
and their own inclinations, the Miller heirs made no division
of the huge 101 Ranch except the mutual agreement with the

[5] The Englands moved to Kansas City a short time after the marriage
where Mr. England practiced law. Later they returned to Ponca City where
Mr. England continued his law practice and served as legal adviser to the ranch
until his death in 1923. The first son, William Henry, Jr., was born May 27,
1906; the second son, George Miller, October 12, 1907; the first daughter, Mary
Ann, September 11, 1910; the second daughter, Eleanor, September 12, 1911;
the third daughter, Louise, November 24, 1913, and the third son, Victor, July
12, 1919.

daughter, Alma, at the time of her marriage whereby she accepted as her share of the estate certain properties not directly connected with the 101 Ranch holdings. The family decided to continue the work so well started, and to direct their united energies to its accomplishment. The oldest son, Joe, naturally assumed the leadership of the family, since he had been *de facto* manager with his father for a long time. It is evident without comment that only one brought up and trained as he to handle wisely the daily problems that arose could have carried on this great enterprise. His splendid physique, the result of outdoor life, his clear eye and quick judgment, his fairness in dealing with men, and his poise under all circumstances, made him an example and leader in anything he undertook. The younger sons, Zack and George, who had varied school and college work with summer work on the ranch, soon assumed positions of responsibility in the various activities of the ranch. Mrs. Miller never relinquished her interest in the affairs of the ranch. She was a remarkable woman in many ways. She possessed exceptional ability and rare judgment regarding the business affairs of the ranch. She was always consulted in regard to the big transactions of the Miller Brothers and their success was due largely to her excellent judgment.

With the development of the ranch the Miller brothers naturally and easily fell into the particular work for which each had the most aptitude. Colonel Joe devoted his time to the general management of the ranch, and the farming enterprises and orchards were his recognized hobbies. He was a natural horticulturist and devoted much of his energies to experiments along that line that were of much value to Oklahoma in future years. He was a man of the southern plantation type and in addition a showman. He was farseeing, liberal, with few equals as a host. In 1915 he was made an honorary colonel on the staff of Governor Robert L. Williams of Oklahoma and was familiarly known as "Colonel Joe." He was married to Miss Lizzie Trosper in 1896 and to them were born two sons, George William and Joseph C., Jr., and one daughter, Alice. His second marriage in 1926 was to Miss Mary Verlin and of this marriage one son was born, Will Brooks Miller.

During Colonel Joe's early manhood an incident occurred that reveals his character. He had attended the Central University at Richmond, Kentucky, for three years, but despite the insistence of his parents, he refused to go back the fourth year. His father told him at the time he would give him a chance to make good. So he handed the young man $10,000 and told him to strike out for himself. With his father's gift added to the accumulations of his own enterprises, Joe turned to Texas as the land offering opportunity. This was in the last years of the drives of the big herds up the trail. To the life of the cow country he was not a stranger in spite of his youth; for many years he had been the constant companion of his father, and more than once had clipped a few weeks from each end of the school year in order to share in the activities of his father's business. His father had made the 101 brand famous over the Southwest in those days of the cattle kings. The long days on the dusty trail, the swimming herds in the swollen streams, the weary hours of night herding, and the headlong dash into the lightning-riven darkness ahead of the thundering stampede was a rough school, but the school which made cowmen, and from this school young Miller could well claim to be a graduate.

Arriving in Texas he deposited his money in a bank, and thinking to try the life of the city he sought employment in a store, but a few days convinced him that his future career did not lie in the mercantile line. Leaving the city he went to Alpine, Texas, where he knew the herds would be gathering for the northern drive. At this time there was in his mind a half formed plan to defer making any permanent investment, and to take service with one of the herds going to Kansas or the Cherokee Strip and work his way north on the trail. As a matter of fact, like many young men he found his new liberty of action not entirely satisfactory and he was homesick for a sight of the Salt Fork, and to ride again a horse with 101 on its left hip.

At Alpine, young Miller found the preparation for the northern drive in full swing and he saw many familiar faces among the cowboys and owners. After many weeks among strangers, the hearty slaps on the shoulder, accompanied with a friendly "Hello, Joe," raised the spirits of the homesick boy. He looked about him with quickened interest; he was in familiar atmosphere. Among the cowmen he heard some talk of the unfortunate illness of Lee Kokernut, his father's friend. Kokernut had gathered a herd of 2,500 head of four- and five-year-old steers, intending to drive them to Montana but had been suddenly stricken with illness, making it impossible for him to accompany his herd. Without any thought that his call would result in his looked-for opportunity, Joe paid a visit to Mr. Kokernut and found him very much concerned over the condition of his business affairs. After some conversation Mr. Kokernut expressed regret that Joe's father had not arrived in Texas so that he could turn over his herd to him. Here was Joe's opportunity and he was quick to take it. One can imagine the surprise of the cowman when the youth offered to take his entire outfit off his hands. Those were the days of the cattle business when the man and not the method was considered; deals involving hundreds of thousands of dollars were decided by the nod of a head, and written agreements were the exception rather than the rule. A few minutes sufficed to close the deal between them, and when Joe left the sick room, he carried a note to Mr. Kokernut's foreman which was the written evidence that he was the owner of the trail herd and outfit.

By the payment of four dollars a head and his verbal promise to pay the balance of the purchase price, Joe became the owner of 2500 head of steers, 136 head of saddle horses, a chuck wagon and mules. The note to the foreman also acted as a transfer of allegiance of a foreman, cook and fourteen cowboys. The cowboys were soldiers of fortune and served the man who paid and fed them. The herd was being held on grazing ground forty miles south of Alpine, trail branded, supplies in the wagon and the cowboys anxious to be on the trail. The morning after Joe arrived at the outfit he sat on one of his newly acquired saddle ponies and watched his herd take shape into a long column of shuffling hoofs and rattling horns and swing its head to the north. His first drive as owner had begun.

Risking stampedes and all the hardships of the border country, young Miller drove the cattle over the trail to his father's ranch south of Hunnewell in the Cherokee Strip. When he arrived his father looked the cattle over and told him he had made a good deal. It developed that he had, because he doubled his money on the cattle. That was in 1887. The next year he made a similar trip and then the Santa Fe built a railroad through that country, which marked the end of driving cattle over the trail from Texas to Oklahoma.

Zachary T. Miller, the second son, was and still is, the cowman, typical of the days of the old West; a wonderful horseman, and like his father, a trader always. For that reason, he naturally devoted his time and energies to the livestock interests of the ranch. His deals in livestock were not limited to those handled on the ranch, but included large wholesale transactions in cattle, mules, and horses which never set foot on the home ranch. It is true that he had the advantage of having grown up in this work under the splendid tutelage of his father, but all men do not improve even under the best of tutors, without natural ability and intelligent application. The trader in Zack is revealed in his purchase of Mexican army supplies.[6]

He was in Texas on a deal for some livestock to be shipped to the 101 Ranch, when he became interested in the situation of General Mercardo, commanding the Mexican Federals besieged by the rebel forces of Villa. Actuated by a desire to see some of the fighting, the young cattleman went to Presidio, Texas, an American town situated directly across the Rio Grande from the beleaguered town. It soon became evident that General Mercardo would be compelled to retire to the American side or face extermination at the hands of General Villa. As the Federal forces consisted almost entirely of cavalry, it meant that a large number of horses and mules would be brought to the American side. When this phase of the situation suggested itself to Mr. Miller, he wired his brother Joseph to join him. Shortly after the arrival of the brother the expected happened, and the beaten Federals swarmed over the river bringing with them horses, mules and transport, arms, artillery and equipment and surrendered to the waiting soldiers of the United States. The situation was without parallel in history. The United States and Mexico not being at war, the horses, arms and accoutrements could not be considered as spoils of war. They were, however, held as being subject to the custom duty imposed on imports. The Mexican consul at Marfa, Texas, received authority from his government to sell the articles if a purchaser could be found to pay the customs duties. The

6 *101 Magazine,* September, 1916.

Miller brothers, representing the 101 Ranch, promptly made an offer to the consul which was accepted and the purchase price paid in cash. Paying the customs charges, they came into possession of all the effects of the defeated army. This was probably the first time that the entire equipment of an army was disposed of in a single sale. The purchase included 3,600 head of horses, mules and pack burros, saddles and bridles, transport wagons and harness, artillery and battery wagons, carbines, revolvers and sabers, ammunition and the general supplies of an army in the field. The removal of the embargo on arms and munitions of war enabled the 101 Ranch to dispose of a greater part of the arms and equipment to their former owners, the Huerta government, who shipped them by rail and water into territory still in their control. Some of the animals were shipped to Texas pastures controlled by the 101 Ranch, and about a thousand head were sent to the ranch in Oklahoma.

In 1923, Governor J. C. Walton of Oklahoma made Zachary T. Miller an honorary colonel on his staff and he is widely known today over the country as "Colonel Zack." He was married twice. His first marriage, in 1906, was to Miss Mabel Pettijohn and there was born one daughter, Virginia. In 1919, the second marriage was with Miss Marguerite Blevins, and to them there was born one son, Zack, Jr., and one daughter, Blevins. Colonel Zack, today, with boots and a wide sombrero remains the typical cowman of the old West.

George L. Miller, the youngest son, was the financial genius of the big ranch, a gentlemanly, and, like his mother, a gracious host. Upon the death of his father, he assumed active direction and management of the financial interests of the family, being in charge of the executive staff and the accounting department of the ranch. The sales and purchases of the ranch reached an enormous total each year. The development of an accounting system whereby a complete check on each of the varied enterprises was possible was the work to which he devoted much of his time and talent.[7] The system he adopted at the 101 Ranch has been pronounced by experts as a model for simplicity and completeness. And today these records tell the detailed financial story of the ranch. The 101 Ranch prospered under his

[7] Margaret M. Tierney to Ellsworth Collings, February 14, 1936.

financial guidance. The big transactions in cattle, horses, mules, wheat, corn, and oil necessitated that he borrow large sums of money. His ability as a financier was recognized throughout Oklahoma, and in 1919, Governor J. B. A. Robertson of Oklahoma made him an honorary colonel on his staff. In contrast to the familiar "Colonel" always attached to his brothers, he was known among a wide circle of friends as plain "George L." In 1908, he married Miss May Porter and to them one daughter, Margaret, was born.

While, as in all great enterprises, each man has his own particular part to carry on and for which he is responsible, yet in an organization such as the 101 Ranch, there must be co-operation in thought and agreement in action, or else a chaotic condition will develop and bring ruin to the whole thing. It was this splendid co-operation and mutual understanding of the Miller brothers that enabled them to bring to realization the vision of their father.

None of the Miller brothers drew any salary for his service. If one wanted money he drew freely on the 101 bank account by an established custom of mutual consent. If Colonel Zack wanted to take a trip to Cuba he placed a 101 check book in his pocket and paid his bills. If Colonel Joe wanted to charter a special train and invite all the editors of Oklahoma down to the ranch for a buffalo barbecue, he did it and no one asked any questions about the cost. If George L. wanted to make a trip to New York, he consulted no one about the expenses. There was no checking up, no questions about doing this or that. Each one did his work whole-heartedly and the profits were the common and joint fund of all. It was an unusual and brotherly arrangement which permitted each man to pursue freely his particular line of work.

It seems unusually fortunate—the farmer, the cowman, the financier within one family—but it is nevertheless true the Miller brothers individually possessed abundant natural aptitudes along these lines, and it was the development of these aptitudes that marked the beginning of the 101 Ranch's greatest growth. They were not afraid to venture along the lines of their particular abilities. When they lost, they tried again. It was that spirit, the spirit of boldness, inherited from their father, that explains the tremendous development of the 101

Ranch along so many lines. And withal they were schooled, from early childhood, in the arts of cowboy life. They grew up in the cattle country as a cattleman's sons, trained to ride, to rope, to brand, and to shoot. A dugout made of sod on the Salt Fork was their first headquarters home; the cowboys and Indians their associates; the plains their life, whereon long-horn steers roved in herds of thousands. They were reared as cowmen and as pioneers. From the very beginning they thought in terms of thousands and ten thousands. The rise of the 101 Ranch under their management to a realization of their father's dream was the logical child of their schooling in the West of the old days.

.   .   .   .

During the early morning of January 14, 1909, a disastrous fire destroyed the big ranch house, together with its contents, including the clothing of the occupants.[8] The fire was discovered at about 2 A.M., when flames had extended practically to all parts of the house and there was only time for the occupants to escape without attempting to save anything except the clothes they had on. The fire was believed to have started in the basement of the building and its origin was unknown. The house was located at some distance from the barns and other buildings on the ranch and none of these was endangered by the flames. "Little Sol," favorite dog of George L. Miller, gave his life in an effort to arouse his master. It was Mrs. Miller who noticed the smoke about fifteen minutes before the walls fell. One trunk and the baggage of some of their guests on the top floor was all that was saved. The ranch house, one of the finest residence buildings in Oklahoma, and its contents were insured for $7,500.

"When they lost, they tried again" seemed the guiding maxim of the Millers, and they always improved their former efforts "when they tried again." Upon destruction by fire of their beautiful headquarters home, they immediately began construction of a new and better home on the same site. The plans called for construction of one of the most ornate, modern and commodious country residences in Oklahoma. Colonel Joe Miller had general superintendency of the preliminary work

[8] *Ponca City Courier*, January 14, 1909.

of construction. When he consulted an architect, he gave orders for a building so absolutely fireproof that if necessary a bonfire could be set in every room without damage to the building. Steel and concrete were used and the only portions that could be burned were the floors, doors, and ornamental woodwork; otherwise the entire building, from cellar to garret, was intact, even the roof being of asbestos material. The plans and specifications contemplated an expenditure of $35,000.

The seventeen-room residence contains every modern convenience and comfort, private plants furnishing electric lights, steam heat, hot and cold water, and hot and cold ventilation. The style of architecture is colonial and with its massive porticoes on two sides, and its porte-cochère, resembles an old-fashioned Southern home. It commands a fine view of the beautiful Salt Fork valley, and from the upper porticoes the winding stream may be followed eastward to where it flows into the Arkansas River, among the blue hills of the Osage country. A spacious yard, landscaped with shrubbery, flowers, trees, and enclosed by an ornate wrought-iron fence, adds beauty to the setting. Surrounding the residence are orchards, vineyards, vast fields of alfalfa, corn, wheat, and farther away the thousands of acres of pasture lands, on which graze thousands of head of cattle and horses. Under the roof, above the halls, the reception rooms, living rooms, and guest rooms, is the billiard parlor. Each room is furnished in a different wood, the walls and ceiling frescoed in individual tints and designs. The entire structure is painted white on the outside and appropriately named the "White House."

The Indians, to whom the Millers had ever been guide and counselor and friend, were elated over the rearing of the new ranch house, for it assured them of the permanency of the Millers in their midst. The ranch had even been their haven, for the improvident Poncas were sure of material help there; the hungry were given food; the ill, medical treatment; the homeless, shelter. Little wonder that the tribe was alarmed over the mere possibility of the Millers deserting them.

The "White House" was the permanent home of Mrs. Miller and her three sons. Here they gave hospitality to the humble and the great of far and near. It was Mrs. Miller's pride that not a day should pass without guests at her table. The utmost harmony prevailed at all times among the members of the family and the home was noted widely for its hospitality.

"Standing on the wide steps leading to the spacious White House, Colonel Joe Miller greets you with typical western style. Where could one hear a kindlier greeting than Colonel Joe, who in his southern drawling voice extends his hand of welcome, saying, 'Come on in, children.' To him all who come are 'children' and his big heart finds room for kindly thoughts for each individual.

"Entering the spacious living room furnished in exquisite taste, polished floors given color by the rare rugs, woven by the Indians, walls adorned with paintings a connoisseur might envy, one is impressed with the feeling of harmony of thought and the realization of ideals. Each piece of furniture is placed to the best advantage and is well chosen for such a home. There is nothing that is not needed, yet beauty is everywhere.

"The first floor of the ranch house is given over to a large living room, library and den, and a large dining room. The kitchen is a model of modern inventions, as is the laundry in the commodious basement. The second floor has nine large bedrooms, each with bath, and a medium sized living room or hall. The real joy is found on the third floor or 'attic' which is one large room, walls adorned with pictures of buffalo and cattle from the ranch herds. Here there are comfortable big four poster beds which furnish sleeping room for one hundred guests, these being filled during the rodeo season when it is the custom of the Miller brothers to take care of the large number of cowboys and others who participate in the events. This attic room is also drawn upon when house parties fill the ranch house proper to overflowing. A screened in porch or balcony opening off this floor gives a view of the country for miles around which would delight the eye of an artist. Ordinarily, when there are no guests at the ranch to remain for more than a day or two the White House kitchen is not used but all go to the ranch café for their meals. Seated at the table with Colonel Joe Miller presiding at the head, one is served with a meal that is perfect in cooking and service, and most wonderful of all each article of food, with the exception of olives, sugar and coffee, is produced and prepared for the table right at the ranch.

[38]

"The day is almost gone and the hours have been so filled with the interesting things that time and thought and the fulfilment of dreams have made, one finds it hard to believe it is time to go. As the golden haze of the sunshine mellows into the line of the western prairie where buffalo once more claim the land as their domain and horses and cattle are at home— fruits and flowers and food in abundance—a little country all its own; not a monarchy but a home of hospitality and love to all who may enter, Colonel Joe and the younger brother George wave a farewell hand—and who can blame the departing guest if he wishes he might return and again hear Colonel Joe's drawling 'Come on in, children.'⁹

Around the "White House" was grouped the settlement known as the headquarters of the Ranch. There was a large store of general merchandise, hotel for employees, café, filling station, blacksmith shop, garage—every convenience for the ranch owners and their employees. There was a modern dairy capable of taking care of the milk from 500 cows, the cows being milked by electricity, that serves the country for miles around as well as a large shipping trade with butter, cream, milk, and cottage cheese. In connection with the dairy there was a modern ice cream plant, ice plants, cold storage and cooling rooms, for the proper handling of the meats and other perishable products of the ranch. An up-to-date meat packing plant with a capacity for dressing five hundred head of cattle and one thousand hogs a month was one of the major enterprises of the ranch. There was a large, two-story structure well built and well equipped for a cider works, and for canning fruits, vegetables, and meats in large quantities. A modern electric light and power plant system extended over the ranch and, in addition, there was a water system with storage tanks, making modern improvements possible. The rodeo arena, the largest and finest in the Southwest, seated 12,000 and was equipped elaborately for bronc riding, steer roping, bull-dogging, and the Wild West Show. There were hundreds of houses, barns, and corrals to supply the needs of man and stock—all constructed on a vast scale because hundreds of head of work stock were required for the operations of the ranch as well as a personnel of several hundred cowboys, workmen, and families

⁹ *Rock Island Magazine,* November, 1926.

maintained on the ranch year in and year out. The 101 Ranch operated a complete oil refinery, making its own gasoline, kerosene, and fuel oil from the crude oil produced from its oil wells. The headquarters was truly a modern city, yet only a speck on the broad and rolling prairies of the 101 Ranch.

In the midst of the ranch's greatest growth, Mrs. Mollie A. Miller, mother of the Miller brothers, died at the "White House," Sunday morning, July 31, 1918, at the age of 72 years.[10] She maintained her interests in the affairs of the ranch at all times and every pleasant day, not given over to her duties as hostess, found her in her automobile visiting some part on the ranch. She was an enthusiastic observer of the motion pictures produced on the ranch and was an interested spectator of the production of all the big scenes. The 101 Ranch Show was always favored with her presence at the opening performance and at some time during the season she visited the show on the road. She traveled in Europe with the show and entertained European royalty.

"Mother" Miller, with snow-white hair, was the name by which she was known to hundreds of cowboys who worked on the big ranch. To any tale of sickness and misfortune she was always a patient and sympathetic listener and was generous with material aid as well as motherly advice. She was gracious, hospitable, and charitable. Her death was a great blow to the cowboys as well as to her famous sons, who now assumed full responsibility in management of the 101 Ranch. She was buried in the I.O.O.F. cemetery in Ponca City.

When Colonel George W. Miller established the 101 Ranch in 1893, it was a ranch and not a farm. For several years, the ranch business was concerned exclusively with cattle. During this time, not a blade of wheat or a stalk of corn was grown. Agriculture was an unknown science on the vast ranges of the 101 Ranch. It was a cattle domain and Colonel Miller was a cattleman. But twenty-five years later, at the time of Mrs. Miller's death, the ranch under the management of the Miller brothers was a veritable agricultural kingdom, as a result of the inevitable march of progress. The age of the buffalo and Indian was followed by the era of the longhorn and the cattleman. Then came the settler and the farmer, which wrought a

10 *Ponca City Courier,* August 1, 1918.

marvelous change in the ranches on the broad and rolling prairies of Oklahoma. The farmer brought the idea of diversified production to the ranchman and thus the shorthorn cattle displaced the longhorns. The Miller brothers, young and alert, followed all these changes in the West of the old days. They established herds of blooded cattle, added a variety of new crops, planted vast orchards, erected modern farm buildings, introduced power machinery, built slaughter and packing houses, put up hundreds of miles of fences, initiated scientific methods in every department of the ranch, and began systematic experiments in an effort to improve what they had. The 101 Ranch's change, in a word, from a cattle domain on the open ranges of Oklahoma to the largest diversified farm in the world, is the result of Miller brothers' efforts to keep pace with the march of civilization. They met, joined, and led this march, thus playing an outstanding part in placing Oklahoma in the front rank of the agricultural and oil producing states of the United States.

III

ITS north boundary the Kansas line, its east the Osage Reservation, and its west the Panhandle of Texas and the "No Man's Land" of western Oklahoma, the Cherokee Strip comprised a vast region of more than six million acres occupying an area fifty-eight miles wide and more than one hundred and eighty miles long. Ideal grazing land, the Strip had been used for a number of years following the Civil War by cattlemen to graze and fatten their herds without payment to the Cherokee Indians, the owners of the Strip. The grass of the Strip shared the rare quality of that in the Osage Reservation, one of the richest grasslands on the continent, and the Texas trail drivers did not fail to observe the fine quality of the grass as they grazed their herds from southern Texas to northern markets. When delayed by swollen streams or by tired and footsore animals, they permitted their herds to scatter for the time on the grass that cost them nothing. And, after the railroads in their westward expansion built loading pens at such places as Arkansas City, Hunnewell, Kiowa, and Caldwell, cattlemen when delayed in loading, as occurred frequently, simply turned their herds loose on the Strip pastures.

From grazing cattle along the trail drives and at the shipping points, it was but a short step to grazing herds in the Cherokee Strip throughout the grazing season. Grazing permits could be secured from the Cherokees for a small consideration, if not free, thus making unnecessary the long and tiresome drives. Consequently, it was only a short time until cattle ranches began to be established in the Strip and before long, it resembled the settled ranges of Texas.

Great herds grazing on the ranges soon attracted the attention of officials of the Cherokee Nation and they accordingly decided to obtain more revenue from the ranches by sending officers to collect a grazing tax of one dollar a head annually on all cattle. When the ranchers protested vigorously, a compromise was agreed to, whereby a grazing tax was imposed of forty cents a head for grown cattle and twenty-five cents a head for all animals less than two years of age, the tax to be paid annually.[1] The Cherokee Strip Livestock Association grew out of this experience, for it was organized at Caldwell, Kansas, March 1883 by ranchers who felt that some form of organization was necessary.[2] Practically all the stockholders in the Association were ranch owners in the Cherokee Strip. The officers immediately set about to secure from the Cherokee Nation a more satisfactory plan of leasing grazing land and succeeded in a short time in leasing the entire unoccupied part of the Cherokee Strip for $100,000 annually for a period of five years. Surveyors were appointed by the Association to determine the boundaries of each ranchowner's range and as a result the Strip was subdivided into slightly more than a hundred ranches. Each ranchman was given a lease on his range by the Association for the entire period of five years at a price of one and a fourth cents an acre every six months. The ranches were fenced by the owners, leaving wide trails for the cattle coming up from Texas.

One of the early ranchmen in the Strip, as we have seen, had been Colonel Miller,[3] whose two tracts—on Deer Creek and on the Salt Fork River—were about equal in size, and included a total of sixty thousand acres.[4] It was on the Deer Creek Ranch that Colonel Miller in 1880 built the first barbed-wire fence in the Cherokee Strip and by 1884 he had seventy-two miles of fence around his pasture.[5]

Although the ranchmen were able to adjust their own difficulties easily through the Cherokee Strip Association, they experienced difficulties outside of their organization that could not be adjusted so easily. Considerable opposition from the farmers along the Kansas line developed because the cattlemen were permitted to occupy the Cherokee Strip while they were

[1] Edward Everett Dale, *The Range Cattle Industry*, p. 47.

[2] *Senate Executive Document*, Forty-eighth Congress, second session, I, 149.

[3] Secretary of Cherokee Strip Livestock Association *Report* of Names of Lessees in the Cherokee Strip, Phillips Collection, University of Oklahoma, Norman.

[4] *Senate Document*, Forth-ninth Congress, first session, p. 309, Phillips Collection, University of Oklahoma, Norman, Oklahoma.

[5] *Senate Executive Document*, No. 54, Forty-eighth Congress, first session, p. 148.

excluded. At the same time there was a general feeling that the Indians had not received full value for the grazing lands and that the Cherokee Strip Livestock Association had resorted to unfair practices in securing the lease. These difficulties, along with the persistent agitation for opening the lands to white settlement, resulted in Congress appointing a commission to purchase the entire Strip from the Cherokees at $1.25 an acre. Matters were complicated by the ranchmen offering to purchase the lands at a price of $3.00 an acre. The Indians naturally refused the government's offer, and, in order to compel them to accept, the Secretary of the Interior advised the President to remove all cattle from the lands and to stop all revenue from the leases. He contended that the lease made by the Cherokee Nation to the Cherokee Strip Livestock Association was void; that the Indians had no authority to lease the lands, and that the President had the power and right to declare the leases in force void. The President accordingly issued a proclamation in 1890 forbidding grazing on the lands of the Cherokee Strip and ordered all cattle to be removed immediately. The removal order was modified but the brief extension of time did not affect the break-up of the big ranches established in the Cherokee Strip.

The Indians, seeing their last hope of revenue from the leases vanishing, yielded to the inevitable, and late in 1891 signed an agreement with the government to sell the entire Cherokee Strip lands for a fraction over $1.40 an acre.[6] The lands were surveyed into homesteads of 160 acres, providing homes for more than forty thousand families. This plan to establish small homes marked the end of the big cattle ranches in the Cherokee Strip, since the very nature of cattle ranching demanded large tracts of grazing lands. Nothing remained for the ranchmen to do but to market such cattle as they could and remove the remainder to other ranges.

Cattlemen, as a class, had little use for the settler in those days. The settler disturbed the freedom of the range and insisted upon planting wheat where nature had sown only grass. But instead of railing at the settler, Colonel Miller saw ahead to the time when the settler would farm the prairie, establish counties, towns, and markets. He began early to lease lands

[6] Edward Everett Dale, *The Range Cattle Industry,* p. 155.

[44]

Upper, second headquarters of the 101 Ranch, 1903; center, the White House of the present 101 Ranch; lower, one of the horse barns of the 101 Ranch

along the Salt Fork River from the Ponca Indians, in preparation for the day when the Cherokee Strip would be thrown open to white settlers. That day came in 1893. Colonel Miller abandoned his Deer Creek and Salt Fork Ranches in the Cherokee Strip and the 101 cattle were moved in the fall of 1892 a few miles down the Salt Fork River to the new range in the Ponca country. On the banks of the Salt Fork, the 101 Ranch became a fact. The leases obtained from the Poncas represent the first lands of the present 101 Ranch. They included vast stretches of rolling prairies, wonderfully rich bottoms, the Salt Fork running through it all, furnishing an ample supply of water. It was a ranch, however, and not a farm. Not a blade of wheat or a stalk of corn grew on the lands. Agriculture to the cattleman was an unknown science. The lands were used exclusively for cattle and Colonel Miller was a cattleman.

When he died in 1903, the 101 lands included fifty thousand acres leased from the Indians.[7] Not one acre was owned. The restrictions required the Indians to secure patents from the Office of Indian Affairs in Washington before selling their lands and, for that reason, Colonel Miller was unable to purchase any of these lands before the time of his death. He succeeded, however, a short time before his death in obtaining options from the Indians on several tracts of land that would come up for sale in a short time. But he never lived to see the actual purchase of any of these tracts. All of the lands under lease at that time were open range in the days when the buffalo roamed at will over the broad and rolling prairies, and were used to graze the cattle moved down from the Salt Fork Ranch in the Cherokee Strip country and for the new herds coming up the trails from Texas.

Before any Indian could sell his land, he was required by the regulations in force at that time to make an application, through the superintendent of his tribe, to the Commissioner of Indian Affairs for a patent in fee to his land. The application had to be made on the Indian's own accord and without any outside inducements. The superintendent of the tribe was required to make a careful examination of the Indian's competency in handling his land and recommend to the Commissioner of Indian Affairs his approval or disapproval of the ap-

[7] *Ponca City Courier*, April 27, 1903.

plication. If the commissioner deemed, upon examination of the application and recommendation, that the Indian was reasonably competent to handle his land, he recommended to the Secretary of the Interior that a simple fee patent be issued to the Indian for the land. The Secretary, following the Commissioner's recommendation, directed the Commissioner of the Land Office to issue the Indian the patent. The patent gave and granted to the Indian and his heirs the land to have and to hold with all rights, privileges, annuities, and appurtenances of whatsoever nature. Upon receiving the patent, the Indian was required to have the patent registered in the county in which the land was located. He was then free to sell the land at any time for any sum, giving the purchaser a regular warranty deed.

Colonel Miller left $30,000 in life insurance to his wife, which she used to purchase the first six sections, 3,720 acres from the Ponca Indians within the fences of the 101 Ranch.[8] The land purchased included the present site of the 101 Ranch headquarters and was the first deeded land owned by the Millers. It was Colonel Miller's life dream to locate his ranch on permanently owned land and this was the first step toward the accomplishment of his wish. The purchase of this land by Mrs. Miller marked the permanent establishment of the 101 Ranch on the Salt Fork. From that time on the Millers continued to purchase land from the Indians. The Indian allotments were usually in small tracts ranging from five to two hundred acres each, and for that reason, the land purchased included many small tracts situated in Kay, Noble, Osage, and Pawnee Counties.

The wishes of Colonel George W. Miller, at the time of his death, that no division of the 101 Ranch lands be made and that the ranch be held forever intact in the Miller family, were faithfully carried out by his widow at the time of her death. The provisions of her last will and testament transferred all of the Ranch holdings to the Miller brothers and designated two of her sons, Zack and George, as executors of her estate.[9] Portions of Mrs. Miller's properties, outside of the 101 Ranch proper, were set aside in her will for her grandchildren, friends, and her daughter, Alma.

[8] *Kansas City Star,* April 27, 1903.
[9] Final Decree in the Matter of the Estate of Mollie A. Miller, County Court, Kay County, Oklahoma, October 17, 1919.

It seems that since the Miller family was operating the Ranch as a unit, very little consideration was given to just which name under which the title to the land was recorded. Apparently most of the land purchased by Mrs. Miller with the life insurance money of her husband was actually taken in patents from the government to two of her sons, Zack and George. Joe was busy with his farming interests and had little mind for the office affairs. In 1917 a disagreement arose between the brothers and Joe's interest was bought by the other two, so that at the time of Mrs. Miller's death, there was none of the land in his name. He was gone from the ranch for two years and returned when Mrs. Miller was dying. Her will, made while Joe was away, naturally named Zack and George as executors. However, on her deathbed she made a codicil, giving Joe the 160 acres in the bend of the river on which he had spent much time developing his big apple orchard and in which he took great pride. While Mrs. Miller was ill, there was a complete reconciliation among the three brothers and a definite agreement among them that Joe was to be considered an equal partner with the other two, one-third interest each, without any payment on his part whatever. For this reason, Mrs. Miller saw no necessity for changing her will other than to give Joe personally his prized apple orchard.

After the reconciliation of the Miller brothers, Mr. England, Alma's husband, as attorney for the ranch, saw the necessity of making some kind of an agreement which would prevent the dissolution of the partnership in case of the death of one, for up to this time the ranch had been operated as a family partnership without any form of written agreement. The question of distributing a one-third interest in the ranch to all kinds of known and unknown heirs would be disastrous. Accordingly, Mr. England worked out a trust agreement, known as the Miller Brothers 101 Ranch Trust.[10] The Miller brothers approved the trust agreement and it became effective September 12, 1921. W. A. Brooks and J. E. Carson were elected trustees to administer the trust agreement. This is the only trust agreement made by the Miller brothers and is the one the 101 Ranch has operated under since 1921. This type of trust

[10] A copy of the Miller Brothers 101 Ranch Trust Agreement is included in the Appendix.

originated in Massachusetts and is generally known as "a Massachusetts Common Law Trust." This type did not need to be organized according to any law, but was formed merely by the appointment of trustees, the deeding of land to these trustees, and the issuance by the trustees of shares to the beneficiaries.

The Miller Brothers 101 Ranch Trust reveals that at the time of its execution, the Ranch included 15,252.97 acres of deeded lands located in Noble, Pawnee, Osage, and Kay Counties, Oklahoma.[11] The Millers continued to purchase lands until they had acquired by 1932 a total of 17,492.31 acres. Since no lands have been purchased since 1932, this represents the greatest total acreage of deeded lands owned by the 101 Ranch.

A large part of the deeded lands was rich bottom land along the Salt Fork River and was used for agricultural purposes. The remainder included high grade pasture land suitable for growing pasture crops and grasses. The acreage alone was appraised at $810,490 during the depression years.

There has been only one disastrous flood and that was in June, 1923, when there was a cloudburst on the head of the Salt Fork River, and at the same time on two of its tributaries. The flood cost the Millers several hundred thousand dollars, as the waters always flooded the choicest agricultural land on the ranch. To prevent further floods, the brothers constructed a levee, several miles in length, along the Salt Fork River, where it took a southward turn just west of the ranch headquarters. This stopped any further floods, since the only flood waters that could overflow the land were those that backed up the Salt Fork from the main Arkansas stream.

The brothers experienced considerable legal difficulties regarding validity of titles to these lands. In 1920 indictments were returned by the Federal grand jury charging them with fraudulently obtaining large tracts of land from the Ponca Indians. The charges were general at first, and for that reason, George Miller demanded that the government furnish a bill of particulars of the alleged fraud. Federal Judge J. H. Cotteral, after hearing the arguments, granted the request and instructed the government to furnish Miller's counsel dates and issue of

[11] For schedule of these lands, see copy of Miller Brothers 101 Ranch Trust in the Appendix.

patents and copies of alleged false reports made by the land superintendent to the Indian Office.[12]

Following Judge Cotteral's decision, the Federal government, through its attorneys, presented forty-eight counts against the Miller brothers. The particular counts alleged that they, first, knowing certain Ponca Indians owning land near the 101 Ranch were incompetent, conspired to induce them to make application for patents to the Secretary of the Interior containing false statements, and, second, obtained deeds from the Indians, who were heavily indebted to them at the time. The case was tried before Federal Judge A. G. C. Bierer at Guthrie, Oklahoma. After hearing the evidence and argument, Judge Bierer rendered a decision in favor of the Miller brothers.[13]

The government appealed the decision of Judge Bierer to the United States Supreme Court. The Court, after hearing the argument, refused October 17, 1932, to review the cases, thus upholding the Federal court which found the Miller brothers had not unfairly induced the Indians to sell their lands.[14]

Thus the long and technical litigation left the Miller brothers in rightful possession of all the 17,492.31 acres of deeded land purchased from the Indians. The land returned to the Indians, as a result of the litigation, was not a part of the 101 Ranch proper but included scattered holdings, ranging in small tracts from twenty to one hundred and sixty acres. The Federal court found that the brothers had not in any instance acted fraudulently and that in only two of the forty-one counts had technical errors occurred in the purchases. The court, however, found that twenty of the Indians, from whom purchases had been made, were incompetent despite government ruling to the contrary at the time the purchases were made. The court, furthermore, ordered that these lands be returned to the Indians with the government paying back in full to the Miller brothers the purchase price of $30,649.90. Judge Bierer, in his decision, blamed the "greater liberalism" policies of the Department of the Interior between 1917 and 1920 for the differences which brought about the litigation. The government policy, during

[12] *Ponca City Courier,* November 18, 1920.
[13] *Daily Oklahoman,* May 27, 1927.
[14] *Kansas City Star,* October 18, 1932.

that time, had been to allow more Indians patents of competency and to allow them to attend to their own affairs as much as possible.

In addition to the deeded lands, the 101 Ranch included many acres of farming and grazing lands leased from the Ponca, Pawnee, Otoe, and Osage Indians in Kay, Noble, Osage and Pawnee Counties, Oklahoma. These lands were checkerboarded with the deeded lands, which made them undesirable for other ranchmen and at the same time gave the Millers control of them at a fair lease price.

Any Indian who was deemed by the Commissioner of Indian Affairs to have the requisite knowledge, experience, and business capacity to negotiate lease contracts could make contracts with the Miller brothers for leasing his own land and the land of his minor children for farming and grazing purposes, and collect the rentals arising under such leases. The lease contracts had to be made on a special contract form provided by the Office of Indian Affairs and were subject only to the approval of the superintendent of the tribe. Indians not deemed competent to manage their own affairs in this respect were required to have their leases made in the office of the superintendent of the tribe. The superintendent negotiated and approved the leases, collected all rentals, and deposited the amount to the credit of the Indians. The money was paid out in accordance with the regulations in force regarding individual Indian moneys.

According to the regulations of the Office of Indian Affairs in force at that time, the Miller brothers could not lease from the Indians more than 640 acres of ordinary agricultural lands for farming purposes. This limit, however, was not strictly enforced and could be waived on authority previously obtained from the Commissioner of Indian Affairs. No limitation was made on the amount of land which could be leased for grazing purposes.

The leased lands were divided into two classifications. One classification included leased Indian lands with preferential rights, which gave the Millers the right to bid above everyone else or to take the lands at others' bid. These lands were used for both farming and grazing purposes. The other classification included lands leased from time to time from individual Indians or leases traded for from other persons holding them. These lands were used almost exclusively for grazing purposes.

The leased lands with preferential rights were contiguous to the deeded lands and, for that reason, the bonus right on these lands was valued at $4.00 an acre during the depression years.[15] The total acreage of these leases was around ten thousand acres; the acreage varied little from year to year. The Miller brothers paid the Indians an annual lease rate of around ninety-eight cents an acre for these lands and the total amount paid in 1930 for 10,509.28 acres was $10,200.44.[16]

It is extremely difficult to state the exact number of acres of leased lands belonging in the second classification. The acreage varied considerably from time to time as a result of the manner in which the leases were obtained. The leases were secured from individual Indians and other parties and were recorded in the Indian agencies in the names of various individuals. The policy of the Office of Indian Affairs in effect at that time looked with disfavor upon extensive tracts leased to individuals and corporations and, for that reason, many of the leases obtained from individual Indians or other parties were recorded in names of persons other than the Miller brothers.[17] Since the records of the Indian agencies handling these leases are incomplete at the present time, the exact number of acres leased in this manner is unknown. Only an estimate of the acreage from individuals associated with the Miller brothers is possible.

The policy of the Millers from the very beginning of the 101 Ranch was to lease extensive tracts of land since they handled annually thousands of cattle, horses, mules, and hogs, requiring huge acreage of farming and grazing lands for feed purposes. W. A. Brooks reports that he assisted at one time in fencing two large tracts of grazing land, one consisting of ten square miles and the other five square miles.[17] These tracts alone totaled seventy thousand acres. Lewis McDonald, a Ponca Indian, who was employed by the Millers for several years to handle the Indian leases, estimates that the 101 Ranch

[15] 101 Ranch Records, December 31, 1930.

[16] An exact schedule of the leased lands with preferential rights is included in the Appendix.

[17] W. A. Brooks to Ellsworth Collings, April 23, 1936.

controlled at one time or another as much as ninety thousand acres of leases, including the preferential leases.[18] Colonel Zack T. Miller states that approximately eighty thousand acres of Indian land was subject to lease and that the 101 Ranch always held large acreages for farming and grazing purposes. In the early days practically all of the Ponca and Otoe reservations were under lease.[19] Many printed sources give 110,000 acres as the total acreage of the 101 Ranch.[20] The 17,492.31 acres of deeded land subtracted from that amount leaves approximately 92,500 acres of lease lands. The differences in these estimates are due, no doubt, to the fact that they are based on different periods in the history of the 101 Ranch. There seems no question that the 101 Ranch included a large acreage of Indian leases for farming and grazing purposes and that the total varied from time to time as a result of the Indians selling or farming their land as the country opened up to settlement.

The lands of the 101 Ranch, then made up a veritable agricultural and livestock kingdom. They embraced an approximate total of 110,000 acres that sprawled like patchwork over the Oklahoma plains in Kay, Noble, Osage, and Pawnee counties. Here is what this vast expanse included: the farming lands comprised fifteen thousand acres planted to grain and cotton crops each season, in addition to garden acreage of cabbage, onions, tomatoes, watermelons, and potatoes.[21] The crop acreage usually included four thousand acres of wheat, twenty-five hundred acres in oats, five thousand acres in corn, and twenty-five hundred acres in cotton. The rest of the fifteen thousand acres of farming land was devoted to alfalfa, cane, kafir, sweet clover, and other short crops for the silos principally. The grazing and pasture lands included the remainder whereon cattle, horses, mules, and hogs roved in herds of thousands. This was fine grazing and pasture land, carpeted with a good quality of native grasses and it provided an excellent range. With the Salt Fork River providing an abundant

[18] Lewis McDonald to Ellsworth Collings, March 6, 1936.

[19] Colonel Zack T. Miller to Ellsworth Collings, December 10, 1935.

[20] Thoburn and Wright, *History of Oklahoma*, pp. 111, 345; *Literary Digest*, August, 1928; *Time*, February 11, 1929.

[21] George L. Miller to the *Daily Oklahoman*, February 6, 1927.

supply of water at all times of the year, it was truly a cattle-man's paradise.

The 101 Ranch lands contained approximately 172 sections. If this amount of land were placed in a strip one mile wide, it would be 127 miles long, or nearly fifteen miles square. Necessarily, several sets of improvements were maintained, so that the employees could be near the work. The Bar L headquarters was such a place. The improvements consisted of a large ranch house for the foreman, barns and corrals, silos, blacksmith shop, and several bunk houses for the cowboys. At this place the cowboys lived throughout the year caring for the livestock and repairing fences of the ranges.

On this vast domain there were located three towns: Marland, Red Rock, and White Eagle, and three hundred miles of fences, costing $50,000 enclosed its tremendous confines.[22] For twenty-two miles U. S. Highway 77 crossed these lands and is paralleled most of the way with the Santa Fe railroad, which has a station at Marland, located three and one-half miles south of the "White House." Large warehouses and shipping pens, accommodating more than two thousand cattle at one time, were located at Marland, the shipping center, and the telephone in the central business office at the headquarters connected with every foreman on the ranch, over thirty-five miles of private wire, and long distance service with cities throughout Oklahoma and the nation. Mail was delivered from Marland to and fro by mounted carriers detailed at all times for this purpose. The 101 Ranch, replete in every way, was truly an empire within itself—the dream of its founder.

[22] 101 Ranch Records, December 31, 1930.

THE YELLOW BACKS

IV

THE first trip into Texas in 1871 revealed to Colonel George W. Miller the opportunity to engage in the cattle business on a big scale. Texas was the grazing grounds for countless thousands of cattle. For these immense herds there was virtually no market and stock cattle on the range only brought from one to two dollars a head and three to four dollars was the top price for selected mature animals.[1] At that very same time round steak was selling in New York at twenty-five cents a pound and cattle on foot in eastern cities at five dollars to ten dollars per hundredweight.[2] Such difference in prices is easily understood when it is remembered that no railroads then extended from the markets to the widespread ranges of Texas.

Peculiarly favorable conditions of the Indian Territory country made it excellent feeding grounds for fattening cattle for the northern markets. The land was within a few miles of railroad yards, and could be leased from the Indians and the government for a very small sum. The native grasses that covered the range for hundreds of miles flourished in abundance and were as nourishing in the winter as in the summer; also there was an ample supply of water. The winters were mild and the summers long and not a fence stood in all the vast country to prevent the herds from grazing at will until the round-up—it was cattle country.

Colonel Miller was familiar with the southern cattle market and quickly grasped the possibilities of developing a cattle business by driving the Texas cattle up the trail to the ranges of Indian Territory, fattening the herds on the native grasses for the northern markets. From the time he drove the first herd of "yellow backs"[3] up the trail from Texas in 1871 to the bus-

[1] Edward Everett Dale, *The Range Cattle Industry,* p. 30.
[2] Edward Everett Dale, "The Passing of the Cattle Industry in Oklahoma," *The Cattleman,* November, 1924, pp. 9-17.
[3] Because of the yellowish color of Texas longhorns, they were familiarly known as "yellow backs" among the cattlemen.

iness panic in 1893, Colonel Miller engaged in the cattle business on a vast scale. For twenty-two years his ranch was a cattle ranch and his business exclusively was cattle.

Colonel Miller's trail herds ranged in number from 1,000 to 1,500 and were driven up a day's journey apart in order to insure adequate water and grass and to avoid stampedes. The total number of trail cattle handled each year was numbered in the thousands.[4] During one year the total reached 25,000, many of which were loaded at Hunnewell, Kansas, for the market.[5] The task of getting these herds from Texas to his ranch in the Indian Territory was one which involved both skill and daring. Only men of unflinching courage and quick movement could succeed in handling the wild cattle. The Texas steer was no respecter of unmounted cowboys, but for the man on horseback he had a wholesome fear. Separately, neither man nor horse had any more chance in the herd, fresh from the open range, than among so many wolves. With their long, sharp-pointed horns these steers rent man or horse with ease and the fights among themselves had all the ferociousness of wild beasts of the jungles.

It usually required about three months for Colonel Miller to drive a herd from Texas to his ranch in the Indian Territory. There were swollen streams to swim, wild runs of cattle to check, bandits or Indians to face, and hardships to endure such as drives all day in the rain and mud, snatches of sleep on the wet ground, tired or sore-footed horses to care for, and bad foods or none at all if brush and wood were soaked with rain. Spring was the usual starting time and May, June, July, August, and September found Colonel Miller on the trail. Once the road-branding was over at the ranches in Texas the cattle were herded into a ragged column and headed northward.[6] The orderly manner in which the herd took its way across the plains was remarkable. A herd of a thousand cattle would string out to a length of two miles, and a larger one still longer. At the start there was hard driving, twenty to thirty miles a day,

[4] Hugo Milde to Ellsworth Collings, March 4, 1936.
[5] *Kansas City Star,* April 27, 1903.
[6] The herd always included cattle of several brands from different ranches and, for that reason, a common brand—a road brand—was needed to prevent confusion.

until the cattle were thoroughly wearied. After that twelve to fifteen miles was considered a good day's drive. The daily program was as regular as that of a regiment on the march.

During the early part of the morning, the herd was "drifted" with little pushing, grazing as it went. By mid-morning, the cowboys urged the cattle closer together and two riders at each side "pointed" the lead steers at a rapid pace while the "swing riders" behind them pushed in the flanks of the herd. Just behind the cattle rode the "tail riders" to keep in the herd the lame and stupid cattle. With the approach of noon, the attention of the cattle turned again to the grass about them, and the "swing riders" had to keep in constant gallop to hold the steers from turning out to graze on the margin of the trail.[7]

The cook went ahead to locate the noon camp at some spot about half a mile from the trail so the cattle would have fresh grass for the hour's grazing. By the time the herd reached the camp, the flap-board on the chuck wagon had been let down and a cold lunch was ready for the cowboys. The cattle by this time were uneasy and were turned again into the trail and walked steadily forward until early twilight, when they were halted for another graze. As darkness came on, they were gathered closer and closer into a compact mass by the cowboys riding steadily in constantly lessening circles around them, until at last they lay down, chewing their cuds and resting from the day's trip. Near midnight they usually got up, stood awhile, and then lay down again, having changed sides. Care was always necessary at this time of night to keep them from wandering off into the darkness. The cowboys sitting on their ponies or riding slowly around and around the reclining cattle, passed the night on sentinel duty, relieving one another at stated intervals. As each rode his arc of the circle about the resting herd, the slow, deep-sounded notes of old songs quieted the cattle and helped the herder to stay awake. A cowboy did not dare let drowsiness overtake him for the cattle did not always lie quietly. Startled by some trifle, the sound of a cracking stick, a flash of lightning, the restlessness of some steer, every head was lifted, and the mass of hair and horns, with fierce, frightened eyes, was off.

[7] Oscar Brewster, old time cowboy on the 101 Ranch, to Ellsworth Collings, July 24, 1936.

Charles W. Hannah describes such an instance on the ranges of the 101 Ranch during the early nineties. "The 101 cattle," says Mr. Hannah, "were peacefully grazing over a wide area when a wagon and horses driven by a man came along through our herd. Under the wagon trotted a small black dog. Some of the unruly longhorn steers, observing the moving wagon, had their curiosity aroused and played alongside of the wagon, now and then getting rather close to the horses. The man, fearing the steers would hook his horses, set his small black dog on them. The steers, naturally wild, became frightened at the dog and ran at top speed out across the prairie, stumbling over a 'sleeper.' The calf jumped up, bawled loudly and started to run. Everything in sight became frightened and, believe me, the stampede was on in a few minutes."[8]

With the first sounds of the stampede the cowboys awoke, mounted their horses they had staked nearby, and rode out to help the night herders in the attempt to break the flight. Getting on one side of the leaders the effort of the riders was to turn them, a little at first, then more and more, until the circumference of a great circle was described. The cattle behind blindly followed, and soon the front and rear joined and "milling" commenced. Round and round the bewildered cattle would race until they were wearied or recovered from their fright. To stop the useless churning and to guard against another wild rush, the cowboys would sing in unison some familiar ballad. It did not matter what they sang so long as there was music to it, and it was not unusual to hear a cowboy begin with "Whoop!" and continue with variations that might have been adopted from a Comanche war yell.

A stampede meant a loss, and Colonel Miller always made a hasty inventory.[9] A sudden swerve of the stampeding cattle might crush to death a cowboy and his horse. A stumbling steer would be tramped on by those behind him and some might be gored by the long horns of those they brushed against. If the riders failed to check the herd and hold it in a mass it might become widely scattered, requiring a delay of days while the

[8] Charles W. Hannah, old time cowboy on the 101 Ranch, to Ellsworth Collings, July 20, 1936.

[9] John Hiatt, old time cowboy on the 101 Ranch, to Ellsworth Collings, September 7, 1936.

remnants were gathered. Another danger was the marauding Indians, who were always feared, and many skirmishes occurred between them and Colonel Miller. An understanding with the chiefs, however, was usually sufficient to insure safety.

Stampedes and Indians were not all the troubles encountered on the trail. Crossing the herd over a swollen stream was a danger escaped only during late summer. The "lead-cattle" instantly feared muddy and swift currents of water and the "point-riders" had hard work to urge them on. Sometimes these cowboys would force their own horses out into the swollen stream to convince the cattle that there was no danger. Once the "lead-cattle" were out to their swimming depth, they usually went on to the opposite bank with the remainder of the herd following. If the leaders became alarmed at the swiftness of the current, they might "mill" in a mad circle, soon becoming a struggling mass as other cattle followed. Then came dangerous work for the cowboys. The cattle in the rear had to be checked immediately, and a "point-rider" had to force his horse into the midst of the panic-stricken cattle, break the mill, and compel some of the cattle to lead off in swimming for the shore. It often required several days to cross a herd over a flooded stream, and as sometimes it rained during all of the time the cowboys didn't get much sleep since they had to stay with the cattle day and night.

Thus accompanied by incidents along the trail that brought into play all the strength and strategy of Colonel Miller and his cowboys, the herd moved on to the ranges of his ranch in the Indian Territory. Reaching the outskirts of the ranch, the cattle were turned loose on the range and allowed to grow and fatten for the markets. Cow camps were built at convenient places, from which the cowboys constantly kept on the outlook for prairie fires, watched closely for cattle thieves, visited the water holes, and guarded in every way the interests of their employer. Later when fences enclosed Colonel Miller's range, these cowboys rode the fences in order to keep them in good repair. Several times during the year these camps were visited by a wagon from headquarters bringing bacon, flour, sugar, coffee, beans, and dried fruits.[10] The life of these cowboys on the

[10] Charles Orr, old time cowboy on the 101 Ranch, to Ellsworth Collings, September 6, 1936.

range was lonely, but the work not especially hard when compared with the work on the trails.

Cattle were always real companions to the cowboys who were doing herd duty through long hours on the range. On a cool, fresh morning the cattle seemed as reluctant to leave their own warm beds on the ground as the cowboys had been to leave their blankets in early morning hours to go on herd duty. The night herders would come in to eat the morning meal and would report "all quiet" to the cowboy at the camp. This was the cue for him to ride forth in early morning light to hunt up the cattle bedded down on the range. When in sight of the herd, he would start singing, continuing until he was riding through the herd as it lay on the ground. While on herd duty, he would usually sit on his pony with one leg over the saddle horn. His body was hunched forward with arms often crossed on his bent knee, leisurely rolling a cigarette. His pony grazed at will while the cattle scattered over a wide area feeding peacefully on the native grasses.

Nothing was more essential to Colonel Miller's cattle business than the cowboys. Approximately fifty were permanently employed on the 101 Ranch at all times. They were true knights of the plains, inured to the hardships of the range. They wore wide-brimmed hats, handkerchiefs around their necks, chaps on their legs, and high-heeled boots. The broad-brimmed hat protected the face from the biting particles of ice in a driving blizzard or from the glare and heat of the sun. The loose handkerchief served as an efficient dust screen when riding behind the herd. Chaps protected the legs from injury from cold and rain. High heels on the boots kept the feet from slipping through the stirrups and provided a brace on the ground when an unruly horse was pulling on the other end of the rope. They could do on horseback anything an ordinary man can do afoot. They could make their cow pony dance, pick up the smallest article from the ground at full speed, and with unerring aim lasso a steer fleeing for dear life.[11]

No adjunct was more necessary in all phases of the cowboy's work than the cow pony. About one hundred were used on the 101 Ranch. These ponies knew the needs and methods of handling cattle as thoroughly as the riders who sat astride

[11] John Hiatt to Ellsworth Collings, September 7, 1936.

[59]

their backs. Without them, the cattle business on the Ranch could not have been carried on successfully, for steers could not have been captured, "cut-out," tied, branded, penned, or shipped.[12]

So familiar were these ponies with the method of pursuit and capture of a running steer, that the guiding hand of the rider was not required. They followed the steer in every turn and brought the cowboy speedily to the most advantageous position for casting his lasso. And when the rope encircled the horns or neck, the ponies understood how best to withstand the physical shock as it grew taut. If the animal was to be tied, they knew the rope must not slaken, for the steer, thrown headlong on the abruptness of its halt, was held prostrate only by the rigid line.

In moving among a herd of cattle these ponies were taught to proceed with furtive movement, for unwonted activity on their part would cause a stampede. If the rider had singled out an individual steer that he wished to "cut-out," the cow pony comprehended instantly the purpose, quietly forced the animal to the outer limits of the herd and then, the danger of commotion over, no longer withheld speed.

The cow ponies would ford or swim a river without hesitation, and seemed to know and avoid quicksand by intuition. They could traverse tracts riddled with prairie dog and gopher holes without once being entrapped. No night was dark enough to hide from their eyes the presence of a wire fence. The rider might never have suspected that strands had been stretched in his path, but the cow ponies always stopped in safety, no matter how fast the gallop. Little wonder, then, that the Millers maintained at all times a permanent staff of cowboys and many cow ponies.

When the skies were clear and the air bracing, the task of herding the cattle on Colonel Miller's range was a pleasant one for the cowboys. But there came stormy days on the great prairies when the cattle were restless and when it was anything but enjoyable to ride through the steady downpour of rain. These storms of the old prairies were unlike any in the settled communities existing today. The lightning with nothing to strike would hit the ground without entering, and gathered into

[12] Charles Orr to Ellsworth Collings, September 6, 1936.

[60]

Upper, large herds fattening on the 101 Ranch; center, cattle round-up on the 101 Ranch; lower, a herd of longhorns on the 101 Ranch

great balls of fire that raced over the prairie for miles and miles bursting with terrific explosion. The flashes of lightning ripping their way from the clouds kept the cowboys and cattle helpless in one spot to be buffeted about by the tornado of wind. The sound of air as it closed in on the vacuum created by the electrical current surpassed all others and was approximated only by the shriek of the wind. The electrical display continued, in most instances, for over an hour and took a long time to die away. The start of the storm came with the suddenness of the rush of the wind, but gradually subsided from its peak of pandemonium and confusion to a peace and quiet enhanced by the purest of air on the range. Charles W. Hannah describes realistically one of these storms on the ranges of the 101 Ranch during the late fall of 1895.

"Thirty-six of us cowboys," says Mr. Hannah, "were holding eight thousand cattle on the open ranges of the 101 Ranch in the vicinity of Red Rock during the late fall of 1895. A big blizzard hit us during the early morning hours one day, and the cattle soon began to run around in a wide circle. We worked all day without rest and food doing our best to keep the herd scattered, for we all knew if the leaders ever got bunched the jig would be up. The cattle were of the mixed longhorn type and, believe me, they sure were plenty wild and unruly, especially during stormy weather. At that time we had no barbed-wire fences and they roamed as they pleased over almost the whole Ponca and Otoe reservations.

"At the height of the storm along late in the afternoon, the mass of milling animals moved about in circles not knowing which way to go. The blinding snow and the biting north wind added to the bellowing of the frightened steers soon brought bedlam and confusion. The crooning songs of the cowboys ceased when they could no longer be heard, but we were still there on the job just the same.

"About seven in the evening the herd broke in the center, and with tails out and extending themselves at fullest speed they ran in a great mad mass. The stampede of unreasoning terror was on, and they ran with the storm for more than twenty-five miles. Recklessly, blindly, in whatever direction fancy led them, over a bluff or into a morass, it mattered not, and fast were the horses that could keep ahead of the leaders.

As the fury of the storm abated, along about midnight, the roar of the herd was the dominant sound. For some time they ran until they tired and slowed down in the early morning hours. Then we rode close to the leaders and by standing in front of them, turned the direct line of travel into a curve. Soon the unruly herd was running in a big circle, then a close mass of milling animals, and the stampede was over about eight that morning.

"The sun soon broke through the clouds in the east and the air was clear and warm as the cold wind slowed down at our backs. All was peace again and the cattle soon fell to feeding about them. As was always the practice of Colonel Miller, we made a hasty inventory. The cowboys all came through alive, but believe me, I was frozen to the bone that morning. We had been in the saddle all night doing our best to turn the leaders of eight thousand frightened cattle. Several times during the night I rubbed my eyes with fresh chewed tobacco to keep from falling asleep. A count of the cattle revealed eight hundred dead as a result of the stampede."[13]

To care for, tally, and market the cattle, Colonel Miller held two round-ups each season. As was a long established custom, he was usually assisted by a combination of ranchers in the locality. The spring or calf round-up was conducted in the spring or early summer, after the season's calves were born, and on this occasion all the unbranded calves were branded with the mark of each outfit taking part. In the fall another was held, known as the beef round-up, at which time the fat beef steers were herded for sale and shipment.[14]

The calf round-up began when the grass came in the spring. A round-up boss, some experienced and respected cowman, was chosen at a meeting of the ranchmen prior to the round-up. Each of these cattlemen furnished cowboys and assumed a share of the expenses in proportion to the number of cattle he owned. A few days before the date set, the outfits would begin to assemble at some agreed place, and each one consisted of some seven or nine extra ponies for each cowboy and a chuck wagon loaded with bedding and food.

As early as four in the morning the day of work would begin

[13] Charles W. Hannah to Ellsworth Collings, July 20, 1936.
[14] Charles Orr to Ellsworth Collings, September 6, 1936.

[62]

with the cook's call for breakfast. The cook's fire blazed near the chuck wagon, and a very few minutes after the call the cowboys would be gathered about, each of them with a tin plate, on which the cook slapped meat and hot biscuits and a tin cup that he filled with steaming coffee.

Oscar Brewster, famous chef in Colonel Miller's camps, claims to have broken the open prairie record, in 1890 when he cooked three meals daily for from forty-five to eighty-five men for a period of twenty-one days, when Colonel Miller was having his annual round-up. During that time three wagons, with sideboards on, loaded with groceries and provisions, were hauled out of Hunnewell, Kansas (then an outfitting point) to Miller's camps.

"There were three divisions of the general round-up in 1890," says Brewster in telling of this occasion. "They were known as the eastern, southwestern, and western. The eastern division included the ranges of the 101 Ranch from the Rock Island Railroad to the Arkansas River, and the captain of this division was Colonel Joe Miller, at that time a young man. There were two or three chuck wagons for each division and Colonel Joe had trouble in getting cooks for his division. I assured him I could take care of his division, although I realized it would be some job cooking for eighty-five hard-working cowboys.

"We outfitted the first day of June at Hunnewell, and our chuck wagons, loaded with groceries, provisions, and bedding, were drawn by four horses across the open ranges. We drove to Bluff Creek the first night and I had forty-five men at supper. The next morning the number increased to fifty-five, and from that time on the men eating at my wagon increased daily for twenty-one days until the last day of the round-up I counted eighty-five men at my chuck wagon, stationed where Ponca City is now located.

"In following up the round-up, it was necessary to move camp each day. We kept a team of horses near-by all the time for that purpose. After breakfast each day we would break up and pull the wagon to the next location, and then I would get the noon day meal, many times without taking time to unhitch the horses from the wagon. Five full loads, with double sideboards of groceries and provisions, were brought to my chuck wagon, and every day for twenty-one days I cooked a

[63]

calf or yearling in addition. Breakfast was cooked in Dutch ovens, buried in long trenches, and the meals were never late, always on time. We had hot biscuits three times a day. Imagine cooking hot biscuits three times a day for twenty-one days for eighty-five men! Our division rounded up twenty-eight thousand cattle that year, and Colonel Joe Miller was the best round-up boss I ever worked for during all my time on the ranges."[15]

Eating breakfast hurriedly, each cowboy roped and saddled his horse from the remuda, which had been driven up to camp as a signal that there was no time to waste in eating. As the cowboys rode away over the prairie for the lurking-places of the cattle, they spread out, breaking up into small groups of "circle riders."

"Oftentimes the cowboys," says Charles W. Hannah, "would ride at full speed along both sides of high elevations waving their yellow slickers frantically at the cattle grazing below them. This would frighten the cattle and, being naturally wild, they would run together and make it easier for the cowboys to round them up for branding. This practice was strictly forbidden by the round-up boss since it made the cattle wilder and often started stampedes. One season the boss would not permit us to use yellow slickers for fear, as we had often done, we would use them in rounding-up the cattle. He supplied us with black ones."[16]

Creeks, shady canyons, and arroyos were searched carefully and after many a chase with unruly calves or sullen steers, a round-up of several hundred cattle was formed near the camp. Around this dusty, milling herd, the cowboys rode to drive back the cattle that turned to dash out from the edges.

Usually four cowboys held the constantly moving cattle, while four others rode through them "culling out" the cows and calves of the 101 outfit. Those cowboys culling turned these cattle over to four other cowboys, who drove them away several hundred yards to another herd, constantly growing and known as "the cut," which was held intact by two or three more cowboys. Not far from them the branding fire for the 101 irons was being prepared.

[15] Oscar Brewster to Ellsworth Collings, July 21, 1936.
[16] Charles W. Hannah to Ellsworth Collings, July 20, 1936.

A cowboy would quietly turn his pony into the herd, mark a cow, work her with her calf out of the herd. Immediately the roper cast his lariat, catching the calf preferably by a hind leg, and dragging it with his horse, brought it up to the branding fire. As it came near, a cowboy would grab it, reach over its back with both arms, seize it under the throat or hind leg, give it a lift so as to swing its legs off the ground and forward and then drop upon it. The cowboy was careful to stick his right knee into its neck, and with an arm, double up and raise its upper front leg as far as possible. The calf in this position was helpless, except for its hind legs. These were cared for by another cowboy, who grabbed the upper leg as he sat down behind the calf and pulled it toward him as he pushed against the lower one with both feet. Then a third cowboy rushed up with the red-hot branding iron, burning the 101 mark on the calf's left side while it bawled and struggled. After all the calves of the round-up had been branded the cattle were freed and allowed to roam at will on the range. Any calves that belonged to neighboring ranches were branded by the cowboys with the irons of these ranches and turned back on the range.

In the fall Colonel Miller's round-up wagon, remuda, and cowboys would leave the ranch headquarters on the beef round-up. The range was "worked" much as it was on the spring branding round-up, except that all of the beef cattle were held in a herd, day and night, and when a sufficient number had been collected they were driven across the country to the railroad. The handling of a trail herd of beef cattle required all of Colonel Miller's years of experience on the range, for a false move would cost his entire year's profits. Fat steers were usually wild and would take flight at the slightest provocation. It was thus that the cowboys would have to bring every resource into action to calm them down and keep them from scattering over the range. The trail to the railroad was always made in a series of short drives, giving the fat cattle plenty of time to graze and water, so that they would be in the best condition when they arrived at the railroad. Upon arriving at the shipping center, they were driven into the stockyards, dragged or coaxed into the cars, and were sent off to meet their fate at the great packing houses. The journey up the trail had been a strange one to them and the end of the trip with close confinement in yard and car, the first they had ever known, was strangest of all.

In 1888 the Santa Fe built a railroad from Texas through the Cherokee Strip country and that marked the end of driving cattle over the trail from Texas to Oklahoma. For seventeen years, 1871-1888, Colonel Miller stocked his ranch in the Indian Territory with cattle driven up the trail from Texas. After that date the cattle were shipped over the Santa Fe Railroad. The years following saw thousands of these cattle shipped into Colonel Miller's ranch during the spring months, fattened on the rich grass, and shipped to the central markets in late summer and early fall.[17]

Under favorable conditions the profits were enormous. During the early seventies, two-year-old steers cost in Texas from $3.00 to $4.00 a head and after grazing a year on the range in the Indian Territory they sold for $40.00 or $50.00 a head on the market.[18] The loss, during favorable winters, was practically nothing and the expense for help amounted to only a few hundred dollars at that time. As the cattle markets extended westward, the profits were not so great, but still good. Two-year-old steers during the eighties sold in Texas for $13.00 a head and fattening on the range the market price remained about the same.[19] During the nineties, these steers sold in Texas for $21.00 a head and after feeding on the range for a season they brought $37.50 a head, a gross profit of $16.50 a steer.[20]

Conditions for profits were not always favorable. From nine to eleven cents a bushel was paid in the early winter of 1886 for corn with which to feed a herd of cattle which Joe Miller bought on the land where the city of Tulsa now stands. The cattle were coming three-year-olds and cost $11.00 a head for the 1100 in the herd. They were rounded-up on the present site of Tulsa, counted, and driven by Miller to his father's ranch. The corn fed to the steers that winter was bought from early day Kansas settlers and they hauled it from twelve to fifteen miles to reach the herd on the Miller ranch. Each farmer was required to hit each ear of corn over the sideboard of his

[17] Hugo Milde to Ellsworth Collings, March 5, 1936.
[18] George Rainey, *The Cherokee Strip*, p. 127.
[19] Ernest Staples Osgood, *The Day of the Cattleman*, p. 52.
[20] Edward Everett Dale, *The Cattleman*, November, 1924, p. 9.

wagon, thus breaking it in two pieces, thereby making the size of the pieces about right for a steer to take in his mouth. At that, the steers failed to bring a profit on the investment.[21]

Nearly all cattlemen found it necessary to borrow considerable money to carry on their business.[22] An incident occurred in this connection during the early nineties that reveals Colonel Miller's sagacity in coping with financial situations.[23] He found it necessary to borrow a sum of money from his banker. The customary practice prevailing was for the ranchman to put up cattle as collateral for loans with little or no investigation on the part of the banker as to number and kind. The reputation of the cattleman for honesty was the main consideration. Because of the risky conditions in the cattle business at that time, the president of the bank deemed it necessary to use caution in making loans, although he did not question the honesty of Colonel Miller. Accordingly, he agreed to advance the loan, provided Miller would give as collateral a sufficient number of his choice steers and stamp them with a new brand in order to designate them from the others in the herd. Although the conditions imposed were unusual, Colonel Miller accepted them without quibbling and accompanied the banker to his herd, selecting the steers that were to be branded as collateral. The banker, satisfied, returned, and Colonel Miller proceeded immediately to choose a new brand for the steers. Somewhat annoyed at the unusual terms of the loan, he ingeniously designed a brand that attracted attention rather humorously to these terms. He selected the brand "10D," which substituted the letter "D," initial of the banker's first name, for the figure "1" in Colonel Miller's "101" brand. The brand was read as "I-Owe-D" and the steers wearing it were always pointed out as the "I-Owe-D" cattle.

The business panic of 1893 was especially disastrous to Colonel Miller's cattle business.[24] A great commission house in Kansas City failed, the house that acted as agent for Colonel Miller in all his cattle transactions. He had a $300,000 credit

21 *101 Magazine,* May, 1927.
22 Edward Everett Dale, "The Passing of the Cattle Industry in Oklahoma," *The Cattleman,* November, 1924.
23 W. A. Brooks to Ellsworth Collings, March 6, 1936.
24 *Time,* February 11, 1929, p. 63.

on the books of that house, money due him for cattle sold. At one stroke this credit was wiped out entirely. In addition, notes aggregating $100,000 held by eastern banks, which the agents of this house should have paid from his credit account, had not been paid. Colonel Miller had seventeen thousand beef cattle on his ranch at that time. He was not only without money, but deeply in debt in a panic year. "The eastern bankers sent in men who took all of our cattle," related Colonel Zack T. Miller.[25] "They took everything but the cripples and the runts. When they got through, all we had left was eighty-eight old horses and a handful of cows. We were as flat as the prairie." Without credit, his vast ranch stripped of its cattle, Colonel Miller's cattle business was practically destroyed. He had a vast cattle range with no cattle to fatten upon its grasses and it was a panic year.

The business crisis of 1893 marked a change in Colonel Miller's ranch, which up to that time had been a cattle range and not a farm. His business during the past twenty-two years had been exclusively cattle. The crisis demanded courage and enterprise and marked the entrance of his sons into the management of the ranch. That winter, in order to get money enough to carry them through, they sold the remaining cows to the Indians and decided to plant wheat. They had the old horses and the homesteaders had proved the fertility of the prairie land. They borrowed money enough to plant five thousand acres of wheat and to buy five hundred yearling calves. They grazed the calves on the growing wheat and the yield was seventy thousand bushels. With wheat selling on the market at a good price, they went on farming, putting in corn, alfalfa, and other crops, as well as wheat. They bought more calves to fatten, and added horses, mules, hogs, geese, ducks, and bison to their flocks. The days of the cattleman were over and the year 1894 marked the change in the 101 Ranch from a cattle range to a diversified farm.

[25] Colonel Zack T. Miller to Charles Lane Callen, *American Magazine*, July, 1928.

BLUE BLOOD
ON THE 101

V

PERHAPS the chief factor contributing to the change in the 101 Ranch from a cattle range to a diversified farm was the coming of a new type of settler to the prairies of northern Oklahoma. "The lean, brown, hard bitten men," says Edward Everett Dale, "who had laid the foundations of the vast cattle empire in northern Oklahoma still remained, but except for the common cow hands who still retained many of the traits of the early cattlemen, they were comparatively few in number. They were giving place to a new group composed of individuals perhaps quite as hardy and vigorous as were the early cattlemen, but who were men of education, broad vision, and intimate contacts with the world outside. Big business was coming to the plains and the new figures in the industry were business farmers in the highest sense of the term.

"It was inevitable that men of this type should see at once the advantages to be derived by improving the breed of their herds and marketing animals at an earlier age. Wild, longhorned Texas steers five or six years old might be sold to the Federal government under beef contracts to feed the Indians, but they did not furnish a quality of beef desired by the markets of the nineties. Much of the American public, particularly in the east, insisted upon better beef than the coarse, stringy product derived from the longhorns. As a result the ranchmen of northern Oklahoma soon began to bring in large numbers of registered or high grade bulls from the corn belt states and even to import a great many breeding animals from Europe."[1]

Not only was better beef demanded by the markets in the early nineties, but changing conditions in the country of northern Oklahoma itself demanded better bred animals on the 101 Ranch. The broad and rolling plains surrounding the ranch, bare of animals for the first few years after the destruction of

[1] Edward Everett Dale, *American Hereford Journal*, December 15, 1936, p. 6.

the buffalo, were now fenced and cultivated by the settlers. Vacant pasture land could no longer be found for the 101 herds outside the boundaries of the ranch. If the cattle business, therefore, was to expand and the value of beef to increase, it had to be accomplished by marketing cattle of higher quality at an earlier age, for it was no longer profitable to keep steers on the ranch until they were four or five years old. This was especially true of the lank, rangy longhorn steers which even at that age were light and yielded a very inferior quality of beef.

As a result of these conditions, Colonel Miller's cattle business changed from grazing longhorns on the ranges to feeding shorthorns on the agricultural products grown on the 101 Ranch. The old range methods of handling cattle, existing on the 101 Ranch prior to this time, underwent considerable modification. The growing of farm products on the fertile lands necessarily required that cattle be held in fenced pastures. This soon brought an end to the old round-up and chuck wagon, since the cattle no longer roved at will on the open range. Instead the cattle grazed in fenced pastures within a few miles of the 101 headquarters or the Bar L camp, where the branding, dehorning, and dipping took place in specially built corrals and chutes. The chuck wagon was no longer the home of the cowboys from which they herded and branded the cattle on the 101 ranges. They lived in bunk houses at the ranch headquarters or the Bar L camp, from which they rode out to repair fences, inspect the water and grass, and look after the cattle, especially the young calves.

Cattle to be branded were driven from the fenced pastures into a large corral at the 101 headquarters or the Bar L camp and then into a small one adjoining the chute. The cowboys, yelling and plying quirts, drove the cattle into the chute until they jammed it full. Branding began when the chute was filled and the bars put up behind the cattle. The branders walked alongside the chute and did nothing but handle the "101" branding irons. Following each brander was a cowboy with a pole, who thrust one end of it under a bar of the chute on the opposite side, and, with a lever thus formed, drew down across the cow's neck to keep her from jumping about when the hot iron was applied to her hip. When all the cattle in the chute were branded, the bars in front were let down, and the cattle

[70]

passed out. The chute daily poured forth its cattle with the 101 stamped on their left hip, while the corrals behind it received more animals from the pastures.

Following the crisis of 1893, Colonel Miller restocked the ranges of the 101 Ranch with improved breeds of cattle. He had handled thousands of the longhorns during his twenty-two years of ranching and fully understood their good qualities. As a product of the open range they did well where purebred cattle would have perished of travel and drouth.[2] In the round-up and on the trail, they were more easily handled than high grade stock, and because of the length of horn, they spaced themselves better under herd and thus traveled with greater ease and less loss of flesh. Their legs were longer, their hoofs tougher, and their endurance greater than blooded cattle. Thus they were able to graze a much wider range, go longer without water, endure more hardships in winter, and take better care of themselves upon the open range than any other breed. But in the fenced pastures of the new farm era these qualities served no longer any useful purpose. And, too, the "yellow backs" did not produce the quality of beef the market of the nineties was coming to demand. Colonel Miller recognized this demand for better beef and adopted the method of "grading up" his herd. When bred to good sires, the longhorn cows produced stock of better beef qualities than the average longhorn steer. Through the use of high grade bulls, the sale of undesirable stock, and the retention of heifer calves from year to year, Colonel Miller had, at the time of his death in 1903, transformed his herd of gaunt and wiry longhorns into cattle of higher beef qualities.

The Miller brothers, active, progressive, alert, followed all these changes, launched huge enterprises, and toiled early and late to bring to fruition diversified farming on the 101 Ranch. They were awake to the opportunities of purebred stock and in a short time their herds of purebred, registered cattle were unsurpassed in all the states, both in number and in blood lines. The first well-bred cattle to be brought to the 101 Ranch were the shorthorns, but it was only a short time until the pure blooded stock of the other breeds were brought in and carefully acclimated to the conditions of northern Oklahoma.

2 J. Evetts Haley, *The XIT Ranch,* p. 182.

The greater business of the Miller brothers in cattle raising was devoted to pure blooded Holsteins, Shorthorns, and Herefords. In the producing of the new breeds, it was necessary to maintain the health of the animals, and every known precaution of science was used to prevent disease among the vast herds of different kinds.

The systematic breeding of the herds was the special work of Colonel Joe Miller, in which he succeeded in doing some very advanced work. Those who are familiar with the change from the old longhorns to the shorthorns and the other breeds of high grade cattle can better appreciate the good judgment needed by a ranchman during these transition periods. This crucial time in cattle raising was weathered with admirable foresight by Colonel Joe Miller and success was due greatly to his constant attempts to bring into existence better cattle than had yet been produced. His scientific accomplishment was brought to such a high standard that many people visited the ranch for the purpose of observing the practical application of his theories of breeding. This work was a benefit, not to the 101 Ranch alone, but to the entire cattle industry throughout the country. The importation of cattle from other countries to cross with other stock was a costly experiment and the pioneer work of Colonel Joe Miller along this line made it possible for hundreds of others to benefit.

"Zack Miller," says Charles Lane Cullen, "took me onto the prairie and showed me one of the strangest cattle herds on this earth. Originally, those great expanses of flat country had belonged to the buffalo. Unattended by man, the buffalo herds had flourished and grown to number millions. The buffalo was hardy, a meat animal, the native of the place chosen by nature herself. The Millers conceived the idea of perpetuating the virtues of the buffalo in a new breed of cattle. So after careful selection, they crossed the buffalo bull with the common range cow. Today they have two hundred of the new cattle, thriving and increasing, the beginning of a herd.

"The success of this 'cross' led to an even odder one. One of the banes of the cattleman is drought. 'Could such a thing as a drought-resisting cattle breed be produced?' asked the Millers. In some parts of the world such breeds existed, but it was impracticable to import them in numbers. It was decided to import a few of a chosen breed and introduce their blood into the herds. The sacred Brahma cattle of distant India were picked for the experiment. Small Brahmas were crossed with the Jersey cow, and big Brahmas with the common cow. The product was not only a drought-resisting animal but a wonderful beef animal. Zack Miller pointed out to me yearlings in the mixed Brahma herd that would bring one hundred dollars on a weight basis as against sixty dollars for a yearling of the common cow."[3]

The purebred stock included three herds: the Holstein, the Shorthorn (Durham), and the Hereford. The Holstein, or dairy herd, numbered five hundred registered and high grade cattle.[4] This herd was headed by the greatest sire of the world, Champion Echo Pontiac No. 359702, Grand Champion of Oklahoma, 1924, who at four years old weighed 2,500 pounds.[5] This great bull was sold as a yearling to the 101 Ranch for $7,200 and one of his brothers sold at auction for $100,000. King Yankee Lefa Segis, No. 286288, was another famous Holstein bull. His sire, King Aggie Segis, sired fifty-four daughters, including the World's Champion under-aged cow, Francher Farm Maxie, with a record of 46 to 86 pounds of butter in seven days. The dam of King Yankee Lefa Segis had a seven day butter record of 32.09 pounds and a milk record of 14,928 pounds. Every cross in this pedigree showed the name of a sire of nation-wide fame, mated with a great producing cow. It was from such blood lines as these that the 101 Ranch Holstein dairy herd was built.

The Shorthorn (Durham) herd of purebred cattle was headed by Maxhall Silver, No. 1056690, one of the world's greatest sires.[6] This herd numbered 350 registered cattle, including Scotch females sired by such noted bulls as Cumberland Gift, Marshal Joffre, Flashing Villager, Imported Baptom Elixir, and Imported Lord Aberdeen.[7] The surplus cattle of the herd not sold for breeding animals were slaughtered at the 101 Ranch packing plant which had a daily capacity of fifty cattle and one hundred hogs.

[3] *American Magazine,* July, 1928.
[4] *Rock Island Magazine,* November, 1926, p. 14.
[5] 101 Ranch Records, July, 1928.
[6] 101 Ranch Records, July, 1925.
[7] *Rock Island Magazine,* November, 1926.

The Hereford (white face) herd was made up of carefully selected cows from the best cattle in the country and the herd bull was purchased after many of the best herds in the country had been visited. The herd included 350 registered cattle, and thousands of high grade beef cattle. Since the Herefords were excellent beef cattle, they supplanted the longhorn stock on the ranges of the 101 Ranch, and for that reason, the herds numbered from five to ten thousand head annually.[8] It is an interesting fact that since that first trip in 1871 when Colonel George W. Miller, the father, drove Texas cattle northward to Oklahoma pastures, there had never been a year that the Miller brothers did not bring cattle north from Texas for their pastures. They had large herds of purebred, registered cattle, but brought up some cattle from Texas annually for grading and grazing purposes. The practice for many years was to raise feed and winter around 2,500 to 4,000 of these cattle, and to buy each spring enough additional cattle to eat up the surplus grass on the ranges of the ranch. The policy was to buy steers in the spring of the year, keep them two summers and one winter, and sell them in the fall when they were coming three years old. In that way all of the surplus feed that grew on the ranch was utilized while producing grain crops.

Under normal conditions the profits from marketing beef cattle fattened on the 101 Ranch amounted to thousands of dollars annually. As might be expected, there were times when the conditions for profits were not always favorable as a result of changing market prices. This was particularly true in the fall of 1918.[9] In 1916 the Miller brothers purchased one thousand head of Hereford calves and pastured them on the Bar L part of the ranch. The cattle were two years old in the spring of 1917 and it was in the fall of that year that Mr. Fern Sanders of a commission house in Kansas City came down to look them over and estimated they would bring $135 a head in Kansas City at that time. However, he advised that the War would bring the price of beef even higher and urged that they be kept over the winter and fed on corn raised on the ranch. Corn was selling at $1.50 a bushel. There is no way to estimate how much corn the cattle ate that winter, but it was typical of

8 Will Brooks to Ellsworth Collings, March 5, 1936.
9 Will Brooks to Ellsworth Collings, March 6, 1936.

Upper, herd of registered Dutch Belted cattle on the 101 Ranch; center, herd of registered hogs (world's largest Duroc breeding farm); lower, herd of spotted ponies raised on the 101 Ranch for the Indians

Colonel Joe Miller that when they were figuring up the losses, he said, "Oh, we can't count the corn because we raised that!" At any rate, when the cattle were shipped to Kansas City the fall of 1918, they brought only $60 a head instead of $135 which could have been gotten the previous fall. This was a direct loss of $75,000, not counting the corn, which was raised on the ranch.

The cattle business of the Miller brothers was not limited to the cattle handled on the 101 Ranch. It included large wholesale transactions in cattle which never set foot on the home ranch in Oklahoma. Thousands of cattle were purchased at one time, shipped to leased lands in Louisiana, Texas, Kansas, Arkansas, and in Old Mexico, and, after fattening, sold in large numbers to eastern markets.

What old-time western cowmen will describe to you as the "greatest single movement of cattle in forty years," and as one of the greatest in the history of the country, took place in Florida during the spring months of 1927 under the direction of the Miller brothers.

That spring, Florida put into effect new and drastic regulations to govern and clean up its previously unregulated cattle industry. Vast expanses of land in the state, unfenced and used for years as open ranges for grazing cattle, were to be subjected to the treatment known as "dipping." Other regulations were imposed, striking panic into the ranks of the state's big cattle raisers, who faced the necessity of expending tens of thousands of dollars. Cattle became a drug on the Florida market, as one big landowner after another quit the business and offered his herds for sale.

At the height of this crisis, two men arrived in Florida. One was big shouldered, browned, and bluff in his manner and speech, and he wore the broad-brimmed felt hat of the western cowman. The other, tall, slender, courteous, business-like, might have been a banker or a corporation president. Yet the two introduced themselves as brothers, Zack and George Miller.

They explained they were just a couple of Oklahoma farmers out to see if they could purchase a few head of cattle. The Florida landowners looked bored. They had trouble enough on their hands without being pestered by a pair of farmers who probably would consider a dozen heifers a big purchase. Florida, that spring, had herds to sell; not cows by the dozens but cows by the thousands.

Still, a buyer was a buyer, so the brothers were shown over the range. They saw young steers which, if fattened and properly marketed, would bring double and treble the price asked. They saw calves and heifers which needed only age to give them value. And they saw these in far-flung herds that numbered tens of thousands! Whole droves were as wild as buffalo, untouched as yet by rope or hand of man. Everywhere cattle were for sale in this state known to the world mainly because of its pleasure resorts.

Then these Oklahoma farmers began to buy. One pasturage contained a thousand cattle; they bought the thousand intact. Another herd was estimated at thrice that number. George Miller, the business-like one of the brothers, handled the financial details, while the big-shouldered Zack picked the cattle. They bought ranges full of cattle, by the hundreds and by the thousands. In one bold stroke they purchased a single herd that numbered nine thousand head, at which even sensation-weary Florida opened its eyes.

The amazed landowners were at a loss to know what the Miller brothers would do with all these cattle and how they would even be able to round them up. Zack Miller's answer was action. He sent a telegram to the 101 Ranch ordering a bunch of cowboys. A few days later a company of lean, tanned men and tough ponies of the Oklahoma prairies unloaded in Florida. The men were spurred and booted, lariats hung from their saddle horns, and bed rolls were strapped to their cantles. It was a hard-riding company, and the round-up began on their arrival.

At Old Town, at Clara, at Cross City, Hines, and Pineland the cattle were assembled. It was like the mobilization of an army, an event unparalleled since the great cattle drives of the Chisholm Trail back in the 1870's. For, when those cattle were counted, it was found that the Millers had purchased thirty-six thousand head!

In the old days of the West such herds were moved overland, feeding off the country as they went. These thirty-six thousand head had to be moved by railroad. Pastures had to be leased for them in which they could fatten, and pastures of

[76]

such size were not to be had offhand. The herd included two thousand cows with spring calves, requiring special handling and pasturage.

An army, indeed, but the Millers, it proved, were capable generals. In the middle of April, as if the whole movement had been carefully rehearsed for months, the cattle began to move westward out of Florida. In Alabama, near Montgomery, seven hundred acres of pasture had been leased for the cows and calves. In Louisiana, Kansas, Arkansas, Texas, and in other states of the South and of the Southwest, and even in Old Mexico, were other huge pasture lands under special lease for the purpose. Toward these scattered points the thousands from the Florida ranges moved by railroad.

They moved eight hundred cattle cars comprising thirty long trains. Animals already prime for the market were segregated and sold in the stockyards of cities through which they routed—sold by the carload, at auction, and invariably at a profit. Ten thousand head were transported to Oklahoma there to be pastured on the 101 Ranch and later transformed into beef in Miller-owned slaughter houses. By the first day of June not one cow, steer, or calf of the original thirty-six thousand was left in Florida—a feat unexcelled, if ever equaled, in the history of American ranching.

True to their Kentucky heritage, the Miller brothers were lovers of fine horses. In horses, as in everything else, they bred nothing but the best. The horse of Colonel Joe Miller was typical of the breeds maintained. "Pedro" was a piebald, a handsome horse, strangely striped black and white, with pink eye-rims and a leonine flowing mane. Colonel Joe related with great pride that he had refused an offer of $25,000 for "Pedro."[10]

After one had looked with some amazement on the beauty of "Pedro," one's eye was caught by the magnificent saddle on the horse's back. What a saddle! It was made of hand-carved leather, with the fanciest pommel imaginable, set off with generous trimmings of silver and gold, which sparkled and glowed with 246 diamonds and rubies. The saddle was a masterpiece of a Texas saddlemaker and cost Colonel Miller $10,000.[11]

[10] *Boston Post*, June 2, 1925.
[11] The S. D. Myres Saddle Company, El Paso, Texas, to Ellsworth Collings, October 17, 1936.

A pure blooded, desert bred Arabian stallion, "Nedjran" by name, was brought in 1907 to the 101 Ranch for experiments in breeding that attracted interest of horsemen throughout the southwest.[12] This stallion was purchased from Homer Davenport, the cartoonist, whose stock farm at Morris, New Jersey, contained many fine Arabians, bought by Davenport on visits to the interior of Arabia.

"Nedjran" was a chestnut, fourteen and a half hands high and twelve years old. He was imported from Arabia by Captain Gainsford of the English army in 1903 and attracted much attention in the international polo games of the English army in that year. In 1904 the horse was brought to America by Mr. Davenport. "Nedjran" was exhibited at the Lewis and Clarke exposition in 1905, and declared a perfect horse. He was chosen for the three thousand mile ride from Silverton, Oregon, to Morris Plains, in an endurance test conducted by officers of the regular army, and was ridden by Second Lieutenant E. R. Warner McCabe of the Sixth United States cavalry.

This stallion was bred to high grade western mares, thus combining the speed and grace of the thoroughbred with the strength and endurance of the western horse. The foals were put into training as soon as they could be saddled and a trainer taught them to follow a polo ball. Many of the ponies showed great aptitude for the game. The particularly intelligent players brought from $500 to $1,000 each on the market.

In addition to "Nedjran," Miller brothers contracted to buy sixteen more of Mr. Davenport's Arabian importations. The Arab sheik from whom Mr. Davenport bought most of his horses came to America as the guest of Mr. Davenport, and the two visited the 101 Ranch, where a display of western horses and western horsemanship was given for the entertainment of the sheik.

The Miller brothers did not engage as extensively in horse breeding as they did in cattle breeding. The horses, ponies, and mules needed to carry on the ranch enterprises were kept and raised for the most part, but many of the finer horses were purchased. The Indians loved spotted horses, and, for that reason, a herd of about two hundred spotted ponies were raised on the

12 *Ponca City Courier*, September 10, 1907.

[78]

ranch to supply that trade. The agricultural crops required four hundred and fifty mules, three hundred horses, while one hundred ponies were used in the cattle business, all exclusive of the horses used in the 101 Ranch show.[13] One hundred fine brood mares and one or more stallions and jacks were maintained for breeding purposes and for replenishing the work stock as a result of physical disability or sales. Huge stables housed the work horses and mules and two blacksmiths were kept busy shoeing them and doing other repair work. The sales were not limited to stock raised on the 101 Ranch, but included many wholesale transactions in horses, ponies, and mules which never set foot on the ranch.

The gross income from sales of beef cattle, horses, and mules amounted to thousands of dollars each year. For the five-year period of 1925 to 1930, the gross receipts from these sources totaled $654,232.38, distributed annually as follows: 1925, $124,524.74; 1926, $91,002.23; 1927, $152,293.34; 1928, $135,098.10; and 1929, $101,302.91.[14] The income from fat beef cattle contributed a large share of this sum. Fattening and marketing around ten thousand beef cattle was featured each year.

The Duroc-Jersey hog herds, several thousand in number, were all purebred and registered. There were hundreds of pens, lots, paddocks, and fields all fenced with woven wire, each containing from one to six or seven hundred head. It was nothing unusual to have from ten to fifteen thousand red hogs on the ranch at one time. The foundation stock of the Durocs was purchased at a cost exceeding $75,000.

In 1928, the 101 Ranch centered on hogs, to a greater extent than ever before. Already there were more than four thousand young pigs on the ranch, farrowed during the first six weeks of that year, and new arrivals made their appearance at the rate of several hundred a day. Ten thousand pigs in 1928 and twenty thousand in 1929, that was the aim of the Miller brothers.[15] They wanted an increased pig production because of the ranch packing house, where twenty thousand could easily be used annually.

[13] *Time,* February 11, 1929.
[14] 101 Ranch Records, 1925-1930.
[15] *Daily Oklahoman,* May 15, 1928.

One thousand sows were bred for farrowing the spring of 1928. That meant five thousand pigs born that springtime and another five thousand later in the season, or two crops of pigs annually. The Millers figured on an average of five pigs to the sow, when figuring on such a big number of sows. They had in 1929 two thousand sows for breeding purposes and raised two litters of pigs each, or a total of twenty thousand for that year.

In order to play a safety first program in raising so many pigs, the Miller brothers arranged five farms, approximately forty acres in size and each fenced with hog wire. One of the five was for pigs when they were weaned and another was used for pigs of the shoat size. Each farm was sown in alfalfa and Johnson grass and the hogs were fattened on these farms for the packing house.

What was claimed to be a record breaker on the 101 Ranch was a litter of thirteen pigs, born to a Duroc-Jersey mother, weighing a total of forty pounds at birth. This was a record by a considerable amount in that the usual weight of a litter was only half that total. Another record, of which Colonel Joe Miller was proud, was a litter of twenty-one pigs, born also to a Duroc-Jersey sow, which he had bought for $1,000. At nursing time, several times a day, the pigs were divided among other sows with pigs in order that all might have sufficient nourishment. The plan worked admirably and the entire litter lived.

Many of the best individuals and pedigrees known to the breed were in the Duroc-Jersey herds on the 101 Ranch. "101 Sensation" was one of the outstanding boars. He was purchased for use on the ranch at $7,500 and was regarded by expert judges as the longest, tallest, and most perfectly formed boar of his kind. Every cross in his pedigree included blood of a famous grand champion. This boar was assisted by another boar, of nation-wide fame, known as "Skyscraper." He was noted as a sire and was a full brother to the World's Grand Champion sow of 1922.

The Duroc-Jersey included a number of famous sows. "Stilts Lucille 5th" was the World's Grand Champion Duroc sow of 1922, Grand Champion National Swine Show, Grand Champion Missouri State Fair, and Grand Champion American Royal Livestock Show. "Miss Skyhigh," another famous sow, was First Junior Sow Pig at the Missouri State Fair in a class of forty-seven. At the 1922 American Royal "Miss Skyhigh" was First Junior Champion. "Skyscraper Queen," likewise, was First Prize Senior Pig of the 1922 American Royal. The herd included many other famous sows but these are typical of the blooded lines maintained on the ranch. Many of the brood sows cost $2,500 for a single animal.

The Miller brothers were successful in the hog business. Through breeding they produced many of the best individuals and pedigrees in the country, as evidenced by the high records achieved at the state and national shows. They were not only successful in breeding, but succeeded in handling an animal market of around twelve thousand Duroc-Jersey hogs. The income from the sales totaled many thousands of dollars annually. From 1925 to 1930, the total gross receipts from this source, exclusive of packing plant sales, amounted to $220,301.75, distributed as follows: 1925, $21,066.27; 1926, $52,560.41; 1927, $22,642.52; 1928, $27,345.63; and 1929, $96,687.12.[16]

The poultry department included ostriches, peafowls, turkeys, geese, guineas, pigeons, and chickens. Large, modern poultry houses, incubators, and brooders, were provided on the chicken ranch, and scientific methods were practiced in hatching, raising the young, and marketing the products. In poultry, as in everything else the Miller brothers bred nothing but the best. The White Leghorn flock was from the finest foundation stock and had been bred and mated by careful and painstaking work. The size of the flock varied in number from year to year. In 1927 it included 1,500 laying hens. Two years before, the number was considerably larger, including 7,500 laying hens, in addition to hundreds of ostriches, peafowls, geese, guineas, pigeons, and turkeys.

"Turkeys," says Colonel Joe Miller, "are the premier money crop of Oklahoma, a fact that is proved by all reports coming in at the Thanksgiving season of the year. In this particular portion of the state there are more turkeys than usual on the farms, although no large flocks excepting that which is raised annually at the 101 Ranch. A thirty-pound turkey is worth anywhere from nine to ten dollars at present. They are

[16] 101 Ranch Records, 1925 to 1930 inclusive.

[81]

hard to raise, but tell me any one line on the farm where the profit is so great.

"It would seem that turkeys can be raised in any and all portions of Oklahoma, the one main thing required being range. Turkeys must be unhampered in being able to cover a considerable territory. It was because of the range offered them that Oklahoma was really the last stamping ground of the wild turkey, and if it were possible for the average farmer to have a considerable field in which the turkeys could range and feed, and at the same time they could be prevented from wandering away, there would not be much difficulty in raising them.

"Old Oklahoma and Indian territories were long the home of the wild turkey, following the settling up of the surrounding states, and it is said by old hunters that the Osage country was the most prolific turkey section that the Southwest has ever known. They were so plentiful throughout the entire territory that frequently they composed all the meat that the army posts had for weeks at a time. When the first Santa Fe train was run through old Oklahoma, following its completion to Purcell, it encountered a flock of wild turkeys in a cut between where Guthrie and Oklahoma City now stand, and a number of the birds were killed under the wheels."[17]

The income from the flocks of chickens, geese, and turkeys amounted to a considerable sum annually. For the five-year period from 1925 to 1930, the total sales amounted to $13,-002.04 distributed as follows: 1925, $4,406.63; 1926, $4,274.-36; 1927, $2,121.61; 1928, $1,772.70; and 1929, $426.74.[18]

The Miller brothers took an active interest in the improvement of livestock in Oklahoma. The service of their purebred sires was at the disposal, free of any charge, of any owner of purebred females. It was their policy to furnish young breeding stock to farmers at popular prices in order to improve the grade of livestock in the immediate and surrounding vicinity, and many of the farmers took advantage of the opportunity to improve their stock.

"We have," wrote Miller brothers, "a herd of about six hundred registered and high grade Holstein cattle. We want to sell about three hundred and fifty of them and thought some

[17] *Daily Oklahoman*, February 6, 1927.
[18] 101 Ranch Records, 1925 to 1930.

[82]

of shipping one or two carloads to a number of different towns and holding small auction sales, but we have decided that it will be best for us to hold a large sale and sell 350 here at the 101 Ranch October 10, 1925, sale commencing at ten o'clock and lasting until after midnight if necessary to sell the cattle.

"In order to put the buyers from a distance on an equal basis with the local buyers we will pay the freight to any station in Oklahoma or Kansas provided any buyer or group of buyers will buy a carload of twenty or more.

"We would like to have you attend the sale and assist the buyers from your county in selecting the cattle. We know your funds available for traveling expenses are not sufficient for you to attend many sales, for that reason we will pay the railroad fare of all Oklahoma and Kansas county agents who attend the sale provided the farmers from their county buy twenty or more. Our cattle are all acclimated, about two hundred are giving milk and all of the others will freshen soon; approximately one hundred of them are two year old bred heifers.

"The sale includes twenty registered cows, ten registered heifers and twenty registered bulls, also three hundred grade cows and heifers. Under the prevailing rules these grade cows cannot be registered, however they are practically pure bred, all of them being sired by registered bulls and their dams for several generations were all sired by registered bulls.

"Every female offered in this sale with the exception of a few that have recently freshened have been bred to registered bulls. This large sale will give your friends a better opportunity to select good Holsteins than they would have in attending a half dozen or more other sales. We will be pleased to have you talk the matter over with your farmers and bring all those interested to the sale. We will send you any number of sale bills that you will post in banks and other public places."[19]

While everything from common farm stock to buffalo and ostriches were raised on the 101 Ranch, the principal income producing livestock were cattle, horses, mules, hogs, and poultry. Cattle and hogs were featured every year and the records indicate they never failed to yield large incomes. Many horses, ponies, and mules were raised annually to carry on the enter-

[19] Letter sent by Miller brothers of 101 Ranch to County Agents of Oklahoma, October 1, 1925.

prises of the ranch. The sales were not limited to stock raised, but included wholesale transactions in horses, ponies, and mules which never set foot on the ranch. While the income from the poultry varied from year to year, the receipts from this source never failed to yield an appreciable sum. The following table indicates the gross profits from livestock for the five year period, 1925-1930.[20]

ANNUAL SALES OF 101 LIVESTOCK FOR THE FIVE YEAR PERIOD, 1925-1930

YEAR	ANNUAL SALES OF LIVESTOCK			TOTAL FOR YEAR
	Cattle-Horses Mules	Hogs	Poultry	
1925	$124,524.74	$21,066.27	$4,406.63	$149,997.64
1926	91,002.23	52,560.41	4,274.36	147,837.00
1927	152,293.34	22,642.52	2,121.61	177,057.47
1928	135,098.10	27,345.63	1,772.70	164,216.43
1929	101,302.91	96,687.12	426.74	198,416.77
Total for Livestock	604,221.32	220,301.95	13,002.04	837,525.31

These figures reveal some interesting facts regarding livestock production on the 101 Ranch. They indicate, in the first place, that the livestock production for the five year period alone amounted to $837,525.31, exclusive of packing plant sales, more than three quarters of a million dollars. The sales totaled annually more than an average of $160,000 for this period. When this amount is considered along with the annual sales of around $175,000 for the meat packing plant, which utilized cattle and hogs raised on the ranch, the huge proportions of livestock production becomes an outstanding feature of the 101 Ranch.

In the second place, the figures of this table reveal constancy of livestock production. While the production in each division of livestock varied slightly from year to year, the in-

[20] 101 Ranch Records, 1925-1930.

[84]

come from sales remained constant for the entire period. For example, the total sales of cattle, horses, mules for the five year period amounted to $604,221.32, each year contributing large sums to this total. The same is equally true in the case of hogs and poultry. These facts indicate the Miller brothers practiced a planned policy with reference to the breeding, fattening, and marketing of livestock on the 101 Ranch.

VI

NOT only were the conditions of panic and the financial difficulties resulting from the failure of the Kansas City commission house forcing the end of the 101 Ranch as a strictly cattle ranch, but the changing nature of the Cherokee Strip foreshadowed the change to a farming region. The fact that the barbed-wire fence made its appearance was indicative that the days of free, unlimited range were almost over. And thus, while creditors were arriving at the ranch and driving away his cattle, Colonel Miller and his sons conferred over the future.

Joe was twenty-four years old at this time, Zack was sixteen, and George was only ten. Young as they were the sons were already the chief lieutenants of their father. They had established a business reputation and they had lost neither courage nor enterprise. That winter, in order to get money enough to carry them through until spring, they had sold their few remaining cows to the Indians, as related in the preceding chapter. During the long winter evenings father and sons sat about the fire and planned. They had the old horses and their acres of leased prairie land as yet untouched by the plow. Homesteaders had already proved the fertility of that prairie land.

And in the course of those conferences around the fire, the idea of a great farm was born. It was not to be the usual type of farm of a few hundred acres; no, it was to be a regal successor to the cattle ranch. Their herds had numbered thousands of head. Why could not their crops mount to thousands of bushels? It required no more knowledge to plow and plant a thousand acres in wheat than it did to plant a hundred, or ten!

They needed implements and seed grain, and money which would supply both. It was known in those parts that the Miller word was good, they paid what they owed, if not in this year then in the next, or the next. When winter broke in 1894, the needed plows were ready, the seed grain was on hand, and workmen waiting. Old Colonel Miller himself stuck the nose of the first plow into the dirt.

There was no time to prepare a variety of crops. In one grand gamble with soil and season they planted wheat. Yet it was not a blind gamble, for wheat had already proved itself the king of crops of the West. The wheat came up, almost five thousand acres of it. By June the harvest was under way, and never before had there been such a harvest in that new country. The prairie acres yielded seventy thousand bushels of wheat— and wheat at Chicago was $1.20 a bushel![1]

With this start the Millers went on farming, putting in corn, oats, alfalfa, and other crops, as well as wheat. They bought calves to fatten, added horses, mules, hogs, geese, ducks and buffalo to their flocks. Every year they extended their operations, and every year they put in some new crop. From that wheat harvest the Cattle Millers became the Farmer Millers. From this time onward the ranch became a diversified farm and everything that soil would bear was grown on its land.

The Miller brothers not only produced extensive agricultural products, but they were scientific along these lines, continually producing new and better types. After turning to the blooded breeds of livestock, they followed breeding only along the best lines of the strongest ancestral record. A new type of corn was produced after long years of experimenting by crossing high grade white corn with the speckled squaw corn, grown extensively in the past by the Indians. A mixture of rye and barley seed was obtained after several seasons of planting barley and rye together, thus producing a brand that provides the best winter pasturage. The Japanese persimmon, the paper shell pecans, and the finer types of mulberries, plums and grapes were grafted on the Oklahoma natives, gradually building up a finer and better line of products that were Oklahoma acclimated. Fruit trees were imported, grafted, and regrafted, and with scientific methods applied every step of the way orchards were developed equal to any found in the recognized fruit belts of the country. The production of new types and breeds was the special work of Colonel Joe Miller, and so great was his achievement along these lines that the Oklahoma State Agri-

[1] *Literary Digest,* August 4, 1928.

cultural and Mechanical College planned as a part of its official agricultural course to have its classes spend at least two weeks annually at the ranch in order to witness the practical application of theories in the production of new types and breeds of farm products.

As a result of the first wheat crop on the 101 Ranch in 1894, northern Oklahoma turned out in a short time to be a great wheat-growing section. Since that year the Millers planted each autumn from two to nine thousand acres. The regular acreage usually included four thousand acres. George L. Miller estimated the total at 126,000 acres up to 1927.[2] Basing the total acreage at this figure in the thirty-two years, and averaging the yield at eight bushels an acre, which George L. Miller believed reasonable, the total number of bushels harvested for that period amounted to 1,008,000, and at an average of seventy-five cents a bushel the Millers received from wheat alone $756,000.

George L. Miller fixed the average price of wheat during the thirty-two years at seventy-five cents a bushel. One season the Millers sold their crop for thirty-five cents a bushel, and one fall they sold for $2.73. When Joseph Leiter made his famous plunge on the Chicago Board of Trade and wheat went from fifty cents to a dollar a bushel, the Millers sold ten carloads produced on the ranch for a dollar a bushel.

The amount of wheat production on the 101 Ranch is indicated by the men, horses, and machinery required to harvest the wheat. Five hundred men, six hundred horses and mules, fifty binders, and ten threshing machines were used by the Millers night and day in harvesting the crop.[3] The ranch has grown in a single season a record crop of more than two-hundred thousand bushels of wheat from nine thousand acres.

In addition to the regular wheat acreage, harvested annually, the Miller brothers always planted at least one-thousand acres additional each autumn for winter and spring pasture. This acreage was, as a rule, plowed under in the spring and planted to other crops. The wheat land was always replanted in short crops each year after the regular wheat crop was taken off, thus making the land bear two crops in one season.

[2] George L. Miller to the *Daily Oklahoman,* February 6, 1927.
[3] 101 Ranch Records, 1925-1930.

Corn was another major cereal crop produced on the 101 Ranch. The crop acreage usually averaged five thousand acres.[4] Under normal conditions the annual yield was around 150,000 bushels.[5] The Millers produced in a single season a record crop of 240,000 bushels of corn from six thousand acres. One cornfield of a thousand acres of fertile land produced annually an estimated yield of 75,000 bushels.[6] The season of 1923 was probably the worst ever experienced. During May and June it rained continually, making it impossible to cultivate the corn properly. Four thousand acres of corn planted on the bottom land were washed out. Then the rain stopped and from early June to the middle of August there was no rain, and fully 90 per cent of the corn in northern Oklahoma was a complete failure on account of dry weather and hot winds. As a result of producing and using seed corn, especially adapted to drouth conditions, the Miller brothers succeeded in growing several hundred acres, averaging from thirty-five to fifty bushels an acre.[7]

Two distinctly new varieties of corn were originated by the Miller brothers. These varieties were especially adapted to the conditions of the Southwest and they attributed their successful corn yields to the use of these varieties. One variety was the White Wonder corn; the other the Improved Indian Squaw corn.

The White Wonder was a large white corn, not deep, but set close together on a large, long cob. Through experiments the Miller brothers demonstrated that a short grain on a large cob would withstand more dry weather than a deep set kernel on a small cob. The explanation is that a long cob holds more sap upon which the grains may draw during the growing season than a small cob does. The foliage of the White Wonder corn was heavy, the stalks were large and soon shaded the ground, thus conserving the moisture and enabling the plant to withstand drouth to a greater extent—a vital requirement in the Southwest. Many varieties of corn were brought from northern seed houses and planted beside plots of the White

[4] 101 Ranch Records, 1923.
[5] George L. Miller to the *Daily Oklahoman,* February 6, 1927.
[6] Colonel Zack T. Miller to Ellsworth Collings, October 24, 1934.
[7] George L. Miller to the *Daily Oklahoman,* May 13, 1928.

[89]

Wonder variety in order to test experimentally the comparative yield. Under exactly the same conditions and care it was found the imported varieties made yields of from five to fifteen bushels less an acre than the White Wonder corn.

The Improved Indian Squaw corn was a hybrid, produced by cross-breeding the White Wonder and a corn which the Indians grew before the coming of white men. When the Millers first settled in Oklahoma they observed the Indians raising a small variety of corn, mottled in color. The Indians merely scratched the ground and planted the corn with a hoe; they did not cultivate the crop at all, yet they always raised sufficient corn for themselves and their ponies. It was remarkable how this corn withstood dry weather. The Indians always had a supply of feed when the settlers in the early days were unable to grow corn at all.

In crossing this variety of corn with the White Wonder, the Miller brothers found experimentally that the new variety retained all the drouth-resisting qualities of the Indian corn and increased its size to almost that of standard varieties. They found that this new type of corn would mature seventy-five days after planting, and make a crop in any season when Kafir corn would grow. They planted the improved Indian Squaw corn in the summer, after a crop of wheat had been harvested from the same ground and when not damaged from chinch bugs it produced seventy-five bushels an acre.

The Miller Brothers contended that in growing corn the first essential was good seed, and then careful and intelligent cultivation. They experimented with seed corn from almost every section of the country, and demonstrated that corn brought from the northern states would not become acclimated the first season, and in some cases would not become acclimated at all. At first, in conducting these experiments, they lost thousands of dollars because of short yields when northern seed was used. Later, they reserved a forty acre plot for a demonstration farm, while their large acreages were planted with proven varieties which prevented further failures.

The reputation of the corn grown by the Miller brothers spread until their seed corn was used widely in Oklahoma and Texas. They erected a large seed-corn elevator at the ranch headquarters and equipped it with all modern cleaning and grading machinery. During the fall and winter months an average of one thousand bushels of finished seed corn passed daily from the elevator to the store rooms. In 1911 one large seed concern in Texas contracted for fifty thousand bushels and many milling and elevator companies in Oklahoma purchased car lots for distribution to the farmers of their locality in order to increase corn production and secure a better quality of corn for milling. The Miller brothers in one season sold 60,000 bushels of selected White Wonder seed corn that was shipped to practically every corn-producing state. They received an average of $3.50 a bushel for the seed corn.[8] They sold no corn on the regular market since they fed thousands of cattle and hogs annually on the ranch. Before feeding operations began each year, they carefully selected every bushel of corn that was to be used for seed, and the cull corn was fed to the stock.

Oats was a third major cereal crop produced annually by the Millers, largely for feed purposes. The acreage usually included 2,500 acres and yielded thousands of bushels. Approximately fifteen hundred acres of grain sorghums were grown, consisting of kafir, milo, and cane; in addition, from three hundred to one thousand acres of barley and rye were planted for pasture and feed.

The annual income from the grain crops was enormous. Since the feed crops, including corn, oats, barley, rye, cane, and milo, were used to feed thousands of hogs and cattle, the income was largely from wheat and seed corn. The ranch sold nothing to the commercial market except livestock and wheat.[9] The rest of the grain crops were fed to the stock on the ranch. For the years 1925 to 1930, the total sales for these crops amounted to $388,364.44, distributed as follows: 1925, $86,-004.73; 1926, $53,526.55; 1927, $61,536.87; 1928, $81,176.-16; and 1929, $106,120.09.[10]

Cotton was produced in large quantities during some seasons, while during others it was not planted or failed to yield

[8] 101 Ranch Records, 1911.

[9] Colonel Joe Miller to *St. Louis Post-Dispatch,* June 11, 1905.

[10] The five year period, 1925-1930, was selected because it represents a normal period of farm crop production, and for that reason reveals the extent of this phase of the 101 Ranch.

[91]

an income. From 1925 to 1930, inclusive, the records indicate income from this source for only two years: 1925, $89.85, and 1926, $31,875.[11] Doubtless large crops were produced prior to this time since reports indicate that 2,500 acres were annually planted to cotton.[12] After years of experimenting, the Miller brothers succeeded in producing an early maturing variety of short staple cotton which they named "Early Bird." This variety produced and matured when planted as late as the middle of June. In addition to this type, a new variety of long staple cotton was developed. This variety was not as early or as quick maturing as the "Early Bird" variety, but produced as many pounds of seed cotton to an acre and ginned 40 per cent lint.

The hay crops consisted of thousands of acres of native grass, two to three hundred acres of sudan, two thousand acres of alfalfa, and four hundred acres of sweet clover. Approximately ten thousand tons of hay were harvested annually, requiring the use of twenty mowing machines.[13] The hay crops were grown for feed purposes and the Miller brothers annually filled eighteen large silos with enough feed to winter several thousand head of cattle.

The garden vegetables were grown on the 101 Ranch in large quantities. Peas, beans, radishes, onions, tomatoes, cabbage, lettuce, turnips, and beets were produced in huge quantities for use on the ranch and for commercial purposes. One hundred thousand Bermuda onions and twenty-five thousand cabbage plants were seeded one year.[14] Large sweet potato hot beds were maintained and as many as twenty-five thousand bushels of sweet potatoes and approximately as many bushels of Irish potatoes were grown annually.[15] Hot and cold storage potato warehouses were erected at the ranch headquarters to store the huge crops of Irish and sweet potatoes. The income from the garden truck amounted to several thousand dollars annually. For the years 1925 to 1930, the total receipts from this source were $27,663.39, distributed as follows: 1925,

11 101 Ranch Records, 1925-1930, inclusive.
12 George L. Miller to the *Daily Oklahoman*, February 6, 1927.
13 Colonel Joe Miller to *St. Louis Post-Dispatch*, June 11, 1905.
14 101 Ranch Records, 1925.
15 Colonel Joe Miller to *St. Louis Post-Dispatch*, June 11, 1905.

Upper, harvesting the wheat crop on the 101 Ranch; center, White Wonder corn on the 101 Ranch; lower, harvesting apples on the 101 Ranch

$3,342.61; 1926, $5,441.51; 1927, $7,396.51; 1928, $5,301.55; and 1929, $6,181.21.

Watermelons, cantaloupes, cucumbers, and pumpkins were grown in large quantities. "The ranch has," reported Colonel Joe Miller, "twenty-five hundred acres in melons this year, which we will ship out by the trainloads. Our watermelons are famous, and the seed alone is worth $2.50 an ounce. My father used to have a sign in the melon patch, 'five dollar fine for anyone who goes through this patch without taking a melon.' That still goes. Anyone can come and eat and carry home all the melons he pleases—or anything else, for that matter."[16]

Large quantities of the vegetables, melons, cantaloupes, and fruits produced on the 101 Ranch were sold at the market maintained at the headquarters. Thousands of tourists stopped to purchase fresh fruits, melons, cantaloupes, and vegetables, which were put up in the canning factory located at the headquarters. The income from the market amounted to a considerable sum annually. For the five year period from 1925 to 1930 the total sales of the market amounted to $29,342.30, distributed as follows: 1925, $1,142.11; 1926, $7,311.01; 1927, $11,107.41; 1928, $3,846.26; and 1929, $5,935.49.

The horticultural production was in keeping with the agricultural. The ranch produced annually an abundance of apples, plums, peaches, pears, and cherries. The apple orchard originally started through an accident. Nearly thirty years ago an enthusiast shipped two carloads of nursery apple trees to Winfield, Kansas, with a view of placing them with the farmers and orchardists of that locality. When the shipment arrived, however, the owner could not pay the freight bill and it looked for a while as though the shipment might be a total loss. Colonel Joe Miller happened to be in Winfield on a business mission and learned of the apple tree shipment. He paid the freight bill and had the trees sent on down to the 101 Ranch. With fifty men under his direction he set out the entire two carloads, working as rapidly as possible in order to save the stock.

In the general mixup that had occurred, the trees had become mixed also, and Colonel Miller could do nothing else but set them out just as he had received them. As a result, various kinds of apples were scattered over the entire orchard, but they

16 Colonel Joe Miller to *St. Louis Post-Dispatch,* June 11, 1905.

happened to be of sufficient varieties so that the orchard produced fruit from June to November every year.

Originally the orchard covered 160 acres. The tract was located on the south bank of Salt Fork River, about two miles east of the "White House." The Salt Fork current happened to strike the high bank when the apple trees were planted, and in the intervening years a considerable portion of the quarter section was eaten away. Today, however, there is a fine orchard of more than one hundred acres and approximately 6,000 trees. The orchard began to yield from a commercial point of view a few years after planting, when the first crop was 3,000 bushels. The yield increased gradually every year thereafter until the annual crop was around 25,000 bushels. Colonel Joe Miller estimated the trees, which he had bought for the freight bill, had brought in money to the ranch a total of $100,000 up to 1927.[17] The trees cost him less than two cents each. The orchard paid him $205 an acre annually and he estimated the value of the orchard at $1,000 an acre.

When the trees were first set out, Colonel Miller had them placed sixteen feet apart in rows that were thirty-two feet apart. He soon came to the conclusion that the trees were too close together and with the use of an eighty horse power tractor, he pulled out every other tree, thus leaving the remaining trees thirty-two feet apart each way. The orchard was sprayed five times during the growing season, and was pruned every winter. The small limbs were cut out only and the large limbs were never molested. That kept the trees strong and healthy.

The 101 Ranch orchard picking started about September 1, and continued to November 1. The entire crop was disposed of at the ranch market. Not an apple was shipped except by local people who purchased a few boxes and sent them away to friends. Many people visited the ranch and bought their winter supplies from the orchard.

The Millers won many prizes and premiums on their apple displays at both county and state fairs, and sometimes in competition with apples from famed districts. "We have," said Colonel Joe Miller, "a hard time of it, sometimes, making people who visit the fairs believe that we actually produced the apples in Oklahoma. It seems difficult for them to believe that

[17] *Daily Oklahoman,* February 6, 1927.

it can be done here."[18] The big orchard was disked to wheat every fall, following the picking season. After the wheat became large enough to afford good pasture, hogs were turned in to fatten on the pasture, and any fallen apples that might have been left. In the spring, the wheat was turned under, thus fertilizing the land.

Joe Miller had his own ideas, gained from experimenting with this big orchard, in regard to what varieties of apples would do best in his section of Oklahoma. Some varieties were much more susceptible to disease than others. Because of having so many varieties scattered throughout the orchard, he was able to pick up what he believed to be the best. In this section, he found the apples to plant were Ben Davis, Grimes Golden, Winesaps, Delicious, and York's Imperial. Other varieties seemingly yielded just as well, but they were more subject to blotch and other diseases.

Blackberries, raspberries, gooseberries, and strawberries were annually produced for ranch and commercial purposes. The vineyard included twelve thousand large producing grapevines. A large part of the horticultural products were used in the 101 Ranch canning factory, which also made peach and apple butter, jellies of all kinds, cider, and vinegar.

The income from the horticultural crops, exclusive of fruits sold at the 101 Ranch market, amounted to several thousand dollars annually. For the years 1925 to 1930, the total receipts from these crops amounted to $59,617.44, distributed as follows: 1925, $10,091.07; 1926, $6,104.15; 1927, $22,842.42; 1928, $9,755.04; and 1929, $10,824.76.[19]

The most immediate results from the extensive grafting experiments on the 101 Ranch were from the persimmon trees on which the Japanese persimmon was grafted. The entire grove of several thousand trees on the ranch was changed from native to the Japanese variety. The bearing wood grew over six feet the entire year and in some instances actually bore fruit the first summer. The almost immediate bearing of the new wood made this variety very profitable.

The experiments proved that the Japanese persimmon withstood the winters in this section of the country, consequently

[18] *Daily Oklahoman,* February 6, 1927.
[19] 101 Ranch Records, 1925-1930, inclusive.

opening up a new source of income for Oklahoma. The persimmon was one of the big native wild crops of the state. George L. Miller estimated that there were 100,000 acres of these trees in the State, with thousands of trees down the Arkansas River valley between Ponca City and Tulsa.[20] The native persimmon had no market value, but the crop from the budded trees sold rapidly and at a price that was in excess of that generally paid for the best acreages.

In addition to success with Japanese persimmons, the Millers had equal success in grafting English walnuts and the finest varieties of black walnuts on native walnut trees. "All the limbs," said Colonel Joe Miller, "were taken from two dozen English walnut trees and grafted on native black walnut trees, and also the same number from the very finest variety of black walnuts were budded on the native trees. The bearing wood that these trees produce will be used to transform the big native walnut grove on the ranch.

"We have been asked why we are budding the black walnut as well as the English variety, and the answer is that the kernels of the black walnut have a greater commercial value than those of the English or any other nuts. The finest variety of black walnut is the result of breeding until a very large walnut has been obtained, the shell of which is not so heavy or thick."[21]

Twenty-five hundred native pecan trees on the 101 Ranch were top-worked one spring, budding them with the soft-shelled variety. It took about five years before these trees produced to any extent. All the limbs were cut off the native tree and one scion of the soft-shelled pecan inserted. "We planted," Colonel Joe Miller said, "25,000 pecans in 1924 and 10,000 walnuts, and when these trees reach sufficient size they will be grafted and eventually we expect to have a big assortment."[22] He was very enthusiastic in regard to the future not only of the pecan, but of the walnuts and persimmons.

Merely as an experiment the Millers grafted the paw-paw onto the native persimmon tree, sending back to Indiana to get scions from paw-paw trees. In accomplishing this grafting, they found the seeds of plants or trees crossed should be simi-

[20] *Daily Oklahoman,* February 6, 1927.
[21] Colonel Joe Miller to the *Daily Oklahoman,* February 6, 1927.
[22] Colonel Joe Miller to the *Daily Oklahoman,* February 6, 1927.

[96]

lar. One of the many particular features achieved in grafting apple trees was in changing the Missouri pippin into Grimes Golden. The Missouri pippin was a fine producer in this climate, but was subject here to blotch and blight, whereas the golden variety was not so affected.

By far the most important forestation program in Oklahoma, and perhaps in the entire Southwest, was undertaken by the Miller brothers in transplanting 50,000 year-old black walnut trees. Colonel Joe Miller directed the work. He used a regular digger machine such as nurserymen use and pulled it with eight horses. This made it possible to uproot the yearlings very rapidly whereas by hand it would have required many men a very long time.

These walnuts, selected nuts, were planted in the fall, and in a year's time the trees were eighteen inches high with roots that extended about three feet from the trunks. The trees were reset along the banks of the Salt Fork and were placed fifteen feet apart in rows that were thirty feet apart. The first row of trees paralleled the river at a point just above the high water mark and another row was planted thirty feet farther away.

Ninety per cent of the trees transplanted lived, since walnuts are not difficult to transplant at that age, although difficult later because of the long tap roots. Several years ago Colonel Miller set out twenty Thomas walnuts, a black variety having considerably more meat. He used the new growth on the Thomas trees to graft on several thousand of the common variety transplanted.

"Very few black walnuts are being planted at present," Colonel Miller said, "although it sells for more than any other kind; with newly patented machines to crack the nuts and extract the kernels, it is not difficult to put the meat on the market."[23]

While everything from common farm crops to figs and okra were grown on the 101 Ranch, the principal income crops were wheat, seed corn, garden vegetables, cotton, fruits, and poultry. Huge quantities of oats, corn, barley, rye, kafir, cane, milo, and hay were produced annually, but these crops were fed to the livestock on the ranch. Wheat was the one major crop grown every year by the Miller brothers and the records indicate it

[23] *Daily Oklahoman,* February 6, 1927.

never failed to yield a large part of the income. The policy of the Miller brothers was to sell only livestock and wheat. Consequently, the income from these sources exceeded all others.

The following table indicates sales of farm products for the five year period, 1925-1930.[24]

ANNUAL SALES OF 101 RANCH FARM CROPS FOR THE FIVE YEAR PERIOD
1925-1930

| YEARS | ANNUAL SALES OF FARM CROPS | | | | | TOTAL FOR YEAR |
	Grain	Fruit	Vegetables	Market	Cotton	
1925	$86,004.75	$10,091.07	$3,342.61	$1,142.11	$ 89.85	$100,570.39
1926	53,526.55	6,104.15	5,441.51	7,311.01	31,775.20	104,158.42
1927	61,536.87	22,842.42	7,396.51	11,107.41		102,883.21
1928	81,176.18	9,755.04	5,301.55	3,846.28		100,079.05
1929	106,120.09	10,824.76	6,181.21	5,935.49		129,061.45
Total for crop	388,364.44	59,617.44	27,663.39	29,342.30	31,865.05	536,852.62

The figures of this table reveal some interesting facts with reference to farm crop production on the 101 Ranch. In the first place, they indicate the farm crop production for the five year period alone amounted to $536,852.62, more than a half-million dollars. The annual income from this source totaled more than one hundred thousand dollars. When this amount is considered, along with the large quantities of corn, oats, barley, rye, kafir, cane, milo, and hay fed annually to the livestock on the ranch, the huge proportions of the farm crop production becomes increasingly evident. In the second place, the figures reveal constancy of farm crop production. While the production in each crop varied slightly, the sales receipts each year remained fairly uniform for the entire period. The same is true of the other farm crops, except cotton. These facts in-

24 101 Ranch Records, 1925-1930.

[98]

dicate the Miller brothers practiced a planned policy with reference to farm crop production on the 101 Ranch.

The Miller brothers used modern equipment and machinery in the production of farm crops on the 101 Ranch. They practiced farm economics and wise plans of diversified farming. There were no waste and slip-shod methods. They applied business methods in every way possible to the farm operations.

"I drove two miles," says M. G. Cunniff, "through a single cornfield, walked through a young peach orchard and saw the 250 bushels of sweet potatoes that had been grown between the rows of peach trees. I admired the economy of planting a pear orchard in the barn yard where the ducks and geese were waddling about. Here was a berry patch of several acres. There a stand of 10,000 ash and sycamore trees, just planted, were facing the approach of their first winter. Everywhere one turned were evidences of progress, of well-thought-out experiments.

"In the ranch-house is the central office of the big farm. It is like a city business office. All documents pertaining to the industry are filed in systematic order—Indian leases, accounts, records. Any paper can be found in a moment. The telephone on the desk connects with every foreman on the ranch over thirty-five miles of private wire, and conversations are frequent with the towns throughout Oklahoma and Indian Territory by long-distance service. Joe Miller has several times telephoned to Chicago. Nor is the business system less orderly than the appointments. Joe Miller attends to the farming operations and does the dealing with his Indian landlords and wards. Zack Miller attends to the cattle, the mules, the hogs, and the horses. George attends to the office routine and the books. But there is no formality. Every brother takes interest in all parts of the business. Tasks are interchangeable and are distributed with fraternal good feeling.

"The three men manage as many as 500 hands in the busiest season. Some little distance to one side of the ranch-house are the bunk-house and cook-house for the employees. Scattered over the ranch are four other similar camps. There are fifty cow-punchers to attend to the 15,000 cattle and 450 mules. Huge stables house as many of the 300 work-horses as are now turned out on the range. Two blacksmiths are kept busy shoe-

[99]

ing horses and repairing farm machinery. One outfit of three men constantly rides the 150 miles of wire fence. There are barns and granaries and tool houses. Yet I was amazed to see an acre field filled with expensive machinery, gang plows, harrows, binders, threshers, exposed to the weather.

" 'It's economy,' said Joe Miller. 'On a farm of ordinary size, one of those would last for years. We use up one in a single season, or in two seasons at most. Then we buy new ones. It would cost more to house them than we could save. And what is more, that big steam plow over there is discarded. We used it for a while, but we found that it was cheaper to plow with mules.'[25] A dozen similar remarks showed that this quiet Oklahoma farmer had studied the science of his business as thoroughly as a Pittsburgh manufacturer studies the cost of steel-making.

"With the steam plow abandoned, spring plowing now goes on with teams of five mules. It gives a vision of farming on the hugest scale to see nine teams move down the long rows of a 9,000 acre field, turning three furrows apiece of the rich red earth. When the hay is ready to cut, twenty machines mow the thousands of acres of grass and the 500 acres of alfalfa. In some places they go five miles before they turn to come back. Ten thousand tons a year is the crop. Forty-two reapers and binders garner the wheat, and it takes five busy steam threshers to thresh it. Binding twine is bought by the carload —$3,000 worth at a time. Last year was a poor one for wheat throughout Oklahoma. The Millers' 9,000 acres produced only 200,000 bushels. Yet so careful are their methods of planting and cultivating that they sold all but 20,000 bushels of this for seed wheat at ninety-five cents a bushel. The average yield of corn in Oklahoma is twenty-five bushels to the acre. The Millers' 3,000 acres of corn produce fifty bushels to the acre, ten of which Joe Miller ascribes to careful seed selection. The wheat and the best of the corn are sold at a high price for seed. The hay, the alfalfa, the oats, and the rest of the corn are fed to the stock. Corn is put into automatic feeding racks, and the hay and the alfalfa are piled in stacks out in the rolling pastures; and the beeves, the mules, and the hogs are permitted to

[25] The ranch in later years used large gasoline tractors in the production of farm crops.

[100]

eat as much as they wish. In addition to this, the stock are turned into the alfalfa fields between the five cuttings and they are grazed also on the growing wheat. What they manage to consume merely thins the growth down to the proper luxuriance. Last year carloads of melons were shipped from the 1,200 acre melon patch, some to be marketed and some to be crushed for the seeds. . . . .

"With all these activities the operating expenses of the ranch amount to about $100,000 a year. The employees range from college men in search of health to cowmen from the Texas Panhandle, and Indians graduated from the Carlisle and Chilocco schools. The work does not stop for Sunday, but is managed on the twenty-six-day system—that is, with a four-days lay-off out of every thirty. In the harvest rush a bonus is given to the men who do not take their lay-off. Frequently $3 or $5 is added to the monthly wages of any man who does especially good work for the month. This keeps them all keyed up. They receive their outfit and their "chuck" or board. Then they are paid according to their efficiency. No questions are asked when a man applies for a job. He is set to work under sharp eyes. He is discharged in short order if he does not "make good" as a capable, orderly worker."[26]

[26] *World's Work,* February, 1906.

VII

IN earlier geological periods, when the ocean covered all or most of the land, the creatures of the sea lived their span of life in the plant life of the sea, and at their death their remains sank to the bottom, which were deposited through ages on the floor of the sea. In time, because of the great pressure of the water, these remains became a part of the enormous deposits of oleaginous shale, with layers of porous sand above and below. Later upheavals brought these beds of shale and sand above the ocean level and folded and bent them, forming hills and valleys, most of which have since been eroded. The larger upheavals formed mountains.

To the untrained individual, the surface gives no indication of the former hills and valleys caused by these upheavals, but a study of the layers of the rock outcropping on the hillsides tells the story of their origin to trained geologists, who call the former upheavals of the earth's surface anticlines, and the valleys between the upheavals, synclines.

When the upheavals were in progress, the pressure on those oil bearing shales became greater, until the oil was pressed from the shales into the porous sands. Since these sands contained salt water from the sea in the synclines, or depressions, the oil naturally sought the highest places in the sand above the water, and the gas, which was generated from the oil, found the top of the anticline, or highest place in the natural reservoir.

Mr. E. W. Marland, who came to Oklahoma from Pennsylvania, discovered in 1908 one of these anticlines on the 101 Ranch lands. By practical application of geological knowledge he had previously discovered an oil field in the east; and he believed he could find other oil fields in the new country. On his way west he stopped in Chicago to visit relatives, and while there he chanced to meet Colonel F. R. Kenney, who had been stationed in Oklahoma in the recruiting service. Colonel Kenney was a friend of George L. Miller and arrangements were soon made for Mr. Marland to visit the 101 Ranch. Together, they came from Chicago to the 101 Ranch and, while visiting there, Mr. Marland tramped the ranch property and the surrounding vicinity. He studied the outcropping of the rocks and walked for miles over the broad and rolling prairie of the 101 Ranch, carefully inspecting the formations. And here is how the anticline was discovered, in the words of Mr. Marland:

"George L. Miller was showing me around the Ranch one day and we rode up a hill to see the cemetery of the Ponca Indians. The Indians placed their dead on wicker platforms above the ground.

"I noticed by the outcropping of the rock on the hill that the hill was not only a topographical high but also a geological high. A little further investigation showed it to be a perfect geological dome."[1]

At that time the 101 Ranch included about one hundred thousand acres. Approximately ten thousand acres were owned outright by the Miller brothers, and the remainder of the lands were held under lease from the Ponca Indians. Convinced that the Indian cemetery was a distinct oil formation, Mr. Marland told George L. Miller he would agree to drill a test well if he would give him a lease on the 101 Ranch lands and help him obtain the necessary leases from the Ponca Indians.

Much time was consumed with the tribesmen in the section when the landowners were known as Running-After-Arrow, Willie-Cries-for-War, Peter-Knows-the-Country, Thomas-on-Two-Lean-Bears'-Ear, and Little-Man-Stands-up. "We had a lot of trouble with the Indians," related Mr. Marland, "before we got a lease on their cemetery and on the surrounding land. But after a lot of palaver, smoking and squatting we got the lands leased up and were ready to drill."[2] In February, 1909, the first location was staked.

The leases obtained included 10,000 acres in the 101 Ranch and 4,800 acres from the Ponca Indians. The Poncas sold a lease on their cemetery tract to George L. Miller, provided he would not drill within the area where they were burying their dead. Miller gave a half interest in the lease to Marland on

[1] *Oklahoma City Times,* July 20, 1934.
[2] *Oklahoma City Times,* July 21, 1934.

the condition that he would do the drilling. It is an interesting fact that this block of leases embraced the entire Ponca field. No other company ever drilled a producer in that field except under sublease from Mr. Marland.

The first well was drilled near the headquarters of the 101 Ranch under the most adverse conditions. There were no heavy draft teams in the country, nothing but light horses and cow ponies. Lumbering teams of oxen with their heavy wooden yokes had to be used to haul rig timbers, tools, boilers, and casings from the railroad at Bliss (the present town of Marland) to the well location. The nearest supply house was at Tulsa, 125 miles distant. The well was drilled with old Manila cable and old-fashioned drills to a depth of 2,700 feet; and was abandoned after locating five different oil and gas sands, all of which were non-producers.

After this failure, a location was made for a second well about five miles from the first, and higher up on the anticline. This location was on land belonging to the 101 Ranch, known as the Iron Thunder tract. The conditions under which this well was drilled were almost as bad as those for the first. At a depth of five hundred feet an extraordinarily large flow of gas was struck in the spring of 1910.[3] The well had a flow of between 11,000,000 and 12,000,000 cubic feet of gas every twenty-four hours. A gas line four miles in length was laid by the Miller brothers between the well and headquarters of the 101 Ranch, piping the gas through wheat and alfalfa fields, leaving pipe connections every one-fourth mile so that the gas could be used as fuel in handling the crops grown on the land.

An old Ponca Indian, whose name was Running-After-Arrow, witnessed the bringing in of the first gas well on the 101 Ranch. He had never seen one before. George L. Miller, who was present, explained to him in the Indian language what a gas well was, but the Indian could not understand the roaring gas coming from the interior of the earth. He looked upon it as an evil omen, as a sign of coming destruction. "Uh-h, no good, no good," he grunted.[4] "Beautiful country all die now. Cattle die. Ponies die. No good, no good. Beautiful country soon all gone."

[3] George L. Miller to F. S. Barde, December 26, 1910.
[4] E. W. Marland to *Oklahoma City Times*, July 21, 1934.

No one realized it then, but the Indian's prophecy soon came true. The plains became spotted with oil derricks, and herds of cattle gradually gave way to huge tank farms. The very site on which the Continental refinery now stands was then occupied by cattle pens.

At about this time, Mr. Marland organized the 101 Ranch Company, in order to develop on a large scale the oil and gas which geological indications made him certain were present. Associated with him in this company were W. H. McFadden, J. C. McCaskey, George L. Miller, Colonel F. R. Kenney, James J. McGraw, and a number of other friends of Pittsburgh, Pennsylvania. This company continued in operation in the Ponca field until 1917, when it was absorbed by the Marland Refining Company.

The Marland interests proceeded to drill other wells in the vicinity of the second one. The third well was drilled 1800 feet southeast of the second one.[5] At 500 feet the same flow of gas was struck as found in the second well. Another large flow of gas was discovered at 930 feet. From the two producing gas wells, there was a flow of 22,000,000 cubic feet from the five hundred foot sand and 10,000,000 cubic feet from the 930 foot sand, aggregating about 30,000,000 cubic feet a day. Of the first eight wells drilled, seven were producing gas wells. The ninth was a producing oil well. From the bottom of that well came oil, and complete justification for Marland's belief in the Mid-Continent field.

The 101 Ranch Oil Company immediately sought a market for its gas supply. At cost of $500,000, it built a pipeline to Tonkawa, fifteen miles west, where it obtained a franchise and installed a domestic gas distributing system. From the promotion of that company and the sale of gas, Mr. Marland secured money to continue his search for oil.

The drilling of the ninth well in June, 1911, which was on the allotment of an Indian named Willie-Cries-for-War, was the beginning of the new oil field in Kay County, known as the Ponca field. The discovery of this field opened up a new empire of production. It was in the heart of this field that the Iron Thunder land of the 101 Ranch—200 acres—lay. The income from royalties from the wells on the 101 Ranch lands

[5] George L. Miller to F. S. Barde, December 26, 1910.

[105]

exceeded $100 a day. Under date of August 15, 1912, the *Ponca City Democrat* wrote:

"The latest oil boom in Oklahoma is about Ponca City, once a border mecca of the cattlemen. The discovery of the field is attributed to E. W. Marland, who came West from Pittsburgh, Pennsylvania, a wealthy man, almost went broke, but now has recouped his finances.

"Marland pioneered the field in 'wild-catting' against the judgment of experts. He came to Ponca City in 1908, ostensibly in search of gas. He found that commodity in plenty, but his lust for wealth led him to sidetrack that industry in the hunt for petroleum.

"His first discovery of indications of oil was on the 101 Ranch. He found gas in plenty, but went after oil at 2,575 feet and spent $18,000 in the venture. He found no oil but did not lose heart.

"Finally, when himself and associates were becoming short of funds, they found petroleum at 1,525 feet, in May, 1911. Since that time he has kept 'hammering away,' and has spent $100,000. But the tide has turned and he has several rich wells. There are nineteen producers in the field and prospectors are preparing to sink many more. . . . .

"The first prospecting was done against the advice of experienced oil men in the rich Mid-Continent field further east in Oklahoma, who held to the old theory that there were no profitable oil fields west of the ninety-sixth meridian or anywhere in the Red Bed formation which begins after passing westward across the Arkansas River.

"But despite this prophecy, oil has been found in paying quantities at a depth of about 1,500 feet. Its gravity is about 44, a grade of such excellence that it is selling at five cents above the market price of seventy cents a barrel.

"For more than two weeks two wells have been flowing 'natural' between 500 and 600 barrels every twenty-four hours. Of the nineteen producing wells of the thirty-one drilled, several are pumping 100 barrels a day.

"A local refinery is building and the Chanute Refinery Company and the Cudahy interests are now building pipelines from the field to their loading stations at Ponca City. The

[106]

Ponca field now has a daily production of about 2,500 barrels. . . . .

"One of the lucky landowners is Mrs. George W. Miller of the 101 Ranch. Mrs. Miller has lived most of her life in the West, and has been acquainted with large business transactions, having dealt heavily in herds of cattle and horses, but she never before enjoyed an income so easily obtained as that which is flowing hour by hour from the three wells on her 200-acre farm in the heart of the Ponca field. Her income from royalties is now $100 a day, to be greatly increased as new wells are brought in."[6]

In the early part of 1915, Dr. D. W. Ohern and Mr. Frank Buttram, geologists, were sent by the Fortuna Oil Company of Oklahoma City to Pawnee County to make a study of oil possibilities in that region.[7] Dr. Ohern soon returned on business to Oklahoma City and left Mr. Buttram to scout for oil structures. In the course of his inspection, Mr. Buttram found a location which he believed to be an oil structure. He immediately called Dr. Ohern and the two rechecked the formation and agreed that indications were favorable. The structure was on the 101 Ranch lands in the neighborhood of where Morrison, Oklahoma, is now located.

The Fortuna Oil Company continued its geological studies in the surrounding country and located four structures which were considered good oil possibilities. They were carefully mapped and plans were made for four fields, known later as the Yale, Cushing, Morrison, and Skeedee fields. Three of these were later found to be richly productive—only the Skeedee proved to be dry.

As soon as leases were obtained from the landowners of the four fields, Mr. A. P. Crockett, President of the Fortuna Oil Company, sought a company to put down a test well. He made a proposition to Mr. Robert Watchorn, President of the Watchorn Oil and Gas Company, at that time located at Ardmore, Oklahoma, in which he offered one-half the acreage included in the four fields in exchange for drilling a test well on any one of the fields Mr. Watchorn might choose. This proposition was

[6] *Ponca City Democrat,* August 15, 1912.

[7] Frank Harper, President, Watchorn Petroleum Company, to Ellsworth Collings, April 31, 1936.

accepted, and in selecting the plat for the test well from the four handed to him, Mr. Watchorn remarked: "Since I don't know anything about the structures in any of these fields, this one looks as good to me as any of the others." The plat selected by chance represented the Morrison field, which included the oil structure of the 101 Ranch lands.

The test well was put down on the 101 Ranch land, and at 2040 feet a rich flow of gas was discovered Christmas Day, 1915. This well failed to produce oil, and a second location was made on eighty acres purchased by the Millers from Bert Diamond, an Otoe Indian. The well was known as the Diamond-Miller No. 1, and gas was struck in it at the same depth as in the first.

In the meantime, the Fortuna Oil Company sold its half-interest in the leases to the Magnolia Company. This company staked a location on the Diamond-Miller tract, known as the Diamond-Miller No. 2, and the well produced 6,500,000 cubic feet of gas at a depth of 2035 feet.

Encouraged by the discovery of gas in large quantities, the Watchorn Company staked its third well, known as the George L. Miller No. 1. In the spring of 1922, this well proved to be an oil producer at a depth of 2740 feet. It produced small quantities of oil for several months, then in the fall of 1923 it was drilled to the Wilcox sand where a rich flow of oil was encountered.

The Magnolia Company drilled a well a short distance from the discovery well, and after going down a considerable depth, abandoned it as a dry hole. The Watchorn Company drilled the well deeper, which resulted in a large oil producer. The discovery of oil in these wells opened up a rich oil and gas field on the lands of the 101 Ranch, known as the Watchorn field.

By 1921, four important oil fields were developing on the ranch lands. Two of these were on the 101 Ranch proper, about five miles northeast of the headquarters; a third was on ranch holdings in the Otoe country, known as the Watchorn field; and the fourth was on the Bar L lands of the ranch, in the Ponca country where the Arkansas River before turning eastward toward Tulsa makes a big horseshoe bend.

By 1923, much of the 101 land was producing oil, and the Miller brothers were regarded as large operators throughout the state. Oil fields dotted the ranch in several directions, and oil derricks formed a wide skyline. There was a daily flow of many thousands of barrels of oil from these wells. The *Ponca City News*, under date of December 13, 1923, wrote of this spread of oil development on the 101 holdings:

"The Miller brothers of the 101 Ranch are interested at the present time in a total of twenty-three producing wells, practically all within the confines of the old Ponca and Otoe Indian reservations and located in three counties of Kay, Noble and Pawnee. They lie within a territory that is approximately twenty-five miles south of Ponca City, east from the town of Marland and Red Rock, and including the town of Watchorn in the Otoe country.

"In only one instance are the Miller brothers alone in a drilling campaign and that is where George W. Miller is drilling the No. 1 George W. Miller in northeast section 6, township 22, range 2 east, Noble County; the casing is being set in this test at 3600 feet. Otherwise in their oil ventures the Millers are aligned at different places with the following companies: Watchorn, Magnolia, Marland, Comar, Texas, Ossie, and Alcorn.

"The present production of the Miller brothers includes eleven wells. The Nos. 3 and 10 George L. Miller are in southwest section 4, township 22, range 3 east at Watchorn. The No. 3 is producing six hundred barrels daily from a sand at 4117 feet and the No. 10 is making seventy-five barrels from a sand at 2678 feet. These are the property of the Watchorn Oil Company. The No. 4 Diamond-Miller of the Watchorn Company is producing twenty barrels at 2600 feet, in the northwest section 4, township 22, range 3.

"The Magnolia Petroleum Company has three producing wells on Miller land at Watchorn, including the No. 2 Diamond-Miller making twenty barrels at 2700 feet, the No. 3 making thirty-five barrels at the same depth, and the No. 4 making forty barrels at 2690 feet. These are in the west half of northwest section 4, township 22, range 3. In the same locality the Alcorn Oil Company's No. 2 Margaret Miller in the northwest section 33, township 23, range 3 is making forty barrels at 2670 feet.

"In the Bar L ranch district, included within 101 Ranch area, the Comar Oil Company's Buffalohead well in southwest section 12, township 24, range 3 east is producing sixty barrels.

"The Marland Refining Company has three producing wells on Miller land in northeast section 19, township 25, range 2 east, in Kay County, southwest of Ponca City. These are the Nos. 1 and 2 Calls-him, making eighty barrels from the 2200 foot sand, and the No. 1 Zack Miller making sixty barrels from the same sand.

"The Marland Company and George L. Miller are fishing for tools in northwest section 20, township 25, 2 east at 3965 feet. There is three thousand feet of oil in the hole from a sand at 3950 feet and it is being drilled on down to the second break in the Mississippi lime. The No. 1 George W. Miller in northeast section 4, township 25, range 2 east is being drilled by the same parties at 2280 feet.

"In the Bar L district, where the Buffalohead is producing sixty barrels, the Texas Company is plugging at 4150 feet on the George L. Miller in southeast section 12, township 24, range 3 east at 800 feet. These wells are in Noble County.

"The Sinclair Oil Company is running one thousand barrels daily at the present time of stored oil from the leases of the Watchorn Oil Company, section 33, township 23, range 3 east at Watchorn. A 55,000 barrel tank has just been completed by Watchorn to store the high gravity oil amounting to six hundred barrels daily from the 5117 foot sand; oil was turned into the tank yesterday. It is the intention of the company to store and keep all this production henceforward.

"The Watchorn Company is now deepening its various wells in the same quarter to the deep sand, including the No. 4 at 2880 feet, the No. 5 at 3100, the No. 6 at 3275, the No. 7 at 2700, and the No. 8 at the same depth. The same company has the No. 2 Diamond-Miller, in northeast section 4, township 22, range 3 east, at 2030 feet with four million feet of gas in the hole, the No. 3 with tools in the hole at 2950 feet, and the rig for a new hole on the No. 1 Brown-Miller in northeast section 33, township 23, range 3, with the present hole at 2100 feet."[8]

The Miller brothers received a large sum annually from the oil and gas production, and from leases on the 101 Ranch. From 1923 up to and including 1930, the income from these sources,

[8] *Ponca City News,* December 13, 1923.

exclusive of the ranch refinery and filling station, totaled $1,-341,756.45, distributed annually as follows: 1923, $61,922.58; 1924, $192,219.91; 1925, $538,749.68; 1926, $300,853.88; 1927, $135,751.85; 1928, $45,960.67; 1929, $41,327.49; and 1930, $25,170.39.[9] These figures indicate that the income from the oil wells on the 101 Ranch lands exceeded an average of $190,000 annually during this period.

Geological reports indicated that the oil possibilities were unlimited, the 101 Ranch having production on all four sides. On the west within a mile and a half was the Tonkawa field, which produced more than $880,000,000 worth of oil in ten years. On the southeast corner of the ranch was the Watchorn field which had produced more than $10,000,000 in ten years. Directly to the north was the Ponca field, which extended into the ranch lands. In this field one well, the George Brett No. 1, produced in 1923 more than $1,000,000 worth of oil. Within two miles of the southern border oil was discovered in 1930 near the Otoe Switch. The first well was brought in as a six hundred barrel producer at approximately 3700 feet. On the east side in the Big Bend on an Indian allotment, within three hundred feet of lands owned by the ranch, a well was drilled in at 3700 feet. This well produced about forty barrels of oil a day for several years.

It was the belief of many prominent oil men of the country that there were at least three more oil structures on the 101 Ranch lands that were equal to the oil formations of the other fields. In 1925, a New York royalty company offered the Miller brothers $1,500,000 for their interest in the Watchorn field, and on November 25, 1931, J. Edward Jones, New York City, offered $1,000,000 for the oil and gas royalty under the lands of the 101 Ranch. The Millers refused all these offers since the productivity of the fields already discovered convinced them that beneath the soil of the 101 Ranch there existed many million barrels of petroleum.

[9] 101 Ranch Records, November 1, 1931.

VIII

NOT only was the 101 Ranch concerned with the production of raw materials but in the manufacture and marketing of them. Especially was this true of agricultural, livestock, dairy, poultry, and fruit products, as well as in great measure in the oil operations of the ranch. Everything grown or produced was utilized in some practical way. Cattle and hogs from the farm were slaughtered in the packing plant and the hides tanned and converted into all kinds of leather goods. Fruit from the orchards was sent to the preserving plant. Grain and other farm crops were stored or sold to the people of the neighborhood, to the employees of the ranch, and to the markets of Marland and of Ponca City.

The ranch produced virtually every kind of raw product—wheat and corn, cattle and horses, hogs and chickens, alfalfa and kafir, fruit and vegetables, buffalo and elephants, camels and longhorns, ostriches and peacocks, work mules and cow ponies; the bizarre and the common. Almost in the shadow of the White House loomed the many derricks denoting production of oil.

The meat packing industry was perhaps the major one on the ranch. Here, in the packing plant, were employed all the modern processes of slaughtering, packing and distributing meat products. It had a capacity daily of a hundred hogs and fifty cattle.[1] It provided huge cold storage and cooling rooms for the proper handling of the meats. The surplus hogs and cattle were slaughtered in the plant and the sugar-cured hams and home cured meats were sold in large quantities. During 1926 twelve thousand hogs and five thousand cattle were handled through the plant.[2] The meat products were sold and delivered by refrigerated trucks within a radius of one hundred miles of the ranch. The plant made a superior grade of ham,

[1] 101 Ranch Records, 1925.
[2] *Rock Island Magazine*, November, 1926.

cured the old-fashioned way—dry cured—that had a wide reputation over the entire Southwest.

Perhaps the annual sales best indicate the volume of the packing plant production. From 1925 to 1930 the gross income from sales amounted to $877,263.74, distributed annually as follows: 1925, $111,696.60; 1926, $167,967.19; 1927, $158,-945.93; 1928, $228,685.25; and 1929, $209,970.77.[3] These figures reveal the magnitude of this industry. The average annual income from this industry exceeded $175,000. While the production varied from year to year, the income from the sales amounted to large sums each year for the entire period.[4] This constancy of income indicates that the packing plant was an important part of the cattle and hog business on the 101 Ranch, since it utilized only cattle and hogs raised on the ranch.

Soon after establishing the packing plant, a large quantity of raw hides accumulated. Since the price offered for them by the tanners seemed to be ridiculously low when compared with the price of finished hides, the Miller brothers built a large tannery close to the packing house. Soon after it was established, however, a cyclone swept it away—leaving only the foundation. A second tannery was immediately built at a cost of $60,000,[5] and operated for only a short time when it, too, was destroyed—this time by fire. But with indomitable persistence the Miller brothers began construction of a third tannery the next morning. In a few weeks the vats and boilers were installed, and raw hides by the hundreds began moving through the tanning process that converted them into leather.

Then the Miller brothers experienced another difficulty. Tanned hides, which had been selling regularly at fifty cents a pound, dropped to three cents a pound, a price much less than the cost of tanning. How this situation was met is described in these lines:

"Beaten? Not these brothers. Away down in Austin, Texas, a wholesale harness house went bankrupt. The news was carried to Zack Miller as a passing bit of gossip. He took the

[3] 101 Ranch Records, 1925-1930.

[4] The five year period, 1925-1930, was selected because it represents a normal period of the packing plant business and for that reason reveals the extent of this phase of the 101 Ranch.

[5] *Literary Digest*, August 4, 1928.

next train to Austin and bought the bankrupt business, lock, stock, and barrel. To friends, the act seemed little short of insanity.

" 'You've got a tannery on hand that's losing money,' they argued. 'Now you up and buy a harness house that experienced harness men couldn't make go. You've gone loco.'

" 'Looks that way, sure enough,' agreed Zack, and began to move the harness-making equipment of the bankrupt business up from Austin to the tannery, which was jammed with unsold hides. There, on the second floor, he set up a harness shop.

"Next, he brought from Austin employees of the smashed concern who were skilled in the art of harness-making. He showed them the stacks of finished hides. 'Go ahead,' he directed, 'and turn this stuff into saddles and sets of harness.'

"A cowboy is particular about his saddle. He likes it to be the best that he can buy. Zack Miller had his Austin workmen turn out saddles to order; he had them turn out work harness. Men came in from more than a hundred miles distance to get saddles made, and they went home with harness, hams, bacon, flour, all their conveyances would carry."[6]

The harness and saddle shop manufactured every article of every description made and sold in a modern leather shop. Besides plain and fancy saddles, the shop made light and heavy harness of many kinds, bridles, halters, rawhide ropes, whips, buffalo and cattle robes, rugs, fur and leather coats, fancy pocket books, suit cases, traveling grips. From 1928 to 1930, the gross income from this source amounted to $22,303.40, distributed annually as follows: 1925, $14,869.94; 1926, $3,-532.46; 1927, $1,990.82; 1928, $1,150; and 1929, $760.18. These figures indicate the average annual income from this industry was around $5,000.

The 101 Ranch dairy was considered the last word in the dairy industry. A modern dairy barn and creamery were built at a cost of $30,000 to house the five hundred registered Holstein cows and to take care of the dairy products. In connection with the dairy there was a modern ice cream plant, cold storage and cooling rooms for the proper handling of the dairy products. The dairy was capable of taking care of the milk

6 *American Magazine*, July, 1928.

Upper left, view of the 101 Ranch meat packing plant; upper center, the 101 Ranch machine shop; upper right, the 101 Ranch store; lower left, view of the 101 Ranch tanning factory; lower center, the 101 Ranch creamery; lower right, the 101 Ranch café

from five hundred cows, the cows being milked by electricity. The milk was made into huge quantities of butter, ice cream, and cottage cheese. The dairy products were sold and delivered by refrigerated trucks for miles around the ranch, including the merchants at Marland and Ponca City. The dairy had, in addition, a large shipping trade in butter, ice cream, and cheese.

The gross income from the dairy sales for the five year period, 1925-1930, totaled $116,554.42, distributed annually as follows: 1925, $18,488.01; 1926, $52,360.41; 1927, $13,820.-63; 1928, $26,359.60; and 1929, $2,436.52.[7] These figures reveal the average annual income exceeded $23,000. While the income varied from year to year, the sales never failed to yield an appreciable sum each year.

The first oil brought in on the 101 Ranch was on the north edge of the ranch about two miles northeast of the "White House." These wells, several in number, produced sufficient oil for the Millers to have an oil refinery of their own at the ranch headquarters. This refinery made one hundred barrels of gasoline daily. The gasoline was sold at the ranch filling station. Large quantities of kerosene and fuel oil sufficient to supply ranch needs were made from the crude oil produced on the ranch.

The sales of oil products manufactured and sold on the 101 Ranch amounted to a considerable sum annually. From 1925 to 1930, the sales of the refinery totaled $96,566.17, distributed annually as follows: 1925, $15,589.18; 1926, $29,090.73; 1927, $20,439.62; 1928, $17,662.18; and 1929, $13,784.46. For the same period, the sales of the filling station totaled $86,349.95, distributed annually as follows: 1925, $5,120.31; 1926, $25,660.83; 1927, $20,991.83; 1928, $18,837.12; and 1929, $15,739.86. The average annual income from these sources combined was approximately $35,000.

The Miller brothers were among the first to produce moving pictures. *Wild West*, a Pathé serial, was produced on the 101 Ranch. It was directed by Robert F. Hill from the scenario of J. F. Nattiford. The story combined all the elements of the wild west and circus life. It necessitated the use of an extensive ranch where there was plenty of room for a stranded tent show to take refuge. It also required the use of trained

[7] 101 Ranch Records, 1925-1930.

[115]

animals, keepers, trainers, wagons, and all other circus paraphernalia. The 101 Ranch had all of these, since it was the winter quarters for the 101 Ranch show. The *Wild West* troupe spent three months on the ranch producing the picture.

Supporting Jack Mulhall and Helen Ferguson were such celebrities of the show world as Nowata Slim Richardson, world's champion bucking horse rider, and Buck Lucas, world's champion bulldogger. There were nine hundred people on the 101 Ranch during the filming of the picture.

The performances in roping, trick riding, bronc riding, and bulldogging for the picture were staged in the 101 Ranch rodeo grounds. Ten trick ropers performed all at once; fifteen trick riders swooped back and forth in acts of skill and daring; dozens of fighting broncos were ridden at the same time. Cowboys leaped from racing horses upon the horns of maddened steers and wrestled them to the ground. Wild, rangy steers were run down, roped, and hog-tied in from twenty to thirty seconds.

The misfortunes, delays, and obstacles in making moving pictures were numerous. "In filming *Trail Dust* on the 101 Ranch," says Gordon Hines, "a star actress was seriously injured two days before the camera work began, thus delaying the company until a substitute could be found and properly costumed. The western village, built on the bare prairie, was blown down three times by fierce Oklahoma winds, and cloudy weather delayed shooting day after day, with each day running up another twelve hundred dollar item against the production cost. Multitudes of small, disagreeable things happened to harass the producers and to add to their heavy expense, but perseverance won and *Trail Dust* was finally in the box and ready for the most tedious work of all—cutting and final titling.

"Imagine a director's disappointment when he has worked for two days to get a satisfactory scene of the very temperamental buffaloes in a wild stampede, only to find, after the film had gone through the laboratory, that a slight detail completely spoils the scene and that it must be retaken.

"When the buffalo stampede was shot for *Trail Dust* the hero and heroine, carefully timing their action, scampered into the branches of a fallen tree barely in time to avoid the onrushing horde of buffalo. The hero, a trifle slow, was seen by a giant bull and charged before he could reach a point of safety. The bull barely missed him, knocking him to the ground and breaking his wrist.

"It would have been a great scene, with a wonderful punch and thrill, but a cowboy, noticing the plight of the leading man and fearing for his safety, rode into the background toward the fallen man. Noticing that the bull had gone on with the herd, he beat a hasty retreat out of the picture and his riding in had not been noticed in the excitement.

"The scene depicts the plight of a man and girl who, alone in the wilderness and unarmed, are charged by the buffalo herd. The cowboy in the background destroyed the entire effect and another tedious 'retake' was necessary—and it took three days this time.

"Old timers, residents of Oklahoma since the 'run,' have been especially interested in the naturalness, the trueness of life, of the wagon train, or 'boomer' scenes, in *Trail Dust*. Such a sequence produced in Hollywood would be made with professional extra people, who try to act all over the place. The director of the picture has no other word but luck to explain his being able to go out on the main highway, near the ranch, and find thirty wagons of modern 'boomers'—folks from the good old state of Arkansas, who had bundled up their kids and their dogs and their cows and started out to make the harvest fields. These people spend their winters at permanent homes, but the first call of the robin finds them hitting the open road for another summer in the great outdoors.

"In one scene an aged woman, who said she was past eighty, drove a spirited mule team down a steep embankment, a pipe drawing with a gurgling noise hung from a corner of her mouth. She insisted that she was 'as good a camp-hand as any man.'

"Another family, in three generations, occupied two wagons, the younger couple being the proud parents of a bright baby girl who had been born in the wagon early in the spring. Their genuine happiness and contentment with their mode of living stamped them as true descendants of pioneer stock. True, they may not be 'successful' as the world regards the matter, but, if you'd ask them, they'd tell you that they were certainly successful, because they had found happiness and freedom in the great outdoors.

"Such real, human 'boomer' folks, living their lives naturally, are transferred to the screen in *Trail Dust* and old timers'
hearts 'warm' to them because they are real folks—not actors.

"The old time Cheyenne and Arapahoe bucks lived over
their raiding, pillaging days of years ago and the younger
braves felt the strange, strong call of heredity when they rode,
shrieking madly, down the street of the burning village during
the filming of *Trail Dust*.

"Night shadows had fallen and the blazing furnace sent
hungry tongues of flame skyward, lighting the prairies for miles
around. It is not strange that the Indians' war whoops were a
bit more blood curdling than their forced attempts for the
rodeo audiences. The excitement of the scene awakened all
their savage instincts and, for a few moments, they were back
in the days of their strongest resistance to the white man's on-
coming—when it seemed that the Indian might yet succeed in
holding his hunting grounds and his wild game for his own use
and pleasure.

"Ready! Action! Camera!

"The music struck up a lively dance air, shouts and laughter rang through the large dance-hall set and the villain strode
down to the center foreground, a leering grin on his face as he
thought of his victory over the hero.

"Then came a flash—a crash of thunder and a long roar as
the heavens opened and water poured through an unfinished
roof upon the actors in the *Trail Dust* production. The wind increased its fury, the camera stopped grinding and, without a
word from anyone, all scampered toward the company's hotel,
where there was shelter and warmth.

"The actors and extra people had barely reached a point of
safety when the Oklahoma twister struck and crashed the unfinished concrete wall of the new studio building in upon the
set which but a moment before had held dozens of people.

"Four thousand dollars worth of high-powered electric
lighting equipment was buried by the concrete blocks, which
by a strange trick of fate, piled up around and over the lights
in such a manner as to leave every big arc and dome un-
scathed."[8]

[8] *101 Ranch Magazine,* March, 1925.

The Miller brothers of the 101 Ranch produced the first pictures at Hollywood and had the first set-up on that now famous ground.[9] They had made some pictures on the ranch, using their wild west show people and equipment, and then decided to winter in Los Angeles, where the weather was better suited for picture making. As a result, they wintered there for a number of years and their outfit was used continuously.

W. A. Brooks of the 101 Ranch, a cousin of the Miller brothers, was their first director, and among the people who helped him and participated with him were many of those who became prominent in the industry. Tom Mix, Helen Gibson, Mabel Normand, Neal Hart, Hoot Gibson, and many others began their careers with the 101 Ranch group.

In her picture *Suzanne,* Mabel Normand did a number of good horseback stunts, showing that she was an equestrienne of experience, yet so far as her horsemanship was concerned, she was a product of the 101 Ranch pictures. The first lesson she ever received in horseback riding was from Will Brooks, who helped her mount the first horse she ever rode.

It was difficult to feed the hundreds of actors at luncheon time, while out on location. Brooks solved the problem and introduced a stunt that is still used frequently. He fed them by placing in paper sacks the noonday lunches, consisting of sandwiches, cakes and fruit. Each sack would contain the same kind and amount of food. These were placed conveniently, and when time for lunch came the people lined up and marched by, each taking a sack. Water, coffee and milk were available for those who might want different drinks.

"The plan worked fine," says W. A. Brooks. "In the line would be cowboys and Indians, and also all the other people, together with Tom Ince and various producers, and in this way we fed them all quickly and satisfactorily. It put everybody on an equal basis and the thing went over big. This method was later adopted by many of the big producing companies."[10]

The 101 Ranch operated a large general store. It was the mercantile center in northern Oklahoma for a number of years. Originally started as a supply place for their large number of

[9] W. A. Brooks to Ellsworth Collings, April 10, 1936.
[10] *Daily Oklahoman,* September 26, 1926.

employees, the Millers eventually expanded until the store became a supply center for fifty miles around.

It was a combined department store, which handled also ranch products of all kinds, and Indian store, operating somewhat as an old time trading post. The sales exceeded an average of $84,000 annually. From 1925 to 1930, the gross income totaled $420,994.53, distributed as follows: 1925, $114,363.-70; 1926, $98,289.19; 1927, $83,106.66; 1928, $67,553.97; and 1929, $57,681.01.[11]

The 101 Ranch café developed from the old "ranch chuck house" where the cowboys answered the call, "come 'nd get it," to a restaurant modern in every respect. The café was well furnished, pleasingly designed and tastefully decorated. The café chefs prepared delicious meals, and every article of food, with the exception of olives, sugar, and coffee, was produced right on the ranch.

Taking care of this modern café, which supplanted the old time chuck table on the ranch, was a big job and there was a well trained staff in charge. They drew their supplies from the big storage plants of the ranch which were filled with potatoes, fresh meats, vegetables, apples, and other articles of food. In addition to providing meals for ranch employees, the café served meals daily to hundreds of visitors. Ordinarily, when there were no guests to remain for more than a day or two, the White House kitchen was not used but all would go to the café for their meals. The income from this source amounted in 1927 to $12,632.47.

A modern laundry was operated by the Miller brothers. It was equipped with modern machinery and did all the laundry work of the ranch, including that for its employees. In addition, it served the needs of the surrounding country, the income amounting to an appreciable sum annually. From 1925 to 1930, the receipts totaled $6,078.54, distributed annually as follows: 1925, $1,070.56; 1926, $1,620.78; 1927, $1,973.06; 1928, $1,114.12; and 1929, $300.[12]

A special building was erected and equipped for the cider and canning industry. Approximately two hundred barrels of cider were manufactured each fall. All of the cider was pas-

[11] 101 Ranch Records, 1925-1930.
[12] 101 Ranch Records, 1925-1930.

teurized, thus keeping it sweet and making it possible to market at any time. Several thousand pounds of apple butter and jelly were manufactured annually.[13] After the cider was made the pomace was placed in barrels and held in water overnight, then run through the press again—from this the jelly was made. On each original package of apple butter was the following guarantee: "This apple butter is guaranteed to keep all winter, if you can keep the children away from it."

The ranch had its own machine, blacksmith, woodwork, and repair shop. The shop was equipped with all the power machinery and tools needed in these lines of work. Two blacksmiths were kept busy shoeing horses and repairing farm machinery. In addition to the ranch work, the shop served the needs of the farmers of the surrounding country.

There was a complete ice plant with a capacity of ten tons daily maintained on the ranch. The plant provided ice for the ranch and its employees as well as the farmers of the community. Three large cold storage plants were provided for the proper handling of the meats and perishable products of the ranch. The ranch had its own electric light plant, system of waterworks, and general power plant.

Perhaps one of the most interesting industries was the novelty factory. All kinds of Indian rugs, beaded belts and clothing, drums, bows and arrows, silver jewelry, etc., were manufactured in this factory by Indians employed by the Miller brothers. In addition, a large assortment of souvenir leather goods, such as cowboy belts, boys' chaps and vests were manufactured and sold along with the Indian articles at the ranch store, which also conducted a large wholesale trade in these articles.

While a great variety of products were manufactured and sold on the 101 Ranch, ranging from petroleum to Indian drums, the principal income-producing industries were the packing plant, harness and saddle shop, dairy, refinery, filling station, laundry, and store. Many moving pictures were produced but no records showing the income from this source are available. The following table indicates the gross incomes from these industries for the five year period, 1925-1930.[14]

[13] *Daily Oklahoman,* February 6, 1927.
[14] 101 Ranch Records, 1925-1930.

ANNUAL SALES OF PRODUCTS MANUFACTURED AND SOLD ON THE 101 RANCH FOR THE FIVE YEAR PERIOD, 1925-1930

YEARS	ANNUAL SALES OF INDUSTRIES							TOTAL FOR YEAR
	Packing Plant	Harness Shop	Dairy	Refinery	Filling Station	Laundry	Store	
1925	$111,696.60	$14,869.94	$18,488.01	$15,589.18	$5,120.31	$1,070.56	$114,363.70	$281,194.30
1926	167,967.19	3,532.46	52,360.41	29,090.73	21,660.83	1,620.78	98,289.19	378,521.59
1927	158,945.93	1,990.82	13,820.63	20,439.62	20,991.83	1,973.06	83,106.66	301,268.55
1928	228,685.25	1,150.00	26,359.60	17,662.18	18,837.12	1,114.12	67,553.97	361,362.24
1929	209,970.77	760.18	2,436.52	13,784.46	15,739.86	300.00	57,681.01	300,672.80
Total for Industry	877,263.74	22,303.40	116,554.42	96,566.17	86,349.95	6,078.54	420,994.53	1,623,019.48

These figures reveal some interesting facts with reference to products manufactured and sold on the ranch. In the first place, they indicate that the gross income from the industries alone amounted to $1,623,019.48 for the five year period, 1925-1930. The annual income from this source exceeded $324,000. In the second place, the figures reveal the constancy of income from this source. While the production for each industry varied from year to year, the income remained constant for the entire period. For example, the total income from the packing plant for the five year period amounted to $877,263.74, each year contributing large sums to this total. The same is likewise true of the other industries. These facts indicate that the manufacture and sale of products was an important phase of the 101 Ranch.

In the management of their diversified enterprises the Miller brothers achieved financial success, but they did it by applying business methods to the ranch operation as a whole. They applied efficient methods toward co-ordinating the processes of production, manufacture, and distribution, to the end that the ranch would produce maximum financial returns as a complete unit.

A special building housed the business offices of the ranch. All documents pertaining to the various ranch enterprises were filed in systematic order: Indian leases, accounts, records. Any paper could be found in a moment. The telephone on the desk connected with every foreman on the ranch—over thirty-five miles of private wire, and conversations were frequent with the towns and cities throughout Oklahoma and the nation by long distance service. Nor was the business system less orderly than the appointments. Colonel Joe attended to the farming operations and, in addition, carried on transactions with his Indian landlords and wards. Colonel Zack attended to the cattle, the mules, the hogs, and the horses. Colonel George attended to the office routine and the books. But there was no formality. Every brother took interest in all parts of the business. Tasks were interchangeable and were distributed with fraternal good feeling.

Twenty-five newspapers came daily to the ranch and several magazines were taken. These, with the constant use of the telephone, kept the ranch office closely in touch with market conditions and opportunities. If the price of beef, hogs, or mules went up in Kansas City, St. Louis, or Chicago, a foreman was called up fifteen miles away, and ordered to round up a herd and drive them over to the railroad. The next moment the railroad was being asked for cattle cars. The following morning the stock pulled into the stockyards. One week Zack Miller would be out in southern California buying up mules, and another week George Miller would be at the New York Horse Show selling polo ponies. One day, just before an important polo match in the east, Joe Miller received a telegram which read: "Send five trained polo ponies by express." In an hour or two they were on the train. In relating this incident he remarked: "If they had been ordered to be sent by first-class mail, special delivery, they would have gone just the same—but the express charges amounted to nearly as much as the price of the ponies."[15]

To give some idea of the business transactions of the 101 Ranch, it might be stated that from 1925 to 1930 there was an annual turnover of nearly a million dollars in livestock, farm crops, industries, oil rents and royalties, exclusive of the 101 Ranch show. The following table indicates the volume of business transacted through the offices of the ranch.[16]

ANNUAL SALES OF 101 RANCH ENTERPRISES FOR THE YEARS 1925-1930

YEARS	RANCH ENTERPRISES				TOTAL FOR YEAR
	Livestock	Farm Crops	Industries	Oil Royalties and Rents	
1925	$149,997.64	$100,570.39	$281,194.30	$538,749.68	$1,070,512.01
1926	147,837.00	104,158.42	378,521.59	300,853.88	931,370.89
1927	177,057.47	102,883.21	301,268.55	135,751.85	716,960.08
1928	164,216.43	100,079.05	361,362.24	45,960.67	671,618.39
1929	198,416.77	129,061.45	300,672.80	41,327.49	669,478.51

With all these enterprises the operating expenses of the ranch amounted to a huge sum annually as the following table indicates.[17]

15 *World's Work*, February, 1906.
16 101 Ranch Records, 1925-1930.
17 101 Ranch Records, 1925-1930.

Enterprises	Years				
	1925	1926	1927	1928	1929
Packing Plant	$16,410.51	17,194.29	$20,194.49	$38,407.45	$34,954.85
Farm Crops	71,755.20	64,068.10	61,216.02	54,534.51	37,399.01
Livestock	21,303.04	19,169.40	15,887.80	34,362.75	32,039.16
Hogs	10,856.99	19,761.58	15,802.75	44,805.94	94,003.14
Store	13,110.15	8,906.93	7,537.67	7,546.17	5,918.25
Filling Station	622.87	1,911.26	1,803.73	2,371.85	2,491.52
Refinery	814.97	1,080.00	.....*.....	2,601.33	2,594.33
Dairy	7,253.01	8,197.79	6,326.17	9,727.59	2,635.93
Orchards	10,031.78	9,720.30	14,057.39	10,094.31	7,940.40
Market	....*....	1,037.11	706.49	400.94	440.46
Poultry	4,662.50	3,850.70	3,934.81	478.01	508.73
Gardens	....*....	5,526.70	7,254.52	1,331.69	161.11
Harness Shop	2,833.26	93.00	324.53	30.00	.....*.....
General Expenses	2,316.81	713.54	15,251.53	1,461.12	657.05
General Salaries	14,966.45	14,763.45	11,457.05	12,604.28	10,113.90
Gross Production Tax	15,732.98	11,214.68	2,976.39	1,308.35	1,001.55
Insurance	4,691.38	12,167.86	11,113.39	5,010.91	.....*.....
Interest and Discount	38,896.40	36,961.87	42,891.94	47,263.98	42,664.49
Leases (Grazing)	14,058.45	7,482.89	13,831.65	5,141.69	3,844.02
Legal	3,391.08	10,715.47	3,327.27	5,496.99	8,779.81
Light and Power	2,104.52	2,139.78	5,479.57	491.29	.....*.....
Office Expenses	2,324.95	1,172.04	1,460.15	1,596.79	1,539.35
Oil and Gas	1,808.75	1,951.50	1,821.40	1,650.00	.....*.....
Repairs	36,835.18	28,453.40	29,818.98	16,730.99	13,481.48
Taxes, County and State	15,360.99	15,380.64	12,646.97	12,245.01	2,024.43
Telephone, Telegraph and Postage	3,415.86	2,485.65	2,016.16	946.85	1,191.42
Hotels	2,833.26	2,847.67	6,522.57	4,574.14	1,369.08
Advertising	5,210.65	2,081.36	3,063.36	1,391.71	491.59
Autos, Tractors, and Trucks	5,388.65	6,681.85	5,908.73	1,271.81	657.32
White House Expenses	3,700.40	5,003.67	....*.....	....*.....	3,776.11
Donations	1,016.95	575.64	507.55	569.00	497.07
Total for Year	320,728.94	323,310.12	325.141.03	326,446.45	313,166.56

* No expenses reported.

In order further to systematize the enterprises of the ranch and bring all the departments into a closer working organization, the Miller brothers organized the Wheel Club. The club was composed of the heads of the departments as active members and the Miller brothers as honorary members. The idea

[125]

of such a club came from Rotary training and association, as the Millers were members of the Ponca City Rotary club.

The wagon wheel was the emblem of the club. Around the rim of the wheel were printed the names of the various departments and the hub represented the 101 Ranch itself. Each member's name was on a spoke, connecting the rim with the hub, and the significance was that these members kept the wheels of the 101 Ranch in motion and connected the individual departments to the main 101 Ranch organization. The purpose of the club, as set out in its constitution, was to encourage and foster between the department heads of the ranch: (a) the most worthy of ideals, that of service; (b) the development of acquaintance as an opportunity for service; (c) the application of the ideals of service by each member toward his department and the business of his employer; (d) co-operation between all departments for the common good; (e) the advancement of understanding, good will, and friendship among the members of the club.

In 1927 the club had representatives from eighteen ranch departments as follows: J. O. Weldon, agriculture; W. A. Brooks, oil and gas; F. H. Hendon, hogs; W. K. Rogers, horses; Thomas R. Brown, cattle; Thomas Crook, dairy; J. J. Vassar, packing plant; J. B. Overton, light and power; Louis McDonald, Indians; J. M. Hogan, poultry; T. O. Manning, accounting; W. E. Seamans, horticulture; Sam Stigall, construction; D. H. Greary, sales and store; F. D. Olmstead, land; George W. Miller, legal; Art Eldridge, show, and J. B. Kent, moving pictures.

IX

WHEN the huge tract of prairie acres, known as the Cherokee Strip, was opened to white settlers in 1893, the lands of the Ponca Indians were not included in the area to which the home-seekers were admitted. The Strip, sandblown and almost treeless, lay along the southern border of Kansas and served as the outlet for the Cherokee Nation. It was a passage through which the tribesmen might pass from their homes in the Indian Territory to their hunting grounds in the Rocky Mountains. With its ten thousand square miles, it was almost as large as the state of Vermont—approximately fifty miles in width, and more than 180 miles in length.

Along the irregular eastern border of the Strip were the lands of the Tonkawas, Otoes, Pawnees, and Poncas. The Tonkawas and Pawnees sold their surplus lands in the reservation, but the Poncas kept theirs. And thus the Poncas owned much of the land of the 101 Ranch.

The ancestral home of the Poncas was along the Niobrara River, near Omaha, Nebraska, and in 1871 the tribe numbered 871. Although their reservation had been guaranteed to them by treaty, they were compelled to surrender it to the Sioux after making it their home for a number of years. It was found the Ponca lands were included in a reservation granted to the Sioux, and for that reason, the government forcibly removed them in 1877 to the Indian Territory, much against their wishes. The resistance of the Indians to the removal is related by Francis LaFlesche of the Bureau of Indian Affairs:

"Standing Bear was a Ponca chief of whom little was known until the removal of his people from northern Nebraska to Indian Territory because the reservation confirmed to them by treaty had been included in land granted to the Sioux. When the order for removal was given, January 15, 1877, Standing Bear strongly opposed it, but in February he and nine other chiefs were taken to choose a reservation. They followed the official but would not select a site. Their wearisome journey brought them to Arkansas City, Kansas, whence they asked to be taken home; being refused, they started back afoot, with a few dollars among them and a blanket each. In forty days they had walked five hundred miles, reaching home April 2, to find the official there unwilling to listen to protest and determined to remove the people. He called the military, and the tribe, losing hope, abandoned their homes in May. Standing Bear could get no response to his demand to know why his people were arrested and treated like criminals when they had done no wrong."

The removal brought much suffering to the Poncas. Within a year approximately one-third of the Indians died and most of the survivors were stricken with sickness as a result of the change in climate. The attendant hardships are described in these lines:

"A son of Standing Bear died. Craving to bury the lad at his old home, the chief determined to defy restraint. He took the bones of his son and with his immediate following turned northward in January, 1879, and in March arrived destitute at the Omaha reservation. Asking to borrow land and seed, his request was granted, and the Poncas were about to put in a crop when soldiers appeared with orders to arrest Standing Bear and his party and return them to Indian Territory. On their way they camped near Omaha, where Standing Bear was interviewed by T. H. Tibbles, a newspaper correspondent, and the accounts of their grievances appeared in the Omaha newspapers, the citizens became actively interested and opened a church where to a crowded house, the chief repeated his story. Messrs. Poppleton and Webster proffered legal service to the prisoners and in their behalf sued out a writ of habeas corpus. The United States denied the prisoners' right to the writ on the ground that they were not persons within the meaning of the law. On April 18, Judge Dundy decided that an Indian is a person within the meaning of the law of the United States, and therefore had a right to the writ when restrained in violation of law; that no rightful authority exists for removing by force any of the prisoners to the Indian Territory, and therefore the prisoners must be discharged from custody."

Many people sympathized with Standing Bear and his followers and wrote to the President and members of Congress protesting against the removal of the Indians from their reservation in Nebraska. In the spring of 1880, the Senate appointed a commission to investigate the removal, the report of which confirmed the contentions of Standing Bear. A satisfactory adjustment of the differences was effected as a result. Poncas wanting to remain in the Indian Territory were given better lands while Standing Bear found a home on the old reservation in Nebraska.

The association of the Millers with the Poncas had begun while the Indians were suffering from the climate and the incursions of whiskey peddlers from Missouri, in their temporary reservation on Quapaw lands near Baxter Springs. An act of Congress of May 27, 1878, removed the Poncas to land purchased from the Cherokees in the Strip. And it was on this land on the Salt Fork River that Colonel George W. Miller established his ranch in 1892, as we learned in an earlier chapter.

Over the vast confines of the 101 Ranch lived the Poncas. A tepee was their earliest home, the Millers were their friends, and the plains were their life. They retained their old time customs and ceremonies. The men remained strangers to work and refused to be introduced. They insisted upon the wife performing all labor—whether there was one wife or three. The squaws carried the baggage, built the fires, erected the tepees, saddled the horses, and were experts at making beadwork. The men made drums, bows and arrows: they would sit for hours carving out some weird design without looking up or saying a word.

The Indians still clung to the old custom of naming persons in connection with some peculiar incident of their lives. Thus, on the ranch there were Mary Buffalo Head, Horse Chief Eagle, Mary Iron Thunder, Alford No Ear, Weak Bone, Sits-on-Hill, White Deer, Eugene Big Goose, Mean Bear, Wolf Robe, Short Tail, Hiding Woman, Red Elk, Girl Bear Head, Big Turkey, Long Pumpkin, White Buffalo, Running-After-Arrow, Willie-Cries-For-War, Little Dance, White Eagle, Peter-Knows-the-Country, Little-Man-Stands-Up, and Thomas-on-Two-Lean-Bear's-Ear.

No Indian wore a beard, for as soon as a hirsute growth appeared, he pulled out the hairs with tweezers. Some of the older men deprived themselves of their eyebrows in this way. They wore long braids of hair which descended from the crown and were plaited with bright ribbons. In war paint and feather head-dresses, they were picturesque and gave the 101 Ranch a western color that was ever a delight to the guests.

The dance was the dominant feature of the Ponca's life. He was born, baptized, married, and died amid the jumble of shuffling feet, gyrating bodies, and the beating of tom-toms. The dance expressed joy, and it was the symbol of grief and bereavement. It was the expression of momentous exploits, and the concomitant of routine duties.

The Indians' wail in honor of the death or burial of one they loved was incomparable with anything of the kind in white man's civilization. The wailing song with its tremulous, wistful, appealing intonations climbed to heights of tremendous emotion. No shrill notes were heard in the wailing song. The songs had their sources deep in the throats of the mourners, and the sound gradually swelled until it passed the half-opened lips and fairly tumbled forth in a trembling, desperate resonance. The thread of the wail, its continuity, was kept intact with a pulsating throb of the tom-tom.

The Indians placed food, clothing, and articles prized by the deceased either into the grave or close beside it, and the custom was to kill the Indian's horse and place its body across the grave. The practice was stopped by the government because of cruelty to animals. The high esteem with which the Indians held this custom is evidenced in the following lines:

"A Ponca chief, a life long friend of Colonel Joe Miller, died and before his death made a special request to Colonel Miller, that his horse be allowed to go with him to the "Happy Hunting Ground." Miller gave his promise though believing that the horse could be led only as far as the grave. As the funeral procession was on the way to the Indian burying ground, near the ranch, the horse dropped dead, and was placed upon the grave of its master.

" 'It was strange that the horse should happen to drop dead at that particular moment,' commented Mr. Miller. But no other explanation was ever forthcoming from the Indians and none was ever known."[1]

[1] *Bristow Record*, October 27, 1927.

All of Colonel Joe Miller's life was spent in intimate association with the tribe, first as a boy at Baxter Springs and then
as a man on the reservation. He spoke the Ponca language with
the fluency of the fullblood. Thoroughly familiar with the sign
language of the Indians, he was never in need of the services of
an interpreter when dealing with them. Conversant with all
their customs and ceremonies, Mr. Miller was punctilious in
his observance of Indian etiquette in all his dealings with them.
His great popularity and influence with the Indians was largely
due to that fact.

The heaviest of Colonel Joe's duties was in looking after the
thousand Indians who owned much of the land of the 101
Ranch and who looked upon him as a father. They called him
at all hours on the telephone, camped in his door yard, brought
their troubles to him, borrowed money from him, made presents to him. They even had a pow-wow and named his baby
for him, giving the name Bright Star to his little son.

According to the regulations of the Office of Indian Affairs,
the rent which the Millers paid for the farming and grazing
leases was turned over to the Indians. Formally, this ended
the relations between the Millers and their landlords. But Indian customs heeded not of pay days and the white man's order
of life. When a Ponca wanted money he borrowed it from Joe
Miller. Whenever an Indian died, the head of the family held
a funeral service, at which, in sign of his grief, he gave away
his personal property, his ponies, his blankets, and his household goods. The next day he was hungry and the next night
he was cold. Of course he must have food, and blankets, and
a pony. He went to Mr. Miller for them, promising to pay
when his lease money came.

The Indians were honest, but their lease money was not
always enough to pay their debts, so the debts continued. They
owed the Millers as much as $22,000 at one time. One In-
dian owed them $200 on a certain settling day; he also owed
another man $200. He was receiving $300 from the agent and
he had immediate need for $100 of it. He kept out his own
$100, and then paid the other man.

"Look here," said Joe Miller, "where is my $200?"

The Indian drew him aside, confidentially, and said: "Me
no like other fellow, bad man. Pay him. He go away. You

stay here, me stay here. You good man. Me pay you some other time."[2]

Many of the Indians regarded their debts in that way. Since both they and the Millers would remain where they were, the money could be paid at any time. The Millers, they reasoned, had possession of their land as security. They felt gratitude, however, for the favors at the hands of the Millers. One time a Ponca chief returned from a visit to a Sioux relative in North Dakota. He brought Joe Miller a beautiful hunting shirt embroidered with stained porcupine quills. It had been given him as a present, but he had no scruples about giving it away again as a token of friendship.

The former war chief of the Poncas was Little Standing Buffalo, second in rank to White Eagle, the head chief and the statesman of the tribe. When Little Standing Buffalo realized that his earthly career was nearing its finish, he called the chiefs and head men of the Poncas into his tepee.

Stating that he realized he was soon to die, the old warrior expressed the wish that "Joe Coga" (Friend Joe) should succeed him as chief. He reminded them of the long ride their friend had made for them as a boy. He called to their attention some of Joe's acts of kindness, and reminded them of the winters when his generosity had saved the tribe from want when the government rations were scarce. Finally he spoke of the increasing perplexities in the business transactions of the tribe. As they always consulted Mr. Miller in these affairs, the old man said that he thought they should give to Mr. Miller's advice the weight of that of a chief.

The old chief spoke to willing hearts, and having secured their promises, Little Standing Buffalo passed to the land beyond. He died content that his place in the council circle was to be filled by a worthy successor. The intention of the Poncas to adopt him and to make him chief was not known to Mr. Miller.

The annual Sun Dance, the big Medicine Dance of the Poncas occurred shortly after the death of Little Standing Buffalo. A delegation of the Indians visited Mr. Miller and requested that he attend the Sun Dance, "just like Indian" as they phrased it.

[2] 101 Ranch Records, 1906.

Left, White Eagle, chief of the Ponca Indian tribe; upper right, Indian marriage ceremony of Colonel Joe C. Miller and bride; scene of the last San Dance on the 101 Ranch

Accordingly Mr. Miller, knowing that his Indian friends would be offended by a refusal of their invitation, arrayed himself in an Indian costume of much splendor. This costume was the gift of a squaw, whose patient hands had wrought each design in beads and colored quills of the porcupine. To complete the effect the cattleman sacrificed his mustache and painted his face. By a fortunate choice he painted his face after the design used by the late Chief Little Standing Buffalo. Mr. Miller learned later that his appearance, decorated with the colors and design of the late chief, was regarded by the Indians as a favorable omen.

Taking with him a number of spotted ponies to be presented to Indians of prominence, and leaving word for several beeves to be driven to the Indian camp, Mr. Miller left the ranch.

His arrival at the Sun Dance camp was the signal for an outburst of savage yells and beating of tom-toms. He made his arrival after the manner of a visiting warrior of note and bestowed his presents and received presents in exchange. The Sun Dance was started and the dancing line of Indian devotees was being ministered to by the medicine man. Everywhere throughout the camp were evidences of the religious frenzy of the Indians. In the center of the camp the tall Sun Dance pole held aloft the offerings of the Indians to the Great Spirit.

The Sun Dance Lodge, sacred to the chiefs and medicine men, occupied a prominent place in the camp. After the exchange of presents the visitor was conducted to the Sun Dance Lodge and was there informed by White Eagle that the tribe had decided to adopt him if he were willing to become a member. This came as a complete surprise to Mr. Miller, but he accepted without hesitation and was placed in the hands of two medicine men, the oldest of the tribe. From the Sun Dance Lodge he was conducted to another tepee and from that time until the completion of the ceremony of adoption he was constantly under the instruction and surveillance of one or the other of the two old medicine men.

He was instructed in the history of the Ponca tribe from the earliest times and was required to memorize and repeat certain songs which told of events famous in tribal annals.

One day and one night he was required to fast, being given

[133]

no food and water during that time. After the night of fasting he was questioned as to the dreams or visions which had come to him in his sleep. On the third night after his arrival in camp Mr. Miller was again conducted to the Sun Dance Lodge, where the ceremony of Blood Brotherhood was performed. After this ceremony he was escorted through the camp and it was announced to the assembled Indians that he had attained warrior rank and had been given the name of Mutha-monta. This name is translated as "going up," indicating that he was progressing or advancing to higher things.

After the ceremonial presentation to the tribe as a warrior Mr. Miller supposed that his experience was at an end, but he was immediately returned to the Sun Dance Lodge, and there for the first time he was informed that he was to become the successor of Little Standing Buffalo and the second chief of the Poncas.

This ceremony required two more days of instruction and ceremonies, and finally he was presented to the Indians as "Waka-huda-nuga-ski," or Big White Chief. Highly appreciating the honor conferred, Mr. Miller sent to the ranch for more beeves, and two days of feasting and dancing terminated the seven days of Sun Dance, which has passed into the history of the Poncas as the Sun Dance of Big White Chief.

Only on ceremonial occasions did the Indians use Mr. Miller's chief name, for to them he was still Friend Joe. The chieftainship was not an empty honor nor without responsibilities. Mr. Miller was summoned to the council whenever matters of moment were to be considered. On several occasions he traveled considerable distances to attend particularly important councils.

The Poncas expressed again their reverence for Colonel Joe Miller by arranging an Indian nuptial ceremony for Colonel and Mrs. Miller. They insisted that he, as an Indian, should have the white man's wedding more completely confirmed by the Indian ceremony. Both Colonel and Mrs. Miller appeared in Indian costume. She wore a very attractive buckskin garment, with appropriate head-dress and moccasins.

Several tepees were pitched between the "White House" and the office building two blocks away. The Indians believed that the tepee itself cut a considerable figure in the program,

[134]

for when the bride-to-be entered the tepee of her intended husband she automatically and immediately became a wife, and according to Indian custom the couple were firmly married.

An Indian barbecue feast served at noon in the ranch rodeo arena, inaugurated the marriage ceremony, a sort of pre-wedding banquet. The ceremony started at two o'clock in the afternoon, when the bride was officially escorted to the scene of the ceremonies by a tribal committee, including Crazy Bear, Good Chief, Big Crow, Good Boy, and Mrs. Crazy Bear.

The prospective bridegroom met his fiancée some distance away and she followed him to his tepee, where his people were waiting to receive her. If she followed him the entire distance, she thereby showed a willingness for the ceremony to proceed, but if she broke line and ran away, this indicated a refusal of the intended husband.

The bridegroom entered the tepee and announced to his people that he had brought with him a maiden, whom he would marry. If his mother was living, she went outside and escorted the waiting fiancée into the tepee, and once the young woman entered, it was too late to repent. The mother greeted her with the term of "daughter-in-law," thus recognizing and consenting to the marriage. A fire was burning in the tepee as a welcome to the bride.

The bridegroom took his place in the center of the tepee with the bride at his left, and the ceremony was completed by the mother-in-law showering the bride with wedding finery. Relatives of the groom were then notified that the wedding was finished, all requirements observed, and that she was now one of the family. All relatives of the groom were supposed to bring wedding gifts.

Among gifts that the Indians always bestowed on the newly married couple was the pipe, with tobacco pouch. This generally was a gift from the chiefs or more prominent men of the tribe. It was to be hung in a convenient place in the new tepee, and each visitor who smoked this pipe indicated his desire for peace and friendship. Good Chief, now blind, presented the pipe and pouch to Colonel and Mrs. Miller. After the bride and groom had been officially received within the tepee by his people, they stepped out in front to receive the gifts from the Indians, which included a beautiful horse given to the bride by Mary Gives Water, while the other women gave calico and blankets.

White Deer was officially in charge of the ceremonies which united "Walking Above," Colonel Miller's Indian name, and his bride, to whom an Indian name, "Sh-shin-ga-ha" or "White Fawn" was given on this occasion. It was White Deer's duty to commend the couple to the Great Spirit above and express the hope that success would come to them and that good health and good fortune would accompany them "in whatever direction of the earth they may walk" or "with whatever wind they may travel."

Following the wedding ceremony, the Poncas assembled in the arena for a celebration, which consisted chiefly of sports. A feature was the attendance of the all-Indian American Legion post, of which Tony Knight was the commander. They presented the soldier or victory dance. While a number of invitations to persons of prominence in the vicinity were sent out by the Indian committee in charge, all citizens were invited to the ranch to witness the ceremony and attend the celebration.

In the autumn of 1883, White Eagle was in Birmingham in company with fifty to a hundred of his people, who were an exhibit at the Alabama State Fair. The Indians had been taken there by Colonel Joe Miller at the solicitation of officers of the fair who believed the Indians would be a great attraction. Colonel Miller and the Indians were given a concession on the fair grounds with permission to charge twenty-five cents admission to the Indian village, where they had their tepees and held their dances.

"It was while we were giving our exhibitions on the fair grounds," says Colonel Joe Miller, "that the invitation came to White Eagle to speak at the First Baptist church, as I now remember it after such a period of years. It was our custom to introduce several of the chiefs outside the village, tell who they were, what they did at home and invite the crowds to come inside the village to see them.

"White Eagle was the tribal chief and, as such, was the one who preached to his own people in regard to their centuries-old religious beliefs. It was in this way that I was accustomed to introduce White Eagle to the crowds on the Alabama State Fair grounds. One afternoon, after I had introduced the chief,

I was approached by a gentleman who introduced himself as pastor of the First Baptist church.

" 'Am I right in asking if White Eagle does preach to his own people at home?' the minister questioned.

" 'That is true,' I replied. 'The Indians meet frequently in their church as do the whites and the chief addresses them in regard to their life and their eventually reaching the happy hunting grounds.'

" 'Do you suppose that White Eagle would preach for me at my church Sunday morning?' was the minister's next query.

" 'I believe he will,' I answered, and then I saw White Eagle, received his consent and carried it to the minister.

"I have seen lots of crowds, but I have never seen anything to equal that which assembled to hear White Eagle preach. It was necessary for the police of Birmingham to attend in squads to handle the crowd, thousands of which could not even get inside the church. The daily papers on Saturday and again on Sunday morning had told of the fact that the Indian would preach and it looked like everyone wanted to hear him.

"White Eagle was equal to the occasion in every respect. He attired himself in the full regalia of his office, with flowing blanket and long head feathers, and wearing his beaded moccasins. He had selected Peter Mitchell (another Poncan) to interpret for him, but at the last minute Mitchell got cold feet when he saw the immense crowd, and the interpreting fell to me. We drove from the fairgrounds to the church in one of those old-fashioned cabs with the top turned back, and when we arrived the police had to separate the crowd to get us through.

"The minister was awaiting us at the door and White Eagle and I went to the pulpit with him. The size and attention of that crowd was enough to make any man quail, but White Eagle never flinched. After the opening service, the minister announced his pleasure at having White Eagle present and that he would now speak. Drawing his blanket around him and holding it in place with his left hand, the chief spoke slowly and deliberately, using his right arm frequently for gestures. He would talk a while, then I would interpret.

"White Eagle explained the religious belief of the red men to some extent. He told them that the Indians have but one church, whereas the white people, even down in Oklahoma, have many churches, one on every corner and each declaring his own way the only true way, whereas the others face eternal hell fire.

"White Eagle said the Indians do not believe in hell; that people have their hell on earth; that when an Indian does wrong it makes his heart hurt and he is sorely troubled, sometimes for a long time, and in this way he experiences his hell. That God is good and that all people, the Indians believe, eventually reach Heaven—the happy hunting ground of the red men.

"When I had finished interpreting White Eagle's final words, and the old chief had taken his seat in one of the pulpit chairs again, the white minister took up the thought of White Eagle's talk and went ahead with a brief sermon of his own, considerably along the same line. Altogether I still remember it as one of the momentous occasions in an entire lifetime. The next morning's daily papers carried pictures of White Chief and many quotations from his sermon."[3]

No cabinet of advisors at the head of any nation exercised more authority or was more attentive to the welfare of its people than were the councilors with which every Indian chief surrounded himself during the days of Indian self-government. The councilors were chosen, as a rule, from among the most noted warriors of the tribe, frequently representing warrior clans—good politics that held together the bands into which almost every tribe was divided.

But with the allotment of lands and with the Federal government supervising the Indians throughout the country, tribal forms of government ceased to function. At present there are living but a very few of the warriors who made up the cabinet of the ruling chieftains. Although these warriors are extremely old, they still possess much of the charm and glamor of their race, and they still command the respect and attention that was accorded them during the days of their authority.

Of such a type was the aged and blind Little Dance, subchief of the Poncas. He had been totally blind for a number of years and relied upon his wife and the young men of the tribe for advice and assistance in looking after the interest of

[3] *Daily Oklahoman*, February 6, 1927.

[138]

his people. He was one of the warriors chosen by White Eagle, the last chief of the Poncas under the old tribal form of government. Little Dance describes the great chief, White Eagle, in this manner:

"White Eagle, as chief, was third in line of the blood clan or band of the Ponca Indians. He was the grandson of Little Bear, and the son of Iron Whip, both chiefs ahead of him. There were seven clans among the Ponca Indians, but the blood clan had not been in power before. It seems that when Little Bear was a young man, he went to war with the then reigning Ponca chief among the Sioux, and the son of the Ponca chief was killed. Little Bear had distinguished himself in battle, and was about the same age as the son of the chief, and it was for that reason that Little Bear was chosen chief, and afterward it was hereditary to his oldest son. The present tribal chief, in name only, is Horse Chief Eagle, the oldest son of White Eagle.

"During the chieftainship of Iron Whip, and when White Eagle was a young man, the treaty of 1865 was entered into with the Federal government, under which the claim of the Ponca Indians for $11,000,000 is now pending before the court of claims at Washington, which amount is the alleged value of land which the Poncas formerly owned in Nebraska, and for which they maintain they never got value from the government.

"White Eagle was chief when the Poncas were moved from Nebraska to northeastern Oklahoma, in the vicinity where Miami now stands. The Poncas did not like that location, and were then moved to their present reservation just south of Ponca City, where the remnants of the tribe now live. White Eagle served as chief for approximately fifty years, and just prior to his death, resigned in favor of Horse Chief Eagle, his son.

"Prior to the Poncas being moved under orders from their reservation in Nebraska to the northeastern corner of Indian Territory, a committee of the tribe including Chief White Eagle and Little Dance, visited the territory for the purpose of selecting a reservation. The chiefs preferred the very location just south of Ponca City, which they are now occupying, but the government agent had arbitrarily chosen the northeastern corner of the territory instead of this one. He was so provoked because the Poncas wanted to locate here instead, that accord-

ing to Little Dance, he deserted them and penniless they had
to walk all the way back to Niobrara, Nebraska, their then
tribal headquarters. Little Dance says that White Eagle paid
the Cherokee Indians $50,000 for the 50,000 acres which still
comprise their lands south of Ponca.

"During the lifetime of White Eagle, he led the Poncas in
their last war with the Sioux and was the last war chieftain
of the Ponca tribe. This was just prior to the tribe being moved
from Nebraska to northeastern Oklahoma in 1877. The head
chief of the tribe was also considered to be the chief medicine
man, in which capacity he acted also as religious advisor.
White Eagle was very progressive, and advocated many of the
advancements of the tribe, including the allotment of lands
here. White Eagle died on February 3, 1914, at the age of 78
years.

"White Eagle understood that the policies dictated by the
Washington government were the better in the long run for his
tribe and he insisted always they should accept and respect
them. A big majority of the Poncas did not want to accept
land allotments, each taking a farm for himself instead of holding the land in common, but White Eagle insisted and allotments were brought about as directed by the government officials.

"There were many sessions of White Eagle's council at
that time, and even some of the councilors were unfavorable
to allotments."[4]

"The Indians," says Corb Sarchet, "were the Millers'
friends. No Indian ever went hungry, none was ever in want
of anything, if the Millers knew it. They participated in the
Indian powwows, taught them how to plant and harvest,
preached their funerals, saw that they had school houses,
worked out their business difficulties for them, were indeed
brothers in every sense."[5] A few years ago, the Miller brothers
rededicated to Chief White Eagle a "signal mound" similar to
the ones used by the Indians in the old days. The mounds consisted of pillars of stone placed on hills about fifteen miles apart,
by which the Indians were guided. About ten miles south
of the White House on Highway 77 one of the pillars was

4 *101 Magazine*, May, 1927.
5 *Daily Oklahoman*, December 16, 1934.

erected and a white eagle, carved in stone, was placed atop the shaft in tribute to the chief. A day of feasting by the Indians marked the dedication. And in turn the Indians not only leased thousands of acres to the Millers, but in full regalia joined heartily in dances and ceremonies at all the wild west functions, giving the 101 Ranch an atmosphere of the West of the old days.

Despite the advantages of civilization, the protection of the government, and the benefits of peace, the Indians of the 101 Ranch will soon be a memory. Swiftly the grim ferryman is beckoning these red men across the dark river to the councils of their forefathers. The handful of Poncas remaining on the ranch today includes nearly all the survivors of this once powerful and populous tribe. "They always have been, and still are," in the words of Hubert Collins, "human beings who act, talk, and think as well as any other human race on the earth."

X

IN the fall of 1882 the citizens of Winfield, Kansas, were planning their first agricultural fair, and they needed some unusual entertainment to attract the necessary crowds. They presented their difficulty to Colonel George W. Miller, who had just finished a cattle drive up the Chisholm Trail, and who still had with him a group of cowboys. With customary ingenuity, the Colonel proposed an exhibition of roping and riding events, which was enthusiastically received by the people of Winfield.

Twenty-two years elapsed before the next round-up show was held. It was also directed by the Millers at the 101 Ranch, and marked the modern beginning of those thrilling displays of western skill and daring—the rodeos. Since then this form of entertainment has been adopted in many places throughout America, and since 1924 an International Rodeo is held in London, England, many of the prizes being won by men who participated annually in the 101 Ranch rodeo arena. The Miller brothers frown upon the use of the word "rodeo," and remain true to "round-up" as the best and most suggestive name for these wild west sports.

In the early part of 1904 Colonel Joe Miller went to St. Louis with Frank Greer of Guthrie and a few other Oklahoma newspapermen to induce the National Editorial Association to hold its 1905 convention in Guthrie. He promised the editors a big wild west show if they would come. Accordingly, in order to prepare for the big event in 1905, the Miller brothers held a round-up in the fall of 1904, just to see whether it could be done. They were gratified with the result.

Then came the National Editorial Association to Guthrie, Oklahoma, June 7, 8, and 9, 1905, and the big round-up June 11, at the 101 Ranch. Geronimo, the old Apache warrior, a government prisoner, came up under guard from Fort Sill and the Poncas on the ranch appeared in full regalia. A huge pasture was fenced off for the sports, and the people came from almost everywhere. Trains began to arrive from all directions and discharging their loads at the exhibition grounds, returned and were sidetracked in the Ponca City yards. Altogether there were thirty regular and special trains, many of them double headers, and all loaded even to the roofs of the cars. One hundred section men looked after the tracks and cars, and the station masters from Newton and Oklahoma City aided the local forces—handling the trains and crowds.

The special trains carrying the National Editorial Association arrived about noon, and so far as could be ascertained nearly every member was present, not even excepting those from Maine and Vermont!

Shortly after two o'clock the procession, nearly a mile in length and escorted by the Miller brothers, came in at the east entrance. In the lead was the cavalry band, behind which came the famous old Indian war chief, Geronimo, hero of a hundred battles with the whites. He bowed and smiled and enjoyed immensely the attention he attracted from the mighty throng of people as he passed around the arena. Following this came other bands and a long precession of cowboys and Indians, the latter wearing their sacred finery. The pioneer wagon train, drawn by oxen, brought up the rear. The parade was a thrilling and spectacular sight such as few people will ever again be permitted to witness in these days, and fortunate indeed were those who were inside the great amphitheater.[1]

After the parade the arena was cleared and the program carried out as had been advertised. The large herd of buffalo, which had been secured at great expense, was turned into the enclosure and representation given of the genuine buffalo hunt, a thing of the past for nearly forty years, and which will probably never again be seen in any country. Buffaloes, which were so numerous on the plains years ago, were now almost extinct, the only large herd in existence being the one on the 101 Ranch. Over two hundred Indians took part in the chase.

Then followed bronco busting, Indian ball, the roping contest and Indian war dance and pow-wow. The performances of Miss Lucile Mulhall and her trained horse attracted the most attention. Miss Mulhall had the reputation of being the best and most daring horsewoman in the world, and her achieve-

[1] 101 Ranch Records, 1905.

[143]

ments aroused a mighty applause from the vast throng. After the program began, one event followed the other in rapid succession and there was not a moment when interest lagged or the crowd became restless. As a closing feature of the day a wagon train was attacked by the Indians on a hill south of the amphitheater, and the spectators were given a chance to see what an Indian raid meant to the pioneers. In the gathering dusk the burning wagons with howling Indians riding fiercely about them, caused a feeling of awe to settle over the entire assembly and there was hardly a person present but felt the blood tingle in his veins at the portrayal.

Those competent to judge say it was the largest crowd ever assembled up to that time in Oklahoma. When the parade began at 1:30 P.M., on Sunday, there were 65,000 people watching and it was an intelligent and good natured crowd, no fault being found with such small and unavoidable inconveniences as always occur where there are large gatherings.

While the round-up was being planned, absurd stories about it became current. One was that Geronimo had offered a prize of $1,000 to anyone who would permit himself to be scalped on the occasion. Another was that the Millers were to sacrifice thirty-five buffalo in one grand battle. The Indians, according to the tale, were to be turned loose among the herd with bows and arrows to show how their ancestors hunted the buffalo. The story reached New York in credible form and, forthwith, Mr. Dan Beard, the well-known editor and lover of wild life, telegraphed to Colonel Joe Miller inquiring if the herd were to be killed by the Indians. Receiving no reply, Beard telegraphed the President requesting him to stop the slaughter, who, in turn, telegraphed the Governor of Oklahoma to send troops up to the 101 Ranch to prevent it. The troops came to the ranch at public expense. And here is Colonel Miller's explanation:

"I had requested the Adjutant-General of Oklahoma to permit two companies of soldiers to come up at my expense, which would have been about $1,000. The soldiers would have been glad to come, but the Adjutant-General refused. I was wondering how I should handle that crowd of 65,000 people without soldiers, when Mr. Beard's telegram came. I saw a way. I said nothing. The troops came at the expense of the territory."

On Saturday afternoon, in presence of the delegates of the National Editorial Association, a single buffalo was killed. It had been the plan of the Millers to kill but one bull, for a feast of buffalo meat, and, to add picturesqueness, to kill him by the chase instead of merely shooting him at the slaughter house. The old bull was driven from the herd and chased by the Indians up in front of the 'White House' where he was finally killed. The editors had buffalo meat for dinner that evening.

From 1904 down through the following years the Miller brothers continued holding the annual round-up at the ranch. A rodeo arena was constructed at the headquarters with a seating capacity of ten thousand and was the finest and largest in the Southwest. The program always included all kinds of roping and riding, bulldogging, Indian dances and other western events.

Because of the fact that the rodeo, as a form of entertainment, originated on the 101 Ranch, and that the best known cowboys of the country have been employed on the ranch at some time, many of them becoming prominent in the moving picture and rodeo world, the Miller brothers felt that the 101 Ranch was the logical place for holding world championship contests. Therefore, beginning with the 1924 round-up the annual winners of the roping and riding contests were proclaimed the world champions and silver medals were awarded to that effect.

The round-up was always scheduled for the early part of September and continued for three days, including Labor Day. It was not put on as a money-making proposition but solely for amusement of friends and also to keep in training a good sized bunch of cowboys and cowgirls, in order that the old régime would not be forgotten.

The 1920 round-up was arranged as a benefit for the Chamber of Commerce band and all the preparations for the event were made by the members of the band committee in conjunction with the Miller brothers. In providing a band for Ponca City and making possible the open air concerts that were being held weekly, the Chamber of Commerce had expended several thousand dollars and it was desired to reimburse this fund, if possible, through the round-up.

[145]

The estimate of moving picture men and others, experts in estimating the size of big crowds, was that more than eleven thousand people attended the round-up Sunday, and that approximately twenty-five hundred automobiles were on the ground; or in other words, there were more than $2,500,000 worth of automobiles in the buffalo park, where the roping arena was built.[2]

The round-up had been widely advertised and people came from many cities. The ticket sellers reported persons from Chicago, Kansas City, St. Joseph, New Orleans, Shreveport, Fort Smith, Dallas, Denver, Wichita Falls, Santa Fe, Omaha and other points, and cars were on the ground from as far west as Anthony, Kansas, Enid and Hennessey; north to Wichita; east to Bartlesville; and south to Oklahoma City, Stillwater and Guthrie. Cars began arriving at eight o'clock in the morning. The Millers were assisted by many notables, including Colonel Zack Mulhall of former show fame; C. K. Williams, the moving picture producer; Henry Grammar, J. H. Cornett, the Shultz brothers, and various others whose names were always read in connection with successful round-ups.

The largest wild west show in the history of the Southwest, celebrating the thirteenth anniversary of the opening of the Cherokee Strip, was held September 16, 1906, at the 101 Ranch. The display of cowboy horsemanship and cattle roping was simply a postscript to a book that had been written. The occasion gave opportunity for a reunion of old-timers, and they came by hundreds. Fully fifty thousand people attended the celebration, twenty excursion trains on the Santa Fe railroad bringing in the crowd. Two thousand people took part in the program, including five hundred cowboys and a thousand Indians.

The Indians smeared themselves with paint, adorned themselves with feathers, glittering armlets and wristlets of German silver, slung their war shields across their shoulders, and armed themselves with spears, bows, arrows, and guns. Among the Indians were men who in younger days had been on the warpath. The younger Indians were mere imitators, trying to do things as the old men had told them they should be done. It was noticeable that the old men painted not only themselves,

2 *Ponca City News,* September 7, 1920.

[146]

but their ponies, which was in accordance with the old custom of the Indian country.

The tepees in the Indian camp at the 101 Ranch were in shape and equipment just the same as they were in former days. Notwithstanding the fact that the Federal government had provided houses for its Indian wards, the latter preferred living in their conical canvas tepees, and remained in them throughout the summer and a greater part of the winter.

The Indian women and children enjoyed the spectacular show with possibly greater interest than did the white persons. They sat in groups in the grandstand and each place was a blaze of brilliant calico dresses and gaudy handkerchiefs. When kodaks were pointed in their direction many of the mothers would hide their babies beneath their shawls. The superstitious Indian fears the kodak for the reason that he believes a photograph steals away at least a portion of the soul of the person whose likeness is taken, and that sickness and death may follow.

The old Indians in Oklahoma had abundant reason for remembering the soldiers of the regular army, and the younger ones had listened to tales of warfare until the sight of soldiers quickly attracted and held their attention. A company of militia from Oklahoma City engaged in a mimic battle with the warriors in the anniversary exhibition. A big Indian, fully armed and wearing a war bonnet, rode cautiously in the direction of the soldiers, dismounted from his pony and crawled through the grass, spying upon the enemy. He took the precaution of hobbling his pony with his bridle rein, to prevent the pony's stampeding should his owner be fired upon.

At the sight of the Indian scout there was a stir among the Indian women. They watched him intently, and when he returned to his comrades and the band of yelling Indians charged upon the soldiers, there was great commotion among the women. Round and round the company of soldiers the Indians circled in their attack, the rifles of the soldiers rattling in volleys. Possibly the Indian women were chagrined when the warriors were repulsed and driven from the field, as they were when they charged a second time. They talked about it in rapid gutturals, and sometimes amplified their conversation by recourse to the sign language.

[147]

One of the exciting features was the roping of wild steers from the open ranges of Texas. Bill Pickett, the originator of bulldogging, rode into the arena on horseback, seized a steer by the nose with his teeth while riding, and, allowing his horse to run from under him, grappled with the steer until it lay helpless and prostrate on the ground.

The reproduction of the race for homes at the opening of the Strip was realistic. Hundreds of men were there who had taken part in the original race. Farmers came in covered wagons from their homes in the surrounding country, bringing their wives and children and their dogs, to participate in the anniversary "run." When the word was given each man struck out for himself, his wagon rumbling and bounding over the prairie, the dogs barking, the bands playing in the grandstand and the fifty thousand spectators shouting. Twice around the arena went the homeseekers.

The winner was "Aunt Eliza" Carpenter, an old Negro woman of Ponca City. She drove two fast ponies to a buggy and stood erect like a Roman charioteer. "Aunt Eliza" was tall and angular, and many persons mistook her for a man with burnt cork on his face and dressed in women's clothes.

This old woman, a native of Virginia, was a well known character in northern Oklahoma. She made the original race and staked a good farm, but lost it, because of describing it inaccurately at the land office. She rode her horse like a man and covered twelve miles in forty-five minutes. For more than thirty years she had owned a number of race horses, and had followed country circuits, winning many races and considerable money.

The Miller brothers gave to the world a new sport—the terrapin derby—an annual event that occurred at the 101 Ranch on Labor Day in connection with the round-up. The idea originated with Colonel Joe Miller in the early summer of 1924, while he was standing talking with Lute Stover, a life long friend, and watching several land turtles crawl about near the 101 Ranch office building.

"Do you remember, Lute," queried Joe, "that old Æsop Fable of the tortoise and the hare and how the tortoise, although so blamed slow, finally won a race between the two because he kept plugging away?"

[148]

OIL PAINTING BY A. L. EAGLESON, OKLAHOMA CITY

The 101 Ranch rodeo in action (bulldogging)

"Yes, I remember," said Lute. "But who ever heard of a turtle of any kind in a race?"

"Well, I don't know that I ever did," answered Colonel Joe, "but I believe it would be an interesting stunt, just the same."[3]

And thus was born in 1924 the idea of the terrapin derby. "Well, we didn't get the idea until pretty late," says George L. Miller, "so there were only 114 terrapins entered in the first derby, but we charged $2.00 entry fee apiece, and decided to give half of it, or $114, for first money, $68 for second, and $46 for third."

"How did you know the terrapins would race?" Mr. Miller was asked.

"We didn't," he replied calmly. "That was half the fun of it all."[4]

Well, everyone who saw the derby declared it was plenty of fun. The 114 terrapins were put in a cage in the center of a large arena at the ranch and a large white circle was drawn in a 100-foot radius from the cage, with lesser circles at the 20, 40, 60, and 80-foot marks. The terrapin who crossed the outside circle first was to be judged the winner, the circle being one hundred feet in any direction from his cage and it being understood, of course, that the terrapins would travel in every conceivable direction once the cage was lifted. For that reason the circle had to be divided into eight or so parts, like a pie, and a judge put at the intersection of each dividing line and finish line.

The next problem was how to make the terrapins race. It was a certainty that they had no competitive instinct. It was equally certain that they could not see food—even luscious peaches, of which terrapins are unusually fond—at a distance of one hundred feet. Did one whistle to terrapins, perhaps? Nothing like it. The Miller brothers and various interested friends spent the greater part of one morning standing one hundred feet away from a group of placid terrapins and alternately whistling, clucking, whinnying, and even mooing to them. It was all to no effect.

The whole plan seemed doomed, when George L. Miller, fooling with one of the terrapins, disconsolately, made a mo-

[3] *Daily Oklahoman,* February 6, 1927.
[4] *Kansas City Star,* August 30, 1925.

mentous discovery. The only thing on earth, apparently, that would give the terrapin a desire to walk was to put it in the sun. It then impatiently, and almost querulously, would waddle to the shade. Mr. Miller, fascinated, picked it up again, put it in the sun again, and once more Mr. Terrapin waddled to the shade, pausing only to take an aggravated nip at Mr. Miller's ankle in passing.

"I've found the answer, men!" Mr. Miller shouted, triumphantly. "Fix it so the cage and the race course are in the sun and the finish line borders in the shade, and we've solved our problem."

"What if it's a cloudy day?" put in Joe Miller, pessimistically.

"Rain insurance," snapped George, with a glare at his brother.

"But suppose they just stay there indefinitely? The whole thing will be an awful flop."

"They won't all stay there," soothed Joe, sagely. "Some of them are bound to amble around and finally cross the line. You'll find terrapins are curious, just like human beings. If it takes them some time to reach the finish, and if they amble around a bit, that all adds to the uncertainty of the race and the interest in it."

The day of the race dawned brilliantly and the afternoon saw five thousand persons in the stands at the ranch arena, all "pulling" mentally and vocally for their favorite entry. Each terrapin had been named by its owner, and each had had a glaring white number painted on its back—in regular racing motor car fashion. Some of the men had trained their own terrapins in their back yards for a couple of weeks, and laid high wagers upon the speed of their animals. A band was playing, visiting Indians were livening things up with their tribal yells, and everybody was highly excited—except the terrapins. They seemed in a placid stupor that worried George L. Miller.

"Supposed they just stay that way after the cage is lifted," he whispered to Joe. "Suppose they don't go anywhere at all?"

"That will be their owners' bad luck," the latter answered blithely.

"Foghorn" Clancy, a gentleman known from the Cherokee Strip to the Rio Grande for the mammoth capacity of his vocal cords, announced the derby in stentorian terms and then Fred Olmstead of the 101 Ranch went out to the cage in the middle of the arena to act as starter. Mr. Olmstead's chore was to see that all the terrapins were comparatively wide awake when the barrier was lifted, or, at least, were on their feet. It instantly developed that he had been given the most onerous task of the day.

Did you ever try to keep 114 terrapins on their feet and off each other's backs and generally in apple-pie racing order? No? Then you have no idea of what Fred Olmstead had on his hands.

"Of all back-breaking, dizzy, impossible jobs that was the worst," he says. "I would get them all set ready to go and then Jenny Lind would take a bite at Marie Antoinette and I would have a first class fight on my hands and have to pull them apart. I would get them straight again and then Star of the Night would fancy he saw a shady spot directly under Easter Bells and would try to burrow down to it.

"Men, I stooped over and picked up terrapins and put them down and turned them over and moved them around until I felt more wilted than my collar! At last I waved my handkerchief, the man on the side line pulled the rope that lifted the cage by a pulley, and the terrapins were free to race."

Then occurred the best and funniest part of the whole affair. There was one terrapin whose owner had trained it painstakingly in the back yard for two weeks and it was supposed to be a "racing fool." That terrapin calmly drew in its head and legs when the carrier went up and went to sleep for the afternoon, refusing to move an inch. Other terrapins got into personal combat with each other and turned the contest from a race to a fight, at least so far as they were concerned. Still other racers hurried around and around the original cage site and would not venture outside its bounds. Still more waddled in good style out to the first white line, became suspicious of the way it glared up at them, and promptly retraced their steps to the society of their companions. A few of the animals—a fairly respectable number at that—ambled steadfastly for the finish line and its inviting border of shade, and these were the ones among whom, it soon appeared, the race lay.

A couple of terrapins got clear to the finish line and became distrustful of it, sitting with their front feet upon it, but refusing to venture over. How like Tantalus they made their owners feel—with victory and a good sized money purse just on the tips of their fingers, and not being able to grasp it!

While these turtles were thinking the matter over, "Shingles," a nondescript-looking animal, entered by Harry Cragin, President of the Ponca City Chamber of Commerce, fairly fell over the finish line and collapsed exhausted, but supremely contented, in the shade.

Close behind him, and to the accompaniment of shrill yells of triumph from all the Indians present, arrived "Ponca Agency," entered by George Hoyo, superintendent of the Ponca Indian agency. Third came lumbering in "Zev," entered by Charles Hurford, a Ponca City merchant. The two terrapins who had been sitting complacently near the line finally decided to cross after these three pioneers, but met only the maledictions and supreme ill-will of their aggravated owners.

Thus ended the first terrapin derby on the 101 Ranch, and it was such a success that the spectators clamored for another one. The second derby was held on a scale that dwarfed its pathfinding parent. Entry blanks were sent out all over the country and entries poured in by the hundreds. At first it seemed as though the several hundred terrapins that were in a stone pit on the ranch would be enough to satisfy all who wanted to enter the derby, but this number was soon exhausted and the Millers had to send out their Indians and cowboys on a terrapin drive to round up more animals.

A visitor to the 101 Ranch was taken to the terrapin pit and given a view of the five hundred animals waiting to have numbers pasted on their backs and be assigned as entries in the terrapin derby. "Pick a turtle and have it run for you," challenged George L. Miller. "The winner is probably right in that bunch, if you have eyes enough to see him."

It was a fascinating thought, at that. There, for $2.00, a man could get a chance that might repay him a thousandfold, and the sporting element of the thing was present, too. "Here goes nothing," sighed the visitor, taking two $1.00 bills out of his pocket, and then he looked around to try to find himself an active terrapin.

The day was dark and humid and the terrapins lay somnolent, none evidently having the least ambition to "go places and see things." The visitor was about to restore his $2.00 to his pocket when a cowboy behind him drawled:

"Hey, mister, one of them there terrapins is about to bite a chunk out of you."

The visitor looked around hurriedly and, sure enough, there at his heel was squatted probably the smallest terrapin in the place, with head extended from his shell, obviously ready to take an aggravated nip at the visitor's sock. He picked the terrapin up and, instead of immediately drawing its head and feet under its shell, as terrapins usually do when molested, it struggled and wrestled around for dear life, moving all four feet in a rapid if ineffectual effort to go somewhere and get there quickly! When he placed the terrapin on the floor, it made tracks for the side of the pit, faster than he had imagined a terrapin could travel. "Hi yi!" shouted the cowboys delightfully. "Look at that old terrapin travel! That's a runnin' fool, mister. He's just as liable to win the derby as not. Grab him off, man!"

The visitor was fascinated. He rescued the terrapin from the side of the pit, put it in the center once more, and once again it lumbered to its retreat. There was another rescue and this time the terrapin, apparently irked exceedingly at the various paces that were being demanded of it, decided to take the matter of warfare into its own hands and proceeded to attempt to ascend the visitor's body between the trousers cuff and the hose, a move that made the visitor go into an eccentric dance that was punctuated by violent kicks with his left leg.

When the terrapin had been routed and the delighted cowboys had stilled their gusty applause, the visitor seized the animal firmly about its middle and marched up to the ranch house with it.

"Here!" he announced to George L. Miller, depositing the terrapin unceremoniously on Mr. Miller's desk. "Write me out a receipt! This is my entry in the derby."

"Good," said Mr. Miller. "What is its name?"

"Bridesmaid," replied the visitor, the name occurring to him on the spur of the moment.

Thus the second derby was run in 1925 with 1,679 entries; the third in 1926 with 2,373 entries, and down through the following years, always with increasing entries. What made the sport popular was the fact that there was no profit in it for anyone. Every dollar of the entrance money was distributed in prizes. No percentage was held for expenses since it was a sporting event entirely, conducted in such a way that no unfair practices of any nature could enter into it. Only land terrapins were permitted in the derby—the kind common throughout the Southwest.

The many diversified resources of the 101 Ranch made it the natural show place of the Southwest. There was ranching in all its old-time picturesqueness. There were thousands of cattle and horses, the unblocked trails and the cattle pastures, the unchanged cowboys, the round-up camps, the rodeo, the corrals, the buffalo, and many tribes of Indians, living undisturbed in wigwams, lodges, or rough houses. And withal there was the western hospitality and cordial generosity of the Millers. They never asked for credentials. They never kept a guard at the door to keep out human hankering for food and good cheer. They had as much use for butlers and servants to formally announce arriving guests as a tamale vender has for a board of directors. "Come one, come all"—that was the hospitality of the Millers at all times.

Because of this hospitality, men, women, and children from all walks of life came in ceaseless numbers to observe the diversified resources of the 101 Ranch and to enjoy its fascinating charms. "It was," says Corb Sarchet, "one continuous entertainment of guests, social, political, business leaders, writers, explorers, actors, the prominent men and women in every line. Presidents of giant railway systems mingled with the cowboys and donned their regalia, pleased at the chance. Admiral Byrd rode the elephants; John Philip Sousa joined the Ponca Indian tribe; Mrs. Mary Roberts Rinehart came for atmosphere when she was ready to write her *Lost Ecstasy;* Walter Teagle sat on the floor with a bust of Geronimo, the Apache chief, in his arms to be enlightened on the price of crude oil; Will Irwin and his wife, Inez Haynes Irwin, came for a day and remained a week; William Jennings Bryan shook hands with Tony, the monkey; Sidney Smith drew Andy Gump on the White House walls; Teddy Roosevelt was delighted; Will Rogers sang cowboy songs all night long with Mrs. Pawnee Bill at the piano;

[154]

Fred Bonfils came to see the terrapin derby; Jack Mulhall was on hand to star in the moving picture—Nancy Astor, John Ringling, Randolph Hearst, William S. Hart, Irvin Cobb, Rex Beach, Richard Bennett, General Bullard, Charles Curtis, William F. Cody (Buffalo Bill), William Allen White, Helen Gibson, Bacon Rind, Art Gobel, Will Hayes, General Savitsky, John D. Rockefeller, Jr., James E. Garman, Warren G. Harding, Roy Howard, Ezra Meeker, Colonel Zack Mulhall—what an array! Unceasingly they came—each found the same welcome, each was enchanted, each had seen a fairyland."[5]

The National Editorial Association, with its several thousand members, visited the ranch twice, in 1905 and 1925. The Oklahoma Press Association members were the ranch guests in 1922. The National Realtors were there in 1926, and the American Association of Petroleum Geologists in 1927. Crippled children workers were there, too. When members of the Oklahoma State Board visited Lew Wentz at Ponca City in 1927, George L. Miller entertained the entire membership at dinner. The state Sunday school convention, the state florists, and many other similar groups were entertained from time to time on the ranch.

The cowboy's occupation in Oklahoma is gone, but the cowboy himself, the genuine, simon pure article, remains the last of his generation and his time. When he takes his final departure down the long, white trail, his campfire will never be relighted. Save in the Texas Panhandle, in limited portions of Western Oklahoma, and in the big grazing pastures of the Osage Indian reservation, the cowboy now lives on a farm. He wears high-heeled boots, spurs, a broad hat, rides a good saddle and carries his lariat, but these things are mostly a matter of old habit.

Perhaps one of the most unusual groups entertained on the 101 Ranch was an organization of these old cowboys, known as the Cherokee Strip Cowpunchers Association. Its members were veterans of the time when it was necessary also for the cowboy to be an Indian fighter whenever the occasion demanded.

There were about four hundred members of the Cherokee Strip Cowpunchers Association in good standing. It was or-

[5] *Daily Oklahoman,* December 16, 1934.

ganized on September 6, 1920, on Cowboy Hill in the buffalo pasture of the 101 Ranch. The majority of the members, of course, were from Arizona, Colorado, Kansas, California, Missouri, Arkansas, Iowa, Oregon, and Washington. Every man was a cowpuncher during the time that the Cherokee Strip was a cattleman's paradise and known in history as one of the greatest cattle domains that ever existed. Reunions were held at Cowboy Hill on the 101 Ranch at the same time the annual round-up and terrapin derby were held.

The association was organized for the purpose of bringing the veterans together annually, thus promoting a better fraternity among those, who in the distant past, prior to 1893, shared their hardships and were brothers to each other under all conditions. A further purpose was to foster that spirit of fellowship by organization, making it possible in the years remaining to meet at least once annually. The first of the members was secured through many difficulties by the secretary, but it was re-arranged and added to gradually, and in addition, the secretary collected all available data about the members, living and dead, and the organization itself, so that he could supply the information to those who desired it.

The reunions of the association were wonderful meetings, where the members brought their equipment for camping out and told tales of things that happened, and sang the songs that they sang while riding the range prior to '93. Each night there was a campfire with plenty of barbecued meat and cider on tap, experience meeting that ran far into the night with stories of the round-up, brushes with the Indians, necktie parties for rustlers, and all the memories that were connected with chaps, lariat, and spur.

Here were assembled the men who had ridden the Chisholm Trail, who knew Pat Hennessey and Bat Masterson and Jesse Chisholm personally, who visited Abilene and Dodge City and Caldwell when they were wide open border towns, who had driven the herds from Texas to Kansas, cut the wire fences of the persistent homesteaders and then protected them against Indian attacks—men who, because of their lives in the open, were still young men in physique despite the fact that they were grizzled veterans.

"No cowboy ever bought a horse blanket in those days,"

was a story told at one of the campfires. "The Ponca Indians buried their dead on top of the ground and they would place beside the body handsome saddle blankets as well as other equipment for the warrior's happy hunting ground. I can tell the world now that very few of them ever used a saddle blanket after death, for the cowboys got them all."

Abe Banta of Billings, Oklahoma, was the first President of the Cowpunchers Association, but at the second meeting, Colonel Joe Miller was unanimously elected president for life, truly a distinction, with Oscar Brewster of Crescent to continue as secretary-treasurer. The association grew to such an extent that it was necessary to name an executive committee to help out with the work, and also a "ladies auxiliary." The old boys had learned the worth of the ladies since the days they "yipped" it across the prairies of the Cherokee Strip. The wives of all the cowboys were eligible to membership. President Joe Miller named Ike Clubb of Kaw City, Hugo Milde of Kaw, Link Barr of Dover, George Laing of Kingfisher, and Monte Tate of Oklahoma City as his executive committee. Some of the members, who attended the reunions, were past eighty years old, having been men of past middle age when the Strip was opened.

When the old cowpunchers met they invariably called upon Oscar Brewster to cook a few dozen pans of biscuits, for Brewster was a famous chef in cowboy camps prior to '93. There never was a cowboy camp in which hot biscuits were not served regularly. "That was because the packages of baking powder put out in those days carried a recipe on the can telling how to make biscuit," said Brewster, "and every fellow that ever cooked in a cowboy camp learned how to make them."

At one of the early reunions, Colonel Zack Miller said: "Boys, the 101 Ranch is yours, anywhere you say, make camp. If you want the White House location, we can move it. We will give you a lifetime lease on as much land as is needed for your accommodation." They selected the site on the bluff on the south side of the Salt Fork River adjacent to the pavement and bridge. The site today is known as "Cowboy Hill" and is set in bermuda grass, shrubbery, and trees. Here the old cowboys held their annual reunion, reliving the old days of the Cherokee Strip.

Young men from the east, whose fathers' wealth ran well into the millions, came to the ranch almost every season as far back as 1905 to spend their vacations, taking this opportunity to learn to ride, to rope, and to take part in the regular ranch activities. The Millers "educated" four hundred such young men during the four summer months, or approximately one hundred each month. They employed all their horses and cowboys in this line of work during the summer months, and the cowboys themselves always expected a regular circus of a time training the tenderfeet. Cowboys came to the 101 Ranch from all parts of the West to be assigned places on the "faculty," and among those who "taught" were several Rough Riders and some of the champion ropers and riders of the country.

"We will furnish them a good mount and saddle," says Colonel Joe Miller, "and put them in camp down along the Salt Fork River. We will let them sleep out of doors, eat from the tail end of a wagon and live the regular cowboy life, but of course without much of the work of it unless they really want to work; then they will be given all they want. We'll send some of the cowboys who are pretty good fellows—good story tellers and all that—over to take care of them, and have a cattle round-up once in a while for their benefit."

Ranged in a circle in a shady grove on the banks of the Salt Fork, near the White House, were a number of comfortable three-room cottages in which the young men lived during their stay on the ranch. They ate their "chuck" in common in a dining hall twenty-four by fifty feet in size, their waiter being an unusually dark complexioned negro. One cottage was used as a library and club room. The apartments were adorned with college pennants, cowboy pictures, and such other things as attracted the fancy of college students. The dude ranch, thus, was a reality on the 101 Ranch from 1905 to 1909.

The cowboy outfit was purchased by the "dudes" and some of the outfits caused old-time cowboys to stand wide-eyed in astonishment. The boys chose their own hours for arising. When ready for the day's jaunt a genuine cowboy would bring a bunch of ponies from which the riders selected their mounts. The Miller brothers trained polo ponies for eastern markets, and in this sport the "dudes" were more proficient than in roping cattle.

For general safety and to insure their return to their parents, each boy, upon his arrival, was photographed for purposes of subsequent identification should he become lost. After he had cast off his "store clothes" and arrayed himself in sombrero, blue flannel shirt, chaps, high heeled boots, and spurs, he was photographed a second time to permit his being traced and located should he wander away in his ranch outfit. The "dudes" were a good natured lot of young men and enjoyed immensely the ranch life provided for them.

Despite the hospitality and cordial generosity of the Miller brothers it was found almost impossible to accommodate the throngs of visitors, tourists, and sightseers who flocked to the 101 Ranch. So eager were they to witness the operations of the vast domain and so absorbed did they become in the sights and scenes that the White House and its adjoining structures were fairly over-run with strangers. Newcomers, finding every living space occupied, sometimes brought along tents and "roughed it."

This overcrowded condition became acute during the summer, but the Millers solved the problem of caring for these annually invading throngs by establishing a camp, operated solely in their behalf and for their comfort and welfare. On the north side of the Salt Fork, a tumbling branch of the Arkansas River, a dozen commodious cottages were erected. Electric light wires were stretched into every room from the central station of the ranch system. Adjoining, an assembly eating hall, in the charge of culinary specialists, was constructed. A clubhouse of ample proportions was placed a few hundred feet away for indoor activities. The Millers called this unusual adjunct, "Riverside Camp."

On the south side of the Salt Fork, opposite the camp, there was a forty acre lake stocked with bass and crappy, known as Red Lake. During the migrating season the lake literally swarmed with ducks and geese, as the Millers always protected them on their flights. There was also a game preserve in which buffalo, elephants, elk, deer, and other wild animals were kept.

Riverside Camp was a success from the start and had devotees and converts to its charm from many sections of the country. Every diversified enterprise of the ranch was opened to their observation and, if they desired, their participation. They participated in the round-ups and rode for miles over interminable prairies with the cowboys; visited the homes and camps of the Indians and watched the performance of strange savage and religious dances and other weird ceremonies and rites; learned how to brand and dehorn and ship cattle by carload to the great stockyards; hunted the furtive coyotes, prairie dogs, wild birds and animals of prairie and forest; watched and sometimes tried the hazardous operations of subduing bucking horses; shot with rifle, shotgun, and pistol at moving and stationary targets; lolled in hammocks under the great spreading shade trees; played polo on the smoothly rolled prairie; gathered in the evening around campfires to tell the romantic doings of the day or sought early rest in the seclusion of their rooms. Everywhere was abounding, buoyant life and vitality, engendered by the health-restoring spirit of the plains.

XI

FOR many years the 101 Ranch had been the wonder spot and show place of Oklahoma. Frequently the Millers gathered their cowboys and horses and steers and buffaloes into a private area, summoned a few score of the Indians, whose primitive homes dotted the grassy bottoms of the ranch, and gave impromptu amateur entertainments. The fame of these spectacular displays soon spread throughout the country. In 1907, when the Jamestown Exposition, Norfolk, Virginia, was promoted, President Theodore Roosevelt invited the Miller brothers, as the most famous representatives of the cattle raising business, to give an arenic display of its features.

That the show from the Oklahoma prairie was the triumph of the fair was remembered by all who attended. The brothers hurried back, recruited another show from the abundant resources of their ranch, and sent it on to Brighton Beach, New York City, where for six weeks it broke metropolitan records. Before the first snow of winter had whitened the 101 Ranch ranges, the Millers and their men and women and livestock were back from what they all called their "spree" with no notion but that their experience as "show people" was over. But the reputation their entertainment had achieved had made too deep an impression. They resisted all overtures, and propositions came to them from many flattering sources, until Edward Arlington placed his plans before them. Then they capitulated and the 101 Ranch wild west show became a permanent factor in the world of amusement.

For years, Colonel Joe Miller had cherished a vision of what he would like to do in the way of preserving frontier customs and conditions. Now he had his chance to realize his dream. "Boys ten years old and younger have never seen a genuine wild west show," said Colonel Joe, "and we are going to make it possible for them to see one." After much thought and planning, he began to prepare a real wild west show, one that would present actual ranch and frontier life as it really existed in the early days, but which was fast passing away. The result of this planning and dreaming was the 101 Ranch wild west show, one of the greatest educational and entertaining enterprises of its kind in the world, and the only one that portrayed ranch and frontier life as it actually existed in the days of the old west. The first exhibition was given in Ponca City, Oklahoma, April 14, 1908.

Mayor Hutchison declared a legal holiday between the hours of 11 A.M. and 6 P.M. in honor of the inaugural performance and the opening of the first annual tour of the Miller brothers 101 Ranch wild west show. The great amusement enterprise gave performances afternoon and evening on the show grounds on Grand avenue and introduced itself to the public in a triumphant street parade.

It was announced by the three Millers and their partner Edward Arlington that all was in readiness for the gala day. The finest circus train in the history of tented amusements was there. Wagons, tents, poles and all the other manifold physical equipment were on the lot; and at the 101 Ranch, performers by the score were awaiting the summons to the full dress rehearsal on Monday evening.

No tented show ever took the road under more happy auspices and felicitous circumstances than this tremendous organization which bore the name of the Miller brothers and was recruited solely from Oklahoma. The eyes of the entire amusement world were focused upon it. From its very nature and source it was the only true typical representative wild west show before the public, and predictions were heard on every hand that its career would be one of uninterrupted patronage and popularity.

Following the engagement in Ponca City the show visited Guthrie, Oklahoma City, Winfield, and Wichita. It then made appearance for two days in Kansas City and followed with an afternoon performance in Fort Madison, Iowa. On the evening of April 23, it began a two-week engagement in the big Coliseum in Chicago. St. Louis was booked for a week and then the show started on a one-day-stand tour for the season.

The Miller brothers ransacked the great Southwest for famous performers in the fields of spectacular western endeavor. Every cowboy, cowgirl, every lasso wielder, every man or woman who aimed a pistol or gun was an admitted champion. The personnel of the arenic department of the organization numbered nearly two hundred persons. Many of them were familiar to the residents of Ponca City for deeds of skill and daring. Colonel Zack T. Miller was in active charge of the performance and no one was better equipped by nature or experience for the important task than he.

One of the feature numbers of the program was a reproduction of the massacre of Pat Hennessey and party, one of the saddest chapters of Oklahoma history. Cheyenne Indians fell upon Hennessey and his companions July 4, 1875, as the freighter was traversing the old Chisholm Trail. Every white traveler had been foully murdered when W. H. Malaley, U.S. marshal, and his band reached the massacre. The 101 Ranch show re-enacted the tragic prairie drama in all its details. To give added realism the Millers secured the presence of Mr. Malaley who went through his movements exactly as performed at the scene of the original massacre. Chief Bull Bear of the Cheyennes was generally accredited with being the author of the murder. He, too, was in the 101 Ranch show arena.

Indian dances and other weird aboriginal rites and ceremonies were one of the features of the show. Scores of red men reached Ponca City at the time of the inaugural performance and took their places in the ranks of the performers—famous old chiefs, warriors, squaws, papooses and pretty dark skinned girls.

Long-horned Texas steers, superb blue-blooded buffaloes came direct from the 101 Ranch. The Millers secured droves of these nearly extinct animals. They were among the four-footed novelties of the show.

One of the principal attractions of the show was Colonel Joe Miller himself. He had been a ranchman for many years before the wild west show was introduced to the public. He was born and brought up on the ranch in the old days. His father went down the trail to Texas in 1871, the first time, covering the whole country from the Rio Grande to North of 36, and on many of these trips was accompanied by the son, Joe. While on these trips with his father, he saw the last of the buffalo on the staked plains of Texas. He saw the country literally covered in places with buffalo bones. He saw the immense herds of cattle grazing throughout the west.

He was unafraid and was one of the cowboys who did things during the border days. Old time cowboys say he never drew a six-shooter in the old days except when necessary, and that he never asked another fellow to ride an outlaw horse that he had not ridden himself. Among all the cowboys there was none who could surpass him in roping a wild steer in a round-up and among the Indians his word was law. It was these experiences in driving cattle continually with his father that made it possible for him, more so than any other living person, to put on the road a wild west show of the character that the 101 Ranch was producing.

It was because Colonel Joe Miller had seen the last of the buffalo herds on the plains and the land covered with buffalo bones that the Miller brothers took such an interest in attempts to preserve the buffalo. They saw the herds vanishing one by one, the prey of ruthless hunters who swarmed from all over the world, and sadly contemplated the approaching extermination of the one distinctive American animal. Through the years the brothers struggled tirelessly to preserve this superb animal and they owned the largest private herd in America. In what was known as "buffalo pasture" on the 101 Ranch, there ranged many of these buffalo, contented and happy, producing the pure-blooded herd used in the wild west show. The "buffalo hunt" was presented in a realistic manner before the people of the country, to millions of whom this event was only romance and fiction.

In the early days of the 101 Ranch, the long-horned steers roamed the ranges by the thousands. But because of the difficulty of fattening them for market, the Millers and other breeders discontinued their production, and the breed vanished quickly. They are today as few in number as the American buffalo. The Miller brothers were among the few persons in the country interested in their perpetuation. They ransacked the Southwest in their quest for the animals, and assembled a large herd on the 101 Ranch. The steers used in the wild west show were the finest specimens of the home herd, with horns as long as six and seven feet. They were the real, lean, rough, bony, untamable cattle typical of the Texas trails of years gone by.

Many of the cowboys with the wild west show were permanent employees of the Miller brothers, hired for their ability on the range and round-up and used in the show arena only at intervals. There was a constant procession of cowboys traveling from the 101 Ranch to the show, and back again. The exuberant young men who struggled with the bucking bronco for the amusement of the public one day might be branding calves on the ranges of the 101 Ranch the next week. They were at once the most daring, most skillful, most graceful, and most useful horsemen in the country.

Accustomed to roam and range upon their wiry, fleet-footed cow ponies, for days and nights over miles of unclaimed country, the cowboy became, perforce, the pilot of the would-be pioneers, the scout of military expeditions, the leader of colonies and boomers, the Nemesis and prosecutor of ferocious Indians bent on devastation and ravage. All of these rôles of the cowboy were depicted realistically in the 101 wild west show arena.

Along with the 101 Ranch men came a company of Mexican cowboys, and appropriately, for the cattle industry in America had its birth in Mexico. The herds of long-horned, wild cattle drifted across the Rio Grande and out upon the Texas plains. One by one the swart-faced Mexican riders dropped aside and adventurous young Americans leaped into the vacated saddles and rode the trails. The Millers brought from the ranches of the sunny southern republic several dozen *vaqueros,* who were the pride of Mexico, to compete with American cowboys in the saddle and with the lariat in the show arena.

Horseback riding was as common and familiar a pastime to the ranch girl as was hoop-rolling to the girl of the east. She went everywhere on horseback. She could execute an equine quadrille or a Virginia reel, and then gallop twenty miles without feeling a suspicion of fatigue. She could rope and tie a steer, ride a bronco, and lodge a bullet in a target bull's eye as she galloped. She "kept company" on horseback and many a piquant retort and pert speech gained point from the accelerated gait or sudden demivolt of her horse, respondent to impatient or emphatic pressure of dainty heel or cut of quirt.

[165]

The cowgirls riding "buckers" and twisting the lariat in the show arena were, like the cowboys, recruited from the 101 Ranch and adjoining ranches. They could rope from horses running at top speed, swing gracefully from the saddle and pick a fallen handkerchief from the ground, mount and subdue bucking horses, and use gun or pistol with the nonchalance and proficiency of the most expert cowboy.

All these girls from the Oklahoma prairies rode astride their horses, the sidesaddle being unknown in the stables of the Miller brothers. The western woman was frequently in saddle for hours at a time. She acted as mail carrier and purchasing agent for the household, and the trading points were generally miles distant from the ranch house. Often she joined in the round-up of the cattle, in which she was as proficient as the cowboy, and it was not unusual for her to take a twenty-mile jaunt for visit or festival of the plains. No woman could have endured these long rides in a sidesaddle, with its impossibility of changing position.

Many of these cowgirls made their first visit to the crowded cities at the time they performed in the show arena. Never did they dream of Dame Fashion's demands, as illustrated by their sisters of the city. Some of these ranch belles had never seen a parasol and could not understand why one should not welcome the tan which accompanied buoyant health. Lorgnettes, vanity bags, dresses entrain, and turban bobs were beyond their puzzled comprehensions. The plaits, coils, and tresses of fashionable coiffure evoked their curious interest, but no desire for emulation.

The fluctuation of the cowboys and cowgirls between prosaic ranch work and show display had the result of making the 101 Ranch a center and school for many arena stars. Best known among these, perhaps, was Tom Mix, a product of the 101 Ranch, where he rode the ranges with the Millers and learned the many stunts and tricks that have since made him famous as a moving picture star. Mix was with the Millers on the ranch a long time and later was with them on the road with the show. Charles (Buck) Jones was another film luminary whose career began on the 101 Ranch. Several years ago the 101 wild west show was playing at Galveston, Texas. A backward country boy, just discharged from the army, approached

Colonel Joe Miller and asked for a job. He was given the only opening—the task of currying horses for the cowboys. Soon an opening occurred in the cowboy "string" and Jones was given an outfit and a horse. He made a splendid arena performer. The list also included Neal Hart, Vester Pegg, Tommy Grimes, Dan Dix, Helen Gibson, Mabel Normand, and other well-known stars of the moving picture world. It can be said without equivocation that the careers of many of the best cowboys and cowgirls appearing in contests throughout the country originated at the 101 Ranch.

Like every other frontier feature of the 101 Ranch wild west show, the bucking broncos were "the real thing," in testimony of which is offered the emergency hospital maintained with the show. Every day in the season from one to a half dozen cowboys or cowgirls were temporary inmates as a result of their struggles with the equine desperadoes. Men and women of less rugged physique and trained endurance would never have survived the fierce combats.

The 101 Ranch show broncos were naturally irreclaimable fighters whose savage and reckless efforts to throw their riders could not be corrected. They might be temporarily conquered after a prolonged and often dangerous struggle, requiring extraordinary agility, skill and courage on the part of their riders, but with every effort to mount came a renewal of the contest between stubbornness and instinct on the one side and brains and nerve on the other, and in it the nobler animal did not always win the spurs.

In the performances of the bucking bronchos no two resorted to the same tactics of defense. One would permit himself to be saddled and mounted before letting out the deviltry with which his hide was stuffed. Another would quietly submit to being saddled, but that was the limit of his sufferance. To still another the very sight of a saddle was the signal for war; he would start off humping his back like a mad cat, and land stiffly on all fours with a force of a pile driver—or he would lie down and stubbornly refuse to budge. Still another would rear and fall backwards with such reckless fury as to sometimes beat out his brains. A fifth would kick, strike, or bite with a savage viciousness rendering him more dangerous than a hungry lion.

And these are but illustrations among innumerable efforts of the 101 Ranch show bronco to escape the ignominy of bearing a cowboy or cowgirl on his back. In some instances, he seemed intent upon injuring the rider only; in others, he aimed to disable himself; and in still others, he seemed frantically bent upon committing suicide. He was a product of the open ranges of the old days and was a natural actor—so full of fiery and furious vim that he played an indispensable rôle in all the western sports of the wild west show.

The 101 Ranch was in the midst of the great plains tribes of Indians. Over its vast acreages once ranged hostile Cheyennes, Arapahoes, Comanches, Kiowas, Pawnees, Sac and Foxes, Poncas, and Osages. Not only were the reservations of these tribes ransacked for papooses and their mothers, radiant belles of the wigwam, wrinkled warriors, and renowned chiefs, but the Millers lured tribesmen from the far southwest and northwest.

Thus, the Indians with the 101 wild west show represented nearly a dozen tribes. They comprised an ethnological study of fascinating interest. Crooked Nose, a stalwart brave, was the champion bow and arrow shot of the Comanches. Flatiron was looked upon as the greatest orator of the Sioux Nation. It was he who harangued the Indians before they went into the Custer fight. He was too old to do active work with the show, but was taken along for good influence among the Indians, seeming to have power to quiet them when they became restless or dissatisfied. Flatiron was a member of the Oglala tribe of the Sioux Nation, and was one of the hereditary chiefs of that tribe.

Three other Indian warriors who had conspicuous parts in the Custer massacre were members of the 101 Ranch aggregation. They were Charlie-Owns-the-Dog, Standing Cloud, and Long Bull. They were always loath to talk of the slaughter. Long Bull was credited with being one of the greatest Indian statesmen of history. He made several journeys to Washington to participate in negotiations with the white men regarding land claims. Standing Cloud, despite his age, was one of the fleetest sprinters with the show. Charlie-Owns-the-Dog was a cousin of Geronimo.

Swift Deer, bowed with age and the responsibilities of his

profession, was the medicine man of the Indians with the show. While the red men were naturally skillful in curing simple ailments, there were many more serious diseases which they did not at all comprehend and for which they had no medical treatment. Such diseases they believed to be caused by evil spirits, which must be driven away by the dream power of the doctor.

Their native dances, ancient ceremonies, and elaborate rituals were the most entertaining part of the performance in the show arena. The war dances performed were those which the government had for years tried unsuccessfully to discourage and check. The Indian children were prohibited by the federal authorities from watching the fantastic, savage evolutions in which the old Indians feigned war, pretending to attack and scalp their enemies, which they entered into with a spirit of grim reality.

The Indian children were one of the interesting sights and studies of the show. The tiniest of them were securely tied to their boards—the primitive cradle—from which they gazed solemnly, with unwinking eyes, upon their new and uncomprehended surroundings. When not slung on the mother's back, this board with its human burden was suspended from a pole or meat-drying scaffold. No attention was paid to the perspiring youngster, save now and then when it whimpered for nourishment. Other children, a little older, were freed from this imprisonment and played on the ground nearby. Despite the irksome confinement of the board, most of them soon became tired of unaccustomed liberty and cried piteously to be restored to its hard surface. They ceased their lamentations only when preparations were made to confine them again.

The children old enough to walk were comical figures, clad in little smocks that reached their knees. Many had a buckskin string about their necks, which carried amber beads or an amulet to keep off disease or the ghost. They ran, played, shouted, and effervesced with life and spirits, like children the world over.

The older boys were armed with bows and headless arrows, and practiced shooting continually—at a mark or for distance, or vertically into the air in an effort to make the arrow land at some particular point. Many of the young braves engaged in sham battles, conducting a mimic fight much after the manner of men, except that they used mud balls. The little girls made dolls and other toys of buckskin, and built playhouses like their white sisters. They were very timid.

In the Indian village that existed in connection with the show, the Indians were seen as they were in the wilds, not alone for exhibition purposes, but because they preferred it. The squaws were expert makers of bead-work, blankets, baskets, and pottery. The bucks made bows and arrows and would sit for hours, carving out some weird design, without looking up, or saying a word. Representatives of every known tribe were in the village and tribes that had waged war dwelled amicably together, not simply because they wanted to, but also because they were compelled to, for the Indians were never left without guards. They had no respect for the white man's law and had a beautiful way of settling their own difficulties if permitted to do so.

Equestrianism in all its reckless and skillful forms was displayed in the arena of the show. Every performer—cowboy, cowgirl, or Indian—was a product of the prairie, except the contingent of Cossacks, under the leadership of Prince Lucca. These members of Russia's noted light cavalry were brought to this country by the Miller brothers to compete in exhibition with the cowboys. The Cossacks did not attempt the bronco riding feats of the cowboys, but they performed acrobatic exploits that for sheer, dare-devil achievement were sensational. Their horses, accompanying them from the steppes of the Siberian border, were lithe and fiery animals of great speed and endurance.

Wild long-horned steer wrestling, or bulldogging, was one of the cowboy sports included in the wild west show. It was considered by many show spectators the most thrilling of these sports. It demanded daring, strength, and speed. The wrestler who threw his steer in the quickest time, while complying with all rules, was declared the winner. The steers were numbered, and before each contest each wrestler selected his steer by lot. When a steer was released from the chute in the show arena, the animal was given a start across the tape or deadline. The wrestler's objective was to ride alongside, leap from the saddle, grasp the steer's horns, put the steer flat on his side while using only his hands, and then raise one hand to signal he had completed his task. His time was computed from the moment he crossed the tape until he raised his hand in signal.

For this event, each contestant had the assistance of a rider, known as a hazer. The hazer's job was to ride parallel to the contestant on the opposite side of the steer, to keep it heading straight down the arena. This assistance was necessary to prevent the steer from turning abruptly away and charging to some distant point at the critical moment when the wrestler made his jump. The hazer gave no assistance in the actual bulldogging.

The steer had to be thrown by hand, "twisted down," after being brought to a stop. If a steer was accidentally knocked down it had to be let up on all four feet and thrown again. Should a steer start running after once being stopped and then thrown by the wrestler putting its horns against the ground, the steer had to be let up and twisted down properly. A steer was considered down when it was flat on its side with all four feet and head straight. A contestant was limited to two minutes. Owing to the size and vicious nature of the long-horned steers used in this contest, any time under twenty-four seconds was considered exceedingly fast.

Colonel Zack Miller credits Bill Pickett, negro cowboy of the 101 Ranch, with being the first bulldogger. "He slid off a horse, hooked a steer with both hands on the horns, twisted its neck and then sunk his teeth in the steer's nostrils to bring him down," is Colonel Miller's version of the Pickett performance. But as he grew older the teeth and nose stunt was eliminated. He started bulldogging down in the mesquite country in Texas, where the wild growth made it impossible to throw a lariat. Pickett was as much an institution with the Millers as the show itself, and not altogether for his bulldogging ability.

Some years ago when the show was in Mexico, the Miller brothers were at a bullfight. There were some tough bulls in the ring and matadors maneuvered carefully. But Pickett maintained he could not only throw one, but could hold him for several minutes. There was a difference of opinion which resulted in some heavy betting. Pickett's responsibility was great, for the Millers had bet the show against $25,000 in gold that he could hold the bull seven and one-half minutes. The bet got noised around and the scene outrivaled the bull battle in

Quo Vadis. Pickett put the bull down, but the Mexicans protested that it wasn't quite done, so he held on grimly for fifteen minutes. There was nothing left finally except to pay off, which the Mexicans did. Bill Pickett, to say the least, was a great bulldogger!

Bill Pickett was born about 1860 and died April 2, 1932, from injuries received while roping a bronc on the 101 Ranch. He was buried at the foot of the White Eagle monument on the 101 Ranch. Members of the Cherokee Strip Cowboy Association erected a stone marker at his grave, September 6, 1936. On the day of his death Colonel Zack T. Miller, who had been his boss for thirty years, wrote the following lines:

Old Bill has died and gone away, over the "Great Divide."
Gone to a place where the preachers say both saint and sinner
will abide.
If they "check his brand" like I think they will it's a runnin'
They'll give to Bill.   *hoss*
And some good wild steers till he gets his fill.
With a great big crowd for him to thrill.
Bill's hide was black but his heart was white,
He'd sit up through the coldest night
To help a "doggie" in a dyin' fight,
To save a dollar for his boss.
And all Bill wanted was a good fast hoss,
Three square meals and a place to lay
His tired self at the end of day.
There's one other thing, since I've come to think,
Bill was always willing to take a drink.
If the job was tough, be it hot or cold,
You could get it done if Bill was told.
He'd fix the fence, or skin a cow,
Or ride a bronc, and EVEN PLOW,
Or do anything, if you told him how.
Like many men in the old-time West,
On any job, he did his best.
He left a blank that's hard to fill
For there'll never be another Bill.
Both White and Black will mourn the day
That the "Biggest Boss" took Bill away.

Calf roping was always considered one of the interesting cowboy performances in the show arena. It was a contest of speed and skill, and was the one sport where a man's working tool, his horse, becomes his athletic paraphernalia as well. The objective was to rope, throw, and tie a calf in the proper manner for branding in the quickest possible time. Under the strictest rules in cowboy sports, this was not as simple as it appears.

The calves were all of average weight, hence there was no advantage in that respect. But no man could say with any assurance which way a loose calf would run. The calf was released from the chute and given a thirty foot running start before the roper could ride across the dead-line in pursuit. The roper would cast his lariat and was allowed to throw two loops to catch the calf. If he missed both, or if the calf escaped after being roped, the roper retired with "no time."

Immediately after the cowboy had roped his calf, he stopped his horse, dismounted, and proceeded hand-over-hand down the rope. He laid the calf on its side, and fastened any three of its feet together in a tie which the judges deemed suitable—one that would hold. Once the roper had signaled he was through, he could not touch the calf again to strengthen the tie. His time was computed from the moment he crossed the dead-line until he signaled "tied."

Strict rules governed every move, but the foregoing were the ones of most interest in following the performance. The roper was responsible not only for his own observance of the rules, but also for his horse abiding by them. A penalty adding to his time was imposed if the horse "busted" the calf. Here was high skill and co-ordination of effort by rider and horse seldom seen in any other sport.

One of the novelties of the show was the picture of western life representing the attack on the prairie schooner. The old wagon, guarded by a typical frontiersman in coonskin cap and buckskin clothes, followed by another old character who looked as if he might have been one of the "forty-niners," was driven slowly across the arena by six steers, where the Indians swooped down. The following gun shots soon set fire to the cloth covering of the wagon, which blazed up brightly, and in the flames and smoke the Indians and pioneers whirled around on their horses, fired blank cartridges, and yelled at the top of their lungs, making a decidedly vivid scene, which was heightened when a troop of cowboys dashed on the scene and put the Indians to flight.

Another valuable part of the performance was an exhibition of the Pony Express, showing how the mail was carried across the plains in the early days. The express rider, armed and mounted like the brave and hardy men who carried the mail before the railroads, slipped off one horse and on another with lightning speed, hardly losing a minute in the change of horses.

The next feature portrayed the lawless days of the West, when it was never safe to travel over the plains, even with guards. In this exhibition one of the original Deadwood stage coaches was used—a battle-scarred vehicle with many bullet holes along its weather-beaten surface. Its driver, no less spectacular, was an old grizzled veteran of the plains. Inside were the passengers, among them several women, and the strong box of the express company. On top were two or three vigilant guards on the lookout for trouble. Suddenly in the distance a band of Mexican outlaws appeared and then began a running fight between these fierce brigands and those in charge of the stage. It was soon settled, however, for amid the puff of smoke and shriek of bullets the brave defenders were soon overcome and the passengers were an easy prey to the Mexicans, who lined them up at the point of their huge six-shooters and relieved them of their valuables. This had hardly been accomplished, however, when a band of husky vigilants appeared, and after a short battle put to flight or captured the desperadoes, and escorted the frightened passengers to safety.

The show was billed a "Real Wild West" and that was exactly what it was in every particular. There was no aerial work, nor were there any trained seals. It was an authentic show of what the 101 Ranch had been for years on the great prairie region of the Southwest. In fact every detail was covered which would properly illustrate life on the great western plains. A. K. Greenland, writing in the *Billboard*, under date of August 15, 1911, described vividly the 101 wild west show in action in the great Boston arena:

"Early in the morning, everybody looked up the line of march in the papers, and eagerly chose the points of vantage in order to observe the Far West procession. As usual, the

Upper, the 101 Ranch terrapin derby; center, 101 Ranch cowboys; lower, Colonel Joe Miller's show horse, Pedro, and his $10,000 diamond-studded saddle

Boston Commons appealed most strongly, so it was there that so many of us stood.

"We heard a trumpet, then a band. The pageant advances, led by the pick of Boston's police department. Next comes a set of lusty ranchmen, characteristically straddling impetuous bronchos. A long train of Indians, bedecked in feathers and brilliant war paint, now jog on before us. Another cowboy band, then a train of big, heavy show wagons, then the cowgirls, gracefully mounted, joyously greet you. Forthwith you begin to picture the West a land of dream and enchantment. The East and historic New England assume a far less superior station in your opinion. Here come the Mexicans, preceded by dusky 'Bill' Pickett. Following them comes the huge, large horned bull, carrying a human load on its back with the most perfect docility. There are the Cossacks, the buffalo, more cowboys and cowgirls, brought to a close by the piping calliope.

"We enter the arch of the arena, and find our good friends all ready for duty. Joseph C., Zack T. and George L. Miller were the first to be greeted. Their genial smiles soon convinced us that all was prepared and every detail looked out for. There are both George and Ed Arlington busy and occupied, as is also Will Brooks, yet ready to chat for a period. As for optimism, George Arlington is ever the champion, and with pleasure he shows us our seats at the edge of the hippodrome.

"The arena tent measures 390 feet in width by 550 feet in length. Three large horse tents, respectively 40x200, 40x80, and 30x60, have been prepared for the accommodations of the equines. The cook tent is a fence-pole top, measuring 60x180. There are 1,100 people and 600 elephants, camels, horses, buffalo, long-horned steers, oxen, mules, and ponies with the 101 show this year.

"The last strains of Director D. La Blanca's well-disciplined aggregation of cowboy musicians fade away in the roomy realms of the Coliseum. We hold our breath and even upbraid one another for disturbing this period of gripping suspense for audible breathing, when forth comes a blast from the horn of La Blanca, and Joseph C. Miller steps triumphantly forth to the heart of the arena. Reverently raising his hat, he introduces his 1911 ensemble to the eagerly hearkening multitude. His introductory speech is concluded; he motions the director, and out comes the host of adventures from all the climes of the Continent.

"Display No. 1 was now actually passing before them. What a gorgeous review of arenic performers marched forth in file, led by Joseph Miller himself on his steed almost white save for some well-placed brown spots on its haunches. Cowboys, cowgirls, Indian braves and their squaws, Cossacks and Mexicans, a stage coach, and a trio of burlesquing harlequins. Soon the arena is cleared for the individual introduction of the participants.

"The bugle blows for Display No. 2 and in they all dash, one after the other, as follows: cowboys from headquarters, Sioux Indians from Pine Ridge, cowboys from Cowskin Camp, band of Cheyenne redskins from Oklahoma, cowboys from Horse Show Bend, Snake Indians from the Creek reservation, a troupe of Russian Imperial Cossacks, followed by Lucca, their prince, a collection of Mexican *vaqueros* and *rurales,* cowgirls, Chief Eagle Feather of the Sioux, Pickett, the Dusky Demon; D. V. Tantlinger, chief of cowboys, and lastly and therefore most important, Joseph C. Miller.

"They all make their bow and hastily race for the exit, then one of the cowboys gives in Display No. 3 a stirring relay exhibition, attired, armed and mounted, a pouch over shoulder, like the brave and hardy pony express rider who sped across the hostile plains ere the shriek of the locomotive had penetrated the Western frontierland.

"Display No. 4 presents some extremely fancy as well as practical demonstrations with the lariat, lassoing horses at full speed, catching runaways, jumping rope, and spinning bizarre figures.

"Display No. 5 depicts the thrilling exploits of some Mexican bandits, who lawlessly hold up, fight and capture an overland stage coach, plunder the passengers, empty the treasure safe and prepare to make away with the booty when they are attacked by a posse of swiftly-pursuing vigilants, *rurales* and cowboys. Great was the hand-clapping when Eagle, a gray cowpony, feigned injury and limped from the field.

"Display No. 7 calls our attention to Pickett, the modern Urus in a demonstration of courage, nerve, strength and agility in which he duplicates his feat of conquering a Spanish bull

[176]

unarmed and unaided, by forcing the largest of bulls to the tanbark of sheer strength.

"Display No. 8 presents the frolics and pastimes of the boys of 101 Ranch in which they gambol and disport with the joy of the school boy. They pick up handkerchiefs and hats while galloping at full speed.

"Display No. 9 is one that attracts the attention of all those assembled, for D. V. Tantlinger, chief of the cowboys demonstrates the use of the boomerang for the hunt, chase and battle.

"Display No. 10 gives the boys and girls of the ranch a chance to execute, a-horse, the intricacies of the quadrille with grace and abandon. Next comes in Display No. 11 a very effective number wherein Edith Tantlinger challenges exhibition with the shotgun. This act is wonderfully clever and on the opening occasion she made every shot count, penetrating a clay bird with each click of the trigger.

"Display No. 12 exemplifies the degree of perfection to which the prairie equine can be educated. This number presents a large number of well trained high-school horses. The act is climaxed by the excellent equestrianism of Madame Marantette and Col. Harris, who exhibit their two high-school horses, Chief Geronimo and Sun Flower, in their latest departures of high-school stepping. The hit of the act is the close when on her jumping horse, St. Patrick, she cleared a structure six feet, four in height and at that nine and one-quarter inches less than the height for which she is willing to take challenges.

"Display No. 13 tells the story of the horse thief of the prairie, disclosing the marauder taking possession of the cowboy's mount, his escape, pursuit, capture and the subsequent treatment accorded any such miscreant.

"Display No. 14 presents cowboys in military tactics wherein they do some of the cleverest riding of the performance, finishing with a Roman three-horse standing mount.

"In Display No. 15, Princess Wenona comes forth to establish her reputation as a peerless horseback rifle shot. No such a hindrance as a bobbing seat a-horse is able to destroy her aim. This is a very commendable act and deserves to be ranked with the best in the business.

"In Display No. 16 the many spectators are treated to an exhibition of football on horse-back as played by the Mexicans and Indians. Trick riding forms the basis of the next displays, Nos. 17 and 18, and some very hazardous bare-back broncho, steer and buffalo mounts are undertaken and successfully accomplished. It is here that Goldie St. Clair performs her perilous feat of riding the bridleless broncho as does also the daring Virgin L. Barnett, well known for his ability in this line. The bridleless bucking buffalo was successfully ridden by cowboy Tex in Display No. 19.

"Display No. 20 afforded C. C. Lee the opportunity of demonstrating his skill at bareback shooting. Display No. 21 depicts with realism the adventures of our pioneer emigrants. The scene reveals their encampment for the night, their attack by the Indians, the ensuing battle, the massacre and the vengeance of the cowboys.

"Music blazes forth a reluctant farewell. We step into the street and solemnly avow that the 101 Ranch wild west show is unexcellable. A well-disciplined host of acts, of pleasing variety and skillful dexterity have been collected for the year of 1911."

During the seasons of 1914, the wild west show was on exhibition for six months at Shepherd's Bush, London, England. To celebrate the century of peace between the English speaking nations, the Anglo-American Exposition was held during that time and was the occasion for the show visiting England. The Miller brothers went to an enormous expense in putting before the English public a show which had never been equalled in the British Isles, for it was wholly realistic, every member of the show being "the thing" at his or her own particular game. The realism of the western sports aroused much interest in the Londoners as indicated in the following lines:

"Quite the most attractive feature of the Anglo-American Exposition at Shepherd's Bush is the performance which is being given twice daily in the Stadium by 'The 101 Ranch Real Wild West.' This representation of life in the prairies is a wonderful spectacle and one which is wholly new to Londoners, and every one of the performers was born and reared on the 101 Ranch, from which the show takes its name. This ranch, which belongs to Messrs. Miller Brothers, is situated at Bliss, Oklahoma, and comprises some thirty square miles, and over this area are herds of horses and cattle belonging to the ranch, under the guardianship of scores of cowboys and cowgirls, who frequently gather together and hold contests among themselves in lariat throwing, 'busting' bronchos, 'bossing' round-ups, and other such pastimes as form part of the daily life of these people of the plains.

"This is the first time they have been out of America, and they only arrived in this country two weeks ago. With them are a number of Indians, who belong to various tribes, having their homes close to the 101 ranch property in Oklahoma. Prominent among the cowboys are Guy Weadick, who, with his wife, gives some wonderful demonstrations of skill with the lariat; Johnny Baker, who is the stage manager, so to speak, of this arenic display; Stack Lee, whose shooting is a thing to wonder at; and Mr. Zack Miller, one of the famous trio of brothers, whose horsemanship is a delight to all beholders; and Chester Byers, the champion roper of the United States. The cowgirls, too, have their champions, and Lucille Mann, the leading broncho 'buster' of the party, has the distinction of being the only woman who is able to ride 'Thunder,' one of the wildest and most stubborn of the 101 Ranch horses, which have been brought over to England, while Alice Lee and Mable Clive can toss a lariat with the best of the cowboy champions.

"Accommodation is provided under cover for no fewer than ten thousand spectators, so that whatever the weather Londoners can witness this alternately thrilling and picturesque performance under the most comfortable conditions. Exhibitions are given twice daily—viz., at 3:30 and 8:30—and the performance, which goes with a swing from start to finish, occupies only about an hour and a half."[1]

The Indians, who were gay with fresh paint—ready to take the "war-path" in the arena—aroused much interest, as did the cowboys, Mexicans, *vaqueros,* and bucking broncos, but the great attraction was the cowgirls from the western prairies. This fascination of the Londoners is expressed rather pointedly in the *Daily Citizen,* under date of July 11, 1914:

"Red Horn Gulch has come to London and settled at the Stadium, Shepherd's Bush, where, among the many inhabitants of the wild and woolly west are a bunch of the most wonderful cowgirls ever seen east of St. Louis.

"Of course, there are cowboys, *vaqueros,* Red Indians,

[1] *Daily Mirror* (London), May 27, 1914.

bucking mustangs, and a hundred and one other centers of interest at the Stadium, but the great attraction is the wiry but pretty girls who, in divided skirts, top boots, and wide, grey felt Stetson hats, make a picture of femininity quite new to this country.

"None of them talks much; the prairies do not encourage conversation. The girls do not like the cities, and during their appearance at the Stadium they intend to camp in the grounds.

"The most important of the cowgirls is Miss Florence Le Due, of Bliss, Oklahoma. 'Say,' she said to a representative of The Daily Citizen, 'I won my title at 'The Stampede,' Calgary, Canada in 1912, and kept it the following year at Winnipeg. This is the belt I won,' she added as she proudly showed an engraved gold belt which encircled her waist.

"Florence is distinctly accomplished in prairie pastimes. She can 'rope' (lasso) a running horse, steer, or even a man with the best cowboy going, and she can make the lariat do all sorts of twists, loops, and turns. And she can shoot 'some.'

"For Alice Lee of Dallas, Texas, it is claimed that she is the champion woman trick rider of the world. Her star turn is to stand in the saddle and gallop at full speed around the arena, and she also makes a specialty of falling off her horse, catching one foot in the stirrup and doing a kind of compulsory frog-march along the ground.

"Lottie Aldridge, of Greeley, Colorado, is addicted to lying flat on her horse's back and firing a Winchester at hordes of imaginary savages.

"Babe Willetts, of Chickasha, Oklahoma, is a cow-puncher, and she backs herself to cut a steer out of a bunch with any cowboy that ever breathed. Mabel Klein, of Pecos City, Texas; Dot Vernon, of Phoenix, Arizona; Ruth Roach, of Ponca City, Oklahoma; and Jane Fuller, of Eagle, New Mexico, are the chief of the other girl champions.

"The majority of the girls are the daughters and sisters of small ranchers, and all the feats they perform are practically part of every-day ranch life."

Queen Alexandra of England accompanied by the Empress Marie of Russia, Princess Royal and her daughter, Princess Maud sat in the royal boxes when the Millers took a bow and then proceeded to stage the most stupendous wild west performance the old world had ever seen. Soon after the royal party arrived dozens of cowboys, cowgirls, and Indians appeared in the arena uttering their wild cries as they cantered round at breakneck pace. Then came pioneer scouts and an emigrant train. Claims were "staked out," and wild west sports took place. A display of riding by the Russian Cossacks particularly pleased the Empress Marie, who pointed out all the details of their costume to her sister. Some remarkable rifle shooting on horseback also excited the admiration of the royal party. Queen Alexandra, who was dressed in black with a small black net hat and a red rose in her blouse, remained for an hour and a half and evidenced much interest in the performances, as the following lines reveal:

"Queen Alexandra yesterday afternoon paid a visit to the Anglo-American Exhibition at Shepherd's-bush for the primary purpose of witnessing the 'Wild West' performance given within the Stadium. In four motor-cars her Majesty and the party by whom she was accompanied set out from Marlborough House shortly after three o'clock. In the first car were Queen Alexandra herself and the Empress Marie of Russia, attended by Sir Colin Keppel; in the second were the Princess Royal and her daughter, Princess Maud, together with the Hon. Violet Vivian; the third car accommodated the Countess of Antrim, Colonel Streatfeild, Prince Chervachidze, and Countess Mengden; and seated in the fourth were General Sir Dighton Probyn and the Hon. Charlotte Knollys.

"On arrival at the Stadium Queen Alexandra was received by the Earl of Lonsdale and Sir John Cockburn, by whom the distinguished party were escorted to the Royal tribune. To the right of her Majesty sat her sister, the Empress Marie, the Princess Royal, and Princess Maud; and immediately on the left of Queen Alexandra was seated Lord Lonsdale. With the greatest interest the Royal visitors followed every detail of the diversified, and in some respects thrilling, programme; and if one may judge by the emphatic approval which Queen Alexandra bestowed on various items, her Majesty thoroughly enjoyed the performance. More than that, Queen Alexandra took so many snapshots during the entertainment that her camera had to be replenished with a fresh spool of films; and before she left the Stadium she specially requested that the entire

[181]

series of photos bearing on the performance should be forwarded to her in order to supplement her own collection. As the Royal party drove off, the members of the company—Indians, cowboys, and all—lined the route and heartily cheered the departing visitors."[2]

It was a big event for the Miller brothers and set the stage for a tour of European countries. But the tour did not happen. Europe and the whole world went to war. To save the horses and mules, worth much money because of their training, Colonel Zack Miller tendered all the show livestock to Great Britain for war purposes, provided the more valuable animals might be sent back to America. England agreed and the wild west show returned to the prairies of Oklahoma. Following is a copy of the Impressment Order of the British Government seizing the horses of the show for war purposes:

National Emergency.　　　　*Impressment Order under Section 115 of the Army Act.*

To Zack T. Miller, 68 Holland Rd. W.

His Majesty, having declared that a national emergency has arisen, the horses and vehicles of the 101 Ranch Show are to be impressed for the public service, if found fit (in accordance with Section 115 of the Army Act), and will be paid for on the spot at the market value to be settled by the purchasing officer. Should you not accept the price paid as fair value, you have the right to appeal to the County Court (in Scotland the Sheriff's Court), but you must not hinder the delivery of the horses and vehicles, etc. The purchasing officer may claim to purchase such harness and stable gear as he may require with the horse or vehicle.

Charles Carpenter, Sergt.
Place *Shepherd's Bush Exhibition*
Date *7th August, 1914.*

During the war period, the Millers devoted their time to furnishing the government with livestock for war purposes and to building up the 101 Ranch. Following the Armistice, they expanded the oil production on the ranch and when the pro-

2 *Daily Chronicle,* London, England, June 26, 1914.

[182]

duction came in to such an extent, Colonel Joe Miller's feet got to itching for the road again. He began dreaming of the big top, a greater big top than ever before. Day by day he counted the ranch oil wells and while building up the ranch, he began quietly building for another show. When the brothers' bank balance was sufficient to build any kind of show he wanted he got busy. That time came in 1924.

Tom S. Tucker, known wherever shows are known, was the man who put the new show on wheels. The Millers told him they wanted the best equipped show of the kind that could be built. They gave him no limit on expenses. Old showmen say frankly there never was a show on the road with such wagons and such railroad cars as the Miller brothers provided for the show. Scores of workmen, skilled in their trades, were assembled at Marland and big buildings were equipped with special machinery. The forty wagons which were used in the parade were all built at Marland. The band wagon, which could not be duplicated at any price, contained on one side life size wood engravings of the *Aztec Sacrifice* and on the other a life size group of the landing of *Ponce De Leon*. It was a work of art done many years ago by a famous German wood carver, and that was the only piece of old equipment about the show. Nothing was old about that wagon but the wood carving. The wheels and all other parts were new.

The thirty railroad cars to haul the show were new. Most of them were steel. Even the stock cars were steel and for that reason were built on the palace car plan. The living cars for the performers and other employees were strictly up to the best construction plans.

But the climax was reached in the private car of the Miller brothers which was the home of Joe, Zack and George Miller while the show was on the road. The car was a veritable palace on wheels. It had baths, electric lights, library, and in fact every convenience that the modern home has. It was artistically designed and furnished.

Almost twice as big as the top of the old 101 Ranch show, the big top and all the canvas were new. Most of the long staple cotton used in making the canvas was raised on the 101 Ranch. The timbers needed were sawed on the ranch and even the stakes and seats were built there.

The cook wagons, carrying ice boxes with a two-day supply of ice capacity, were marvels of construction. They had been built so that forty minutes after the wagons got on the lot, meals for five hundred persons would be ready.

The lighting was another unusual feature. Never before had such a lighting system been built for a show. The lights were so powerful that it was possible to see a pin in any part of the tent when they were on in full force and still there was no glare. The electric switchboard had been arranged to give as good a lighting effect for the spectacles as could be given on the most modern stage in the country.

Arabia was the opening spectacle. It was the story of the pilgrimage of Fatima, wife of Ali the Fourth, caliph of Egypt. There was displayed an array of dancers that had never before been under canvas. They were chosen from the leading dancing schools of the world. They had been trained for many weeks for their part in the spectacle. The camels, the slaves, and, in fact, as complete a caravan as could be reproduced was used in the opening. The setting was especially designed and was entirely different from the usual circus spectacle.

Such famous trick riders, ropers, bulldoggers as Mamie Francis, California Frank, Hank Durnall, Reine Hafley, Tad Lucas, Mildred Douglas, Buck Lucas, Buff Brady, Joss Darrera, Milt Kinkle, Cotton Ashley, Fred Carter and scores of others comprised the wild west performers. Then there were the famous clowns, Dan Mix and Joe Lewis, with their mule acts. Ezra Meeker and his ox-drawn prairie schooner were with the show.

But it is the ballet and the far east acts that constituted the side departure from the old line of show. Joe Miller went personally to New York and other cities while Zack Miller went to Mexico City, New Orleans, and Cuba and their agents scoured the Orient to get the dancers they wanted.

None of the old time circus side show performers were included. Youth, beauty and grace were the prime requisites of those who wanted to get on the show. Girls from Ziegfeld's Follies, dancers from the famous theaters of Mexico City and Buenos Aires and Slayman's famous troop of Arabs were brought in to the show. An entire troop of Russian Cossack riders and dancers were imported. And they were the best Joe

Miller could find in Russia. They were all young and trained under the new conception of art rather than the old circus idea.

Among the Indians were John Last Man, Two Dog, Yellow Boy and few others who were with the original 101 show. But there were scores of others. They were mostly Sioux and Cheyenne. The Osage and Poncas were not good show Indians because, as Joe Miller said, they were too independent. Most of them tire of show life. If he had taken them along he would more than likely have waked up some morning and found his Indians had broken camp by night and gone back home.

Two troupes of trained elephants and trained camels, buffalo and elk constituted the animal section of the show, except, of course, the horses and steers. The horses used in the wild west performance for riding were selected over a period of months. They were outlaws that would buck when they smelled leather. Any horse that could be tamed was not taken. That was the reason it took several months to pick them. The same was true of the steers. From the Brahamas on down, they were a wild bunch that no amount of riding would tame. The Millers started out to make the wild west section a real wild west show and nothing tame was connected with the wild west section.

The side shows were so different from the old side lines that there was no comparison. They were absolutely clean and nothing on the order of the old "for men only" joints was tolerated. There was not a show on the lot that would offend the most exacting critic of morality. But there was youth, beauty, and art.

Through all of the building of the big show, there was a great deal of fun and hard work. The hundreds of people gathered at the ranch from all parts of the world to help put on the exhibition and played their parts well. Life on the 101 Ranch during this time was more like a street scene in some foreign city where all the nations of the world were represented.

The big 101 super-wild west show opened in Oklahoma City, April 21, 1925. The opening exhibition was dedicated to the Eighty-nine celebration. The Miller brothers were known all over Oklahoma long before the big "run." They were frontiersmen and with them in the show were others of their type who braved the hardships long before the opening of territorial lands to colonization.

The old show was operated successfully from the fall of 1908 to the fall of 1916, during which time it made a net profit, after paying for the entire equipment of over $800,000.[3] After reorganization in 1925, the new show did not do so well financially in spite of the fact it met with tremendous approval of the people. The show met the greatest opposition any business ever met, namely: the three cornered fight—the Barnum and Bailey, Ringling interest on one side, and the American Circus Corporation on the other. It was a fight to the finish, but the Millers always held their own in the eyes of the people. The opposition, however, was a heavy drain on the income of the new show.

In addition, the expenses in operating the new super-wild west show were enormous as a result of the high class performances added in the reorganization. The income declined increasingly each season, largely because of business conditions, to such an extent that in 1926 the season closed with a loss of around $119,000.[4] With grim determination to succeed, the Millers continued the show on the road until it finally stranded in Washington, D. C., August 5, 1931, following financial difficulties which led to court action.

For the 1931 season, Colonel Zack Miller started the show out with meager funds with the hope of renewing interest once shown by the American Circus Corporation in buying it. The show left Marland, Oklahoma, with only a small sum in the cash box, struck two or three big days near home and was able to continue on a schedule that really had not been seriously planned. During the summer, Colonel Miller was called back to the ranch for the conference with creditors which preceded the appointment of the ranch receiver, leaving the show run by paid employees.

The advance man always makes or breaks a show. He is out ahead of the show about two weeks and makes all the contracts. Without question the advance man broke the 101 Ranch show during the 1931 season. Whether he was paid to

3 101 Ranch Records, 1925.
4 W. A. Brooks to Ellsworth Collings, March 7, 1936.

do it by some other show corporation, it is not known, but he would send the show on a 250 mile jump one night (freight $900) and the next night 250 miles back to within 50 miles of where the show had previously been. He would route the show into towns where the police and firemen were having benefit rodeos or into towns where most of the population was out on strike from the mills and factories. Colonel Miller was informed of the deplorable situation but was too busy at the ranch with the receivership negotiations to pay much attention and the needless expense and loss in ticket receipts continued.

As a result, the management, in time, was unable to meet some of the outside obligations and financial difficulties reached a critical point when a creditor attempted to attach the ticket wagon receipts on several occasions. This, of course, completely demoralized the finances and when the show reached Washington, D.C., the situation had become so serious that the management could not pay the show employees. A big business was expected in Washington but, when the show arrived, the management discovered the advance man had neglected the billing and that the citizens hardly knew the show was coming. The Washington appearance was a dismal failure.

"Then the whole thing went haywire," explains Colonel Zack Miller. "Led by the very men and women who owed the greatest loyalty to me and the 101 Ranch, the 392 employees became obstreperous and it became impossible for the managing executives to protect and preserve the show property or to accomplish anything that would relieve the situation."

The employees refused to permit the show to be moved back to the 101 Ranch before they received their back pay, and W. E. Rice, ranch trustee, under a mortgage of $150,000 received on the show's property, asked the district supreme court, Washington, to issue an injunction without notice to the employees, forbidding them to interfere with the shipment of the show back to Oklahoma. The application alleged that the show had already suffered damages, and that more were threatened unless the court intervened; that the claims of the employees for back wages could not be enforced against the show equipment because of the mortgage; that the 101 Ranch had offered to transport the employees back to Oklahoma if they would pack the show up, and they had refused; and that the

[187]

employees had threatened to, and they would, unless restrained, destroy the property. The court denied the application, but ordered the employees to appear in court the next
day to show cause why the injunction should not be issued.

The employees opposed vigorously the application and,
after some delay, the court granted the injunction, and, without waiting for an additional court order to prevent interfer-
ence by the unpaid troupers, the management of the show se-
cretly imported a crew of sixty men from Baltimore to pack up
the show, preparatory to shipment back to the 101 Ranch.
The importation of the moving crew from Baltimore caught the
troupers by surprise. The show people stood watching, but no
effort was made to interfere with the labor, other than dropping caustic jibes here and there.

Thus, sad elephants, sadder Indians, cowboys and cowgirls,
sideshow folk, spangles, bit tops; wagons and musicless bands
—the famous 101 Ranch wild west show moved back to the
prairies of Oklahoma. Money for the gloomy ride was furnished by Colonel Zack Miller and the unpaid employees were
invited to return with the show to the 101 Ranch. In the meantime, Colonel Miller issued the following statement, putting an
end to the show that had entertained queens and shown in
every city of the United States with a population of 25,000 and
over.

"Oklahoma's 101 Ranch Wild West Show is through. It is
through, at least, as a unit of the Miller Brothers' 101 Ranch.
Colonel Zack T. Miller made that assertion Monday at the 101
White House during a conference of creditors of the ranch-
farm institution. If the circus, one of the leaders in its day,
ever goes out again, it will be under another owner or under a
complete lease. The 101 Ranch will not operate it again. If
no other disposition is made it will be dropped, said Colonel
Miller."[5]

[5] *Daily Oklahoman,* August 11, 1931.

THE 101 ON THE AUCTION
BLOCK

XII

FOR fifty-seven years the 101 Ranch had prospered: first under the shrewd management of Colonel George W. Miller who built a great cattle ranch; then under the combined genius of the three brothers who wrought a vast empire of diversified industry. But, in 1927 misfortune beset its progress.

First, there was the accidental death of Joe Miller. He died October 21, 1927, the victim of deadly carbon monoxide gas poisoning. He was found in his garage by Mr. W. A. Brooks, who had been looking for him because some old friends had called at the ranch to see him. He was last seen at the ranch about ten o'clock the day of his death, when he put some groceries in his automobile to take to his home about five miles north of the ranch, in preparation for the homecoming of his wife. She had been on the road with Colonel Miller nearly all summer with the ranch show, and had gone with their infant son, Will Brooks Miller, to her old home in Grand Rapids, Michigan, for a few days' visit.

Colonel Miller's car was giving him some trouble when he left the ranch, and upon returning home, he drove the car into his garage, and was apparently working on it at the time of his death. The garage doors were partly opened; the hood of the car was up and on the running board were his pocket knife, which he had been using as a screw driver, and several screws which he had loosened from the motor. He had started the car to ascertain just what the difficulty was. Evidently after working over it for some time he straightened up for some reason, was stricken immediately by the poison gas and fell dead instantly. It had come so quickly and was so deadly that he did not even use his hands to protect himself in the fall; his arms were crumpled underneath him; evidently life had passed before he fell. Attending physicians, who were called, said without doubt and without hesitation, death was caused by monoxide gas poisoning thrown off by the running car.

The oldest of the three brothers, his was the duty of holding the guiding hand—the kindly spirit over all. For every stranger calling upon Colonel Joe Miller there was a friendly word and a smiling greeting that at once made the stranger feel the warm touch of his interest. He was a typical example of the southern planter. His snowy white hair and mustache, his twinkling eyes, courtly manners and southern drawl, made him seem naturally the master of a Kentucky plantation. As he invited the stranger into the great ranch White House to receive old fashioned hospitality, one felt he was truly a friendly man. Upon leaving after a visit, one carried the memory of kindly words: "Come back again soon and stay all day."

Joe Miller was alert and active in his constant endeavor to find new and better methods of farming. Hundreds of experiments were tried out on the 101 Ranch under his personal supervision. Field crops, vegetables, and fruits were given opportunity to show their possibilities under southwestern conditions. Livestock breeding was carried on. Modern machinery was put in operation over all the ranch. Not a few of the innovations in southwestern farming of the past several years may be traced to the influence of the valuable work done along these lines. As illustrations, mention may be made of the use of the combine in harvesting small grains; storing of green feed in silos; wide growth and modern storage of sweet potatoes; large scale production of apples; general diversification of crop growing; and the bringing in of some of the best blood obtainable in hogs, poultry, and cattle.

Colonel Joe Miller was the "farmer," as he called himself, of the 101 Ranch, and he gave his ideas freely to anyone interested in modern farming. The experiments in field crops, stock breeding, and horticulture were not attempted on a small scale. When he was interested in anything new he gave it every chance to prove itself. In his death, the farmer of the southwest lost a valuable friend, one ready to give a trial, working with his own hands and regardless of expenses, to anything suggesting a gain for the improvement of agriculture.

It is evident that Joe Miller possessed rare ability as a farm manager—ability which was indispensable in directing the 101 Ranch agricultural enterprises. The ranch expressed magnificently, at the time of his death, the West of today.

It grew out of the West of yesterday, and represented an institution of growth whose destiny was guided by the hand of a man with vision, personal charm, and friendly manner. It expressed the soul of Colonel Joe Miller.

It was, no doubt, the accidental death of Colonel Joe Miller that started the downfall of the 101 Ranch. It was not apparent at first, not for some time afterwards, but it had a deep effect on the ranch. The ranch continued operations just the same for some time following his death, but still it was not the same. There was something lacking; the guiding hand of Colonel Joe Miller was badly needed.

Colonel George L. Miller stressed his oil business chiefly, bringing in more money to meet financial obligations, and he kept the ranch up to standard in operation after the death of his brother. During the winter of 1929 he went to Texas to look over his oil holdings and had just returned home from a week's business trip at Big Springs and other cities in southwestern Texas, where he was drilling a wildcat well in Sterling County. The day he returned, February 1, 1929, was dismal, sleety, blizzardy. Returning home about midnight of that day from Ponca City, his automobile skidded on the slippery pavement and crashed on the side of the road. The accident happened about two o'clock, but it was four o'clock before help arrived. Oscar Clemmer found George Miller crushed and pinned beneath a front wheel, which suggested he had attempted to jump when he lost control of the heavy car on the slippery road. He was rushed to Ponca City, but died before reaching the hospital.

George L. Miller was extremely jealous of the 101 Ranch and the name of the Miller brothers. His greatest desire was that the ranch should be a genuinely outstanding institution, successfully operated, with a name that in itself should be a guarantee. This was his pride and it was demonstrated only a short time before his death.

The Miller brothers had sold the 101 wild west show, with every detail agreed upon, and they had assembled to sign the contract. At the last moment, the purchasers demanded they be permitted to use the name of the Miller brothers on stock certificates that would be sold to finance the corporation. Immediately George L. Miller, although very anxious to sell the show so he could devote his time to ranch and oil affairs, called off the deal, asserting the name of the Miller brothers could not be used in any such financing scheme.

For a number of years he had been financial head of the 101 Ranch. His smooth and efficient management had been a mainspring in the development of the ranch. His shrewd financial judgment was devoted toward perpetuating the integrity of the Miller enterprises. His death was an irreparable loss to the 101 Ranch.

When the oldest brother, Colonel Joe Miller, was accidentally killed in October, 1927, George L. Miller assembled the other members of the family in a business conference and outlined the policy whereby the ranch could be held intact. Immediately he started the training of his two nephews, George W. and Joe C., Jr., sons of Colonel Joe Miller, so that they could follow in his footsteps whenever it might be necessary. Frequently, he spoke of the splendid manner in which the younger men had accepted responsibility and were making good. It was a source of great pride to him. With his death February 2, 1929, the management of the ranch passed to the surviving brother, Colonel Zack Miller, and to these young Miller boys.

In a short time after Colonel Zack Miller and his nephews took over the management of the 101 Ranch, the world's greatest economic upheaval came late in 1929. The bottom dropped out of the oil business. Livestock sold at its lowest figure. Agricultural and horticultural products brought practically nothing. Judging that the economic depression was only temporary, the Millers secured a mortgage of over half a million dollars in order to finance the ranch operations. Conditions failed to improve as anticipated through 1930—they even grew worse. At the close of the year the ranch suffered a net loss of $301,064.08 for that year.

The mortgages, notes, taxes, interest became due in the regular course of time, but there was no cash reserve stored away to meet such an emergency. There were thousands of bushels of corn in the bins, vast acres of alfalfa, huge crops of oats, sweet potatoes, producing oil wells, but no markets, no sales, no net profits. The ranch operations came to a standstill and the indebtedness mounted.

It was impossible to refinance, seemingly impossible to do anything, yet the ranch assets trebled the liabilities as the following figures indicate:[1]

Assets and Liabilities of the 101 Ranch as of November 1, 1931
Ranch Assets
Cash and Accounts:

Cash on Hand and in Banks:		$	1,634.01
Accounts Receivable:	$ 76,070.34		
Notes Receivable:	9,322.42		
Mortgages Receivable	8,168.16	$	93,560.92

Real Estate:

10,000 Acres @ $75.00			
Farming Lands	$750,000.00		
7,000 Acres @ $25.00			
Pasture Lands	175,000.00		
480 Acres @ $10.00			
Osage Lands	4,800.00		
12,000 Acres @ $4.00			
Leased Lands	48,000.00	$	977,800.00
Watchorn Royalties:		$	150,000.00

Fixed Assets:

Auto, Trucks, Tractors	$ 6,000.00		
Buildings on Ranch Property	248,615.23		
Furniture and Fixtures	16,000.00		
Fences and Pens	31,815.00		
Farm Implements and Tools	14,000.00		
Show Equipment	212,000.00		
Machinery	21,000.00		
Refinery, Filling Station,			
Pipe Lines	9,135.70	$	558,565.93

Inventories:

Farm Products	$ 67,906.13		
Livestock	24,207.00	$	92,113.13

Total:

Liquidating Assets	$1,873,673.99

[1] The Receiver's Report to the Kay County Court, September, 1931.

Ranch Liabilities

Mortgages, Taxes, Interest:

Albright Title and Trust Co., Newkirk, Oklahoma	$100,000.00
John Hancock Life Ins. Co., Boston, Massachusetts	141,200.00
Passumptic Savings Bank, Baltimore, Maryland	50,000.00
Federal Land Bank, Wichita, Kansas	27,615.78
Kansas City Joint Stock Bank, Kansas City, Missouri	39,190.69
Commissioner of Land Office, Oklahoma City, Oklahoma	4,200.00
First Trust Company, Wichita, Kansas	1,300.00
Wentz, L. H.	146,800.00
Collins Mortgage Company, Assigned to L. H. Wentz	5,500.00
Taxes and Interest	62,776.68

Total: Mortgages Payable,
Interest and Taxes $ 567,942.18

Notes and Interest:

Exchange National Bank, Tulsa, Oklahoma	$108,850.00
First National Bank, Ponca City, Oklahoma	4,547.00
Security Bank and Trust Co., Ponca City, Oklahoma	26,661.80
Harbough Cline Tractor Co., Enid, Oklahoma	2,154.20
Interest	12,095.00

Total: Notes and
Interest Payable $ 154,310.70

Current Items:

Accounts Payable	$ 11,386.57
Accrued Taxes	18,722.71
Accrued Interest	11,555.49
Accrued Pay Roll	3,556.65
Miller, Colonel Zack T.	59,288.03

Total: Current Items	$ 104,309.45
Total: Liabilities	$ 626,762.33

Creditors stepped in. They did not want the ranch, but they insisted on something to satisfy their loans. Colonel Zack Miller remembered how the ranch had weathered the panic of 1893. He was confident it could be done again and insisted the creditors would be paid one hundred per cent on the dollar, if they would only give him a little time. He toiled early and late in a disturbed world in search of a way out. No doubt a way would have been found could he have had the able assistance of his dead brother, George L. Miller. But he was a cowman and not a financial wizard. Individuals with sufficient capital to refinance the enterprise refused to advance the money unless they were given controlling interest; in fact, they demanded management of the ranch. Colonel Zack Miller stubbornly resisted all such proffers; he insisted on retaining the controlling interest and protested vigorously any thought of assuming a minor rôle in the affairs of an institution that he and his brothers had built on the prairies of Oklahoma. This action closed all the gates of refinancing, and set in action a long legal struggle in the state and federal courts.

Colonel Miller thought the show might get a break on the road, but instead it broke in Washington. This was but added disaster. He called a conference of all the creditors at the White House, August 10, 1931, to consider the situation. "Save the ranch, preserve its traditions," was the cry and the hope of the seventy-five creditors and visitors who crowded into the room, but there was a mountain of debt to climb or go around.

The conference with Colonel Zack T. Miller and his associates brought out these facts:

1. The ranch's indebtedness, much of which was past due with interest and penalties piling up steadily, was $626,762.33.

2. The estimated value of the farm crops produced on the ranch that season was $231,734, which, with the estimated value of $977,800 for the 101 Ranch lands, gave total potential assets of more than $1,000,000.

3. Colonel Miller requested a moratorium of six months, asking that no new suits be filed by creditors, and that all court action pending be suspended during that period; he proposed to bring in new money to pay back-due taxes and to restock the ranch with livestock.

4. Bankers and other creditors expressed a willingness to give him the extra time, but also expressed doubt that he could interest new capital due to the financial condition in which the ranch had been plunged, due to the depression and continued losses by the 101 circus.

5. The ranch either would be able to see financial daylight within sixty days, or it would be taken over by the creditors under a federal receivership by that time.

"I believe all I need is six months' time in which to begin to see the light," Colonel Miller said. "If the creditors will stop bringing lawsuits against the ranch and if the threats of federal receivership will cease, then I can get enough money to clear up the situation, buy some livestock and get started again. But I must have assurance before I can get any money that some creditor won't pop up with another lawsuit and call for a receiver."

Miller told of having put $268,000 of his personal funds into the ranch trying to save it in the last two years. Many of his friends suggested he settle with all creditors on the basis of 60 cents on the dollar.

"But I won't do that. I am going to pay 100 cents on the dollar or go down with the whole thing," Miller declared.

He said when he took over the management of the ranch early in 1931, it was like "piloting a sinking ship across an uncharted sea."

He declared that he was a cowman and not a "financial wizard" and suggested that any reorganization plan should include the employment of a business manager. However, he said, the ranch had suffered from mismanagement for two years before he took charge.

L. K. Meek, Ponca City banker, sounded a blue note at

[196]

Herd of buffalo on the 101 Ranch

OIL PAINTING BY ROBERT LINDNEUX, DENVER

.the meeting. Meek said that it would take about $250,000 to restock the ranch and square the delinquent taxes and some of the delinquent interest items against the property now.

"And I don't know where you could go to get that money to put in at this time."

It was brought out at the meeting that in the event the ranch was forced to the wall every creditor would be paid in full. It was estimated that 3,500 acres of the land could be sold readily at $100 an acre; 5,000 acres at $50 an acre, and the remainder at an average of $30 an acre even on a depressed market.

The value of the land alone would pay off all of the secured and unsecured creditors, it was stated, and the machinery, live-stock and crops grown that year would bring a large sum. But in that case the ranch would be gone, the name of the famous 101 would sink into oblivion.

Judge W. E. Rice, Ponca City, acting for the trustees, who presided at the conference, suggested that the unsecured cred-itors hold a separate meeting and agree, if possible, not to file any more suits against the ranch for a period of six months. They met and appointed a committee of three to get in touch with all others and give an answer within thirty days.

The two other parties in the ranch trust, heirs of the late George L. and Joe Miller, were represented by George W. Mil-ler, Ponca City, son of Joe Miller, and Joe Chambers of the Exchange Trust Company, Tulsa. They gave no expression regarding Colonel Zack's proposal to "put all the trust shares into one pot and 'sink or swim.' "

Following upon the heels of the conference a receivership was unexpectedly filed, August 27, 1931, in the district court of Kay County. That was the beginning of the long, legal battles that have torn asunder the 101 Ranch. Declaring that the estate of the late George L. Miller was being depreciated because of conditions at the ranch, the Exchange Trust Com-pany of Tulsa and George W. Miller, son of Colonel Joe Mil-ler, as executors of the George L. Miller estate, filed the peti-tions asking that an operating receiver be appointed. The pe-tition set forth that originally the 101 Ranch trust was owned equally by the Millers, Joe C., George L., and Zack T. There was a total of 100,000 shares, of which Joe C. and Zack T.

owned 33,333 shares each and George L. 33,334 shares, or one more than either of the other two brothers. On this basis the executors made claim of authority to ask for a receiver and prevent the depreciating of properties and securities. The John Hancock Life Insurance Company and the Passumptic Savings Bank of Maryland filed similar petitions in the Kay County Court, and after considerable discussion the creditors finally agreed in conference at the ranch White House upon Mr. Fred C. Clarke, ranchman, near Winfield, Kansas, as general operating receiver. Judge John S. Burger of Kay County district court confirmed the appointment, September 16, 1931, and the 101 Ranch passed for the first time in its long history from the control of the Millers. It marked the beginning of the end of the famous ranch, although at the time the step was designed to put the ranch on a paying basis.

Clarke's bond was fixed at $50,000 by the court, with the stipulation that the bonding company making it must be legally doing business in Oklahoma and must show the name of its service agent.

A restraining order was issued by Judge Burger preventing any suit or execution against the ranch involving crop or other property, or filing foreclosure actions. Judge W. E. Rice, trustee of the ranch, was ordered to turn over all records to Clarke.

The John Hancock Life Insurance Company and the Passumptic Savings Bank of Maryland withdrew their petitions for a special receiver and agreed with other creditors on Clarke, with the understanding that later these companies eventually could foreclose on the acreage covered by their mortgages, but that no such action would be taken prior to January 1, 1933.

All actions taken by the court looked to the rehabilitation of the ranch and its continuation as a unit and really constituted the moratorium that had been sought for some time to give opportunity for such a rehabilitation program. Clarke assumed his duties immediately. It was the hope of Colonel Zack Miller that he might have a prominent part in the ranch program under the receivership of assisting in carrying on the various departments and chiefly that of livestock.

With the appointment September 16, 1931, of the general operating receiver, Mr. Fred C. Clarke, the rehabilitation of the 101 Ranch and its continuation as a unit was the hope and wish of its creditors and friends. Because of a lack of funds, and perhaps requisite experience, Mr. Clarke was greatly handicapped in this undertaking, and soon abandoned the plan to restock the ranch and set into action the other huge enterprises. As an alternative, he chose to lease the ranch and farm property to individual farmers and to dispose of all the personal properties of the ranch, much to the displeasure of Colonel Zack Miller. Accordingly, on March 24, 1932, Mr. Clarke advertised a sale of the personal properties. Everything from hogs to buffalo and from saddles and harness to grain combines was offered to the public. The sadness marking that occasion is described realistically in the following lines.

"There were sad doings here Thursday, marking the passing of a great Oklahoma institution, the 101 Ranch, internationally famous symbol of a young state that rides 'em cowboy. A picturesque crowd of more than 3,000 persons turned out for the receiver's sale of all the property of the Miller brothers 101 Ranch Trust, a few coming to buy, but a vast majority simply to walk stolidly along the dusty lanes and watch with calm solicitude the disintegration of the greatest show place in the west. Over in the historic White House of the ranch, Colonel Zack Miller, sole survivor of the trio of brothers which made the place famous, roared defiance to the world, threatened to blow up the mansion, and even fired a shotgun in the direction of attorneys seeking a conference with him. He termed the sale a 'legal robbery.'

"In his sorrow this booted and spurred old showman feels there are few persons he can trust. They are tearing asunder his beloved ranch, and it has aroused in him the fighting spirit of the western rancher. Let them take care was his ultimatum, and although the White House was surrounded by half a dozen deputies of Sheriff Joe Cooper, none disturbed the belligerent colonel.

"While this tense drama was being enacted at the ranch house the auctioning of the livestock, farm implements and other properties proceeded to the fascination of the dust-covered spectators. A quartet of robust auctioneers raised pudgy, socratic fingers over bucking bronchos, work horses, hogs and cattle by the hundreds. They labored indefatigably. Their necks wrapped in flambouyant handkerchiefs, their nasal exhortations bringing chuckles to papooses strapped to their mothers' backs, and blond urban infants brought out specially for the occasion.

"The four 'colonels' took an hour off for a well-earned luncheon, and the crowd spread over the immense pastures in picnic groups.

"On all sides there were loud lamentations at the passing of the great ranch, which in its halcyon days was visited by more than 100,000 persons every year.

"Not so long ago this was the connecting link between the old west and the new. Rollicking cowboys nonchalantly roped firebreathing steers for the edification of properly awed dry goods merchants from New England. Tourists were astonished by the sight of the buffalo herd, elk, camels, elephants and other elements of the famous wild west show operated in connection with the ranch.

"Huge herds of cattle roamed the 110,000 acres which made up the great ranch, lights twinkled in a hundred cabins, Indian braves stalked proudly in gay blankets, and in the White House there was light and laughter.

"Oil wells spouted wealth, crops were diversified, range cattle gave way to pure bred stock, and the 101 Ranch was considered a permanent monument to the heroism of western pioneers.

"George Washington Miller, who established it in 1879, was a man of prodigious pride, who made business executives of his sons when they were not yet ten years old. He expected them to carry on from generation to generation, and that is one reason for Colonel Zack's distraction.

"When George Washington Miller established the ranch, buffalo grazed placidly on these rolling prairies and it was in all respects a happy hunting ground. First the cattlemen became too numerous, and then the inevitable advancement brought the farmer. The west became no more glamorous than main street in Peoria, but to the preservation of its ideals the Miller family dedicated the infinity of its possessions, all its wealth and strength, even its life.

"Now that it is gone everyone realizes that there never can be another 101 Ranch. And it was particularly a source of regret to the Oklahomans who gathered in this funeral atmosphere Thursday. The scene was one of astonishment and confusion, with no comedy relief anywhere.

"Practically all the land is leased in small tracts to neighboring farmers. The ranch store, which handles everything from moccasins to celluloid collars, is being operated in receivership. The buffalo are to be sold privately to the highest bidders, and the rows upon rows of farm machinery will be sold or junked.

"Perhaps in a year or so conditions will be so changed hereabouts that there will be nothing to distinguish the vast expanse of the ranch from a group of prosaic Iowa farms.

"Little boys will have nothing to inspire them to play cowboy and Indian any more and will have to be content with mimicking traffic cops and impulsive governors.

"The lonely man there in the famous White House, living among his dead hopes, bellowing defiance from his sickbed, simply typified the already half-forgotten, glorious yesterdays of Oklahoma."[2]

Piece by piece, part at a time, livestock, implements, the buffalo herd, even harness, saddles, and feed, everything but the White House and its furnishings went on the auction block. And the White House was under heavy mortgage. That was a memorable day, when Colonel Zack Miller, heart-broken, mentally broken, sick in body and soul, attempted with his six-shooter to stop the sale of the personal properties of the ranch. He heatedly declared the auction of the ranch properties was "legal robbery." Eventually he was calmed after he had discharged a shotgun in the direction of two of the receiver's attorneys seeking a conference with him. But he faced criminal prosecution for his armed defiance of the auctioneer's hammer as it was lifted over his beloved empire. His defiance of the auction block was followed by court actions, by charges and countercharges, even by imprisonment. Yes, Zack Miller, the last of a dynasty of plainsmen, was confined in the limits of four barred walls. Zack Miller was a prisoner in jail by decrees of the laws of a state which he helped nurse into existence. Then the Governor of Oklahoma, William H. Murray, through the use of the state militia, released Colonel Miller from prison

[2] *Daily Oklahoman,* March 25, 1932.

in the Kay County Oklahoma, jail. The military order of the governor, given below, sets forth the charges and counter-charges leading up to the imprisonment of Colonel Miller.

STATE OF OKLAHOMA
EXECUTIVE DEPARTMENT

EXECUTIVE—MILITARY ORDER

FOR THE RELEASE OF COLONEL ZACK T. MILLER FROM FALSE IMPRISONMENT BY JUDGE CLAUDE DUVAL

TO ANY DISTRICT JUDGE OR COURT, ANY SHERIFF OR HIS DEPUTY, MARSHAL, TURNKEY, JAILOR OR GUARD, OF NEWKIRK, AND OF KAY COUNTY, OKLAHOMA; AND,

TO BRIGADIER GENERAL CHARLES F. BARRETT, ADJUTANT GENERAL, AND TO ALL CONCERNED HEREIN, GREETING:

WHEREAS, the controversies between citizens in civil or other private matters are not the concern of the Chief Magistrate, but the false imprisonment and liberty of the citizen are his concern, particularly as appears in this case, where it seems that, through conspiracies of creditors and the grasping cupidity of such creditors, aided through a series of rulings by the Court, a citizen is wrongfully restrained of his liberty, it becames the duty of the Chief Magistrate to liberate him from such wrongful imprisonment; and, therefore Colonel Zack T. Miller is hereby ordered released permanently from imprisonment in Newkirk, and Kay County, Oklahoma, because of the arbitrary and apparent conspiracy on the part of his creditors, joined by the Court, to dispoil him of his property and patrimony and home, constructed through the efforts of his father and brothers, representing a lifetime of labor: the reasons therefore are contained in the sequel hereof:

It appears from documentary evidence that Colonel Zack T. Miller sued his former wife, Margaret Blevins-Miller, in the Seventh Judicial District Court in Catahoula Parish, State of Louisiana, for a decree of divorce and possession of their two minor children, and that, on the 21st day of March, 1931, His Honor, F. E. Jones, District Judge of said Parish, did enter a decree granting permanent divorce to the said Miller, and the custody of the said minor children, assessing the costs against the defendant: this after regular hearing in which both plaintiff and defendant were present in open court, and represented by counsel:

[202]

It further appears that subsequent thereto, the said defendant appealed to the Supreme Court of the State of Louisiana, where the case is now pending;

It also further appears that for a number of years the said Miller has had difficulties with his creditors for the payment of loans secured on the 101 Ranch, in Kay County, Oklahoma; that during this time, the said Colonel Zack T. Miller has sought to secure loans in order to extinguish his obligations to his creditors, and the same was made known to the undersigned in the fall of 1930, on an appeal for assistance, and that in every effort to secure a loan, certain creditors living in Ponca City had communications made to a proposed new creditor that Miller was irresponsible, and that the loan would not be safe, evidently with a desire to foreclose and secure ownership and possession of this world-known home and patrimony of Colonel Zack T. Miller, builded through a lifetime of effort of himself, his brothers and father; and that the Court of Kay County, Oklahoma, through the action of Judge Claude Duval, has acted in that effort in that a receiver was appointed, who, instead of making a business and honest effort to extinguish the debts, has, with apparent purpose, dissipated the personal property, disposing of the same for an inadequate consideration. Fine registered Holstein cattle that cost from $1,000.00 to $11,000.00 two years prior to the sale were sold for $45.00;

That when said sale was ordered, Miller asked for an order to separate and segregate from the herds in the pasture certain personal stock known to belong to him and not to the 101 Ranch Trust, whereupon the said Judge Duval gave him twenty-four hours; in the meantime, the said Miller was enjoined by the said Duval from going on the Ranch, to the barn, or any of the premises outside of the "Big House," known as the home, and to the road. The said Miller then entrusted the work of separation and segregation to a negro attendant who had served him for many years, by the name of Bill Pickett; and, when the said attendant undertook to separate said property, a wild horse reared and struck the said Bill Pickett in the head, inflicting death wounds;

Colonel Miller then applied to the Court for an extension of twenty-four hours in which to segregate his personal goods and animals from the 101 Ranch Trust Sale, and was denied by the Court, resulting in the sale of this property, along with the residue of the 101 Ranch property by the receiver;

In the meantime, it would appear that the creditors induced the former wife of Miller, from whom he had been divorced by the Louisiana Court, to come to the 101 Ranch, to harass Colonel Miller, whereupon the said Miller asked of the Court, Judge Duval, a restraining order against her molestation of his home. The Court ruled he had no jurisdiction, since the case was pending in the State Courts of Louisiana, but, subsequent thereto, his former wife, in September last, filed a petition in the District Court of Kay County, Oklahoma, asking for separate maintenance and partial custody of the children; and, in an ex parte hearing, the said Judge Duval assumed jurisdiction, nothwithstanding the case in Louisiana, and issued an order directing Colonel Miller to pay One Hundred ($100.00) Dollars to her attorney, and Forty ($40.00) Dollars a month to herself and Ten ($10.00) Dollars of costs:

A motion to dismiss was filed by Miller, based upon the fact that the Court of Oklahoma had no jurisdiction, and that was over-ruled by the said Duval; and, on November 22, Miller was cited for contempt, and convicted, for refusing to make this payment, and, at the same time, was not permitted to go to the barn or to any part of his own property, or to dispose of any of the property with which to make the payment, and he offered evidence, undisputed, that he was unable to make payments; and that, in fact, the groceries for his meals were paid for by a friend, Gordon Hines, sojourning temporarily at the home of the said Miller;

It also appears that the receiver of the 101 Ranch Trust Estate has gathered and sold the crops from Indian lands leased by the said Miller and belonging to him individually, selling the corn to a son-in-law in Ponca City, at eight to twelve cents a bushel less than the same could be sold for at Marland,—a six mile closer haul,—and the same was approved by the said Judge Duval;

It also appears that one L. K. Meek, acting as President of the Security State Bank of Ponca City, had been permitted, through the action of the said Judge Duval, to swindle Miller out of the sum of $9,000.00 by allowing him to purchase a note alleged to have been secured by chattels mortgaged by one individual whose wife later recovered the chattels as proper owner, the Court refusing to grant judgment to Miller against the said L. K. Meek or his bank.

These acts, together with others, as detailed to the Chief Executive from time to time since the fall of 1930, would make it clearly appear that there is a collusion and conspiracy between the said creditors, L. K. Meek, L. H. Wentz and certain loan companies, aided and abetted by the said Duval, acting as Judge, using Miller's divorced wife further to harass him with the apparent purpose of wrecking Miller and taking from him the world-known estate, the 101 Ranch, by denying him access to his own property, or the sale of any part thereof; and then executing an order compelling him to pay alimony and attorney's fees, which was impossible for him to do; and then imprisoning him as a culmination of the design of wrecking Miller and his estate; and,

WHEREAS, the governmental decrees making for justice in civil matters between citizens is the concern of the Courts, even though they may err from ignorance, design, or venality, nevertheless, the liberty of a citizen is of vital concern and within the authority and challenges the duty of the Chief Magistrate; and,

[204]

Whereas, under the Bill of Rights of the State Constitution no man can be imprisoned for debt, where the obligation is agreed to and acknowledged, hence how much less authority has a court to imprison a citizen for something over which he has no control and for acts placing him in a position whereby conspiracies, corrupt combination and design on the part of creditors, aided and abetted by the Court of Justice: therefore, it does become the duty and the obligation of the Chief Magistrate to liberate such person from such false imprisonment;

Searching through the records in this case, the mind but compares Colonel Miller to Victor Hugo's Jean Val Jean, and the acts of Judge Duval recall those of Judge Jeffries of England:

NOW, THEREFORE, I, Wm. H. Murray, The Governor of the State of Oklahoma, do hereby pardon the said Colonel Zack T. Miller of any and all offenses for which he stands convicted and all orders and decrees of the said Judge Duval, or any other Court in Kay County, Oklahoma, and do hereby order his permanent release, and do hereby direct the Adjutant General, Charles F. Barrett, to see that this order is executed, using such force as may be necessary for the execution of the same.

Done, on this, the 28th day of November, A.D., 1932, and the Seal of the State is caused to be attached hereto.

By the Governor of the State of Oklahoma
WM. H. MURRAY
Commander-in-Chief of the State Militia.

Attest:
R. A. Sneed
Secretary of State
By:
Una Lee Roberts
Assistant Secretary of State

Dismissal of Fred C. Clarke as operating receiver for the 101 Ranch was sought September 19, 1932 in a petition filed in Kay County district court by Colonel Zack Miller. The petition charged Clarke had been guilty of gross neglect and prejudice against Colonel Miller and the interest of the ranch. It set forth that the fields had not been cultivated and that the buildings had been allowed to fall to a state of ruin. The motion sought the appointment of a new receiver.

Unable to get an immediate consideration of the petition, Colonel Miller set about working out a new reorganization plan with the creditors. The plan agreed to by the creditors included a two year operating lease on all ranch land, heretofore fore-closed and sold, with an option to repurchase it within the two-year period. Certificates of indebtedness were to be issued to all creditors and were to become due at the expiration of the two-year lease, January 1, 1935. The Kay County district court approved, March 25, 1933, the reorganization plan, dis-missed Fred C. Clarke, as operating receiver, and returned the management of the ranch to Colonel Zack Miller and two trustees for a two year period, ending January 1, 1935.

Thus, the moratorium in which to redeem the ranch, sought so long by Colonel Zack Miller, was finally wrung from the creditors. The operating receiver had been discharged and Colonel Miller was once more manager of the ranch. It would take approximately $700,000 to redeem the loans. Many ef-forts were made to raise that sum. Some looked at times as if they would be successful, but $700,000 was a huge amount of money during the depression times. Even the notorious Al Capone was interested. But nothing developed from any of these efforts. Many of the prominent financial friends, who were at their zenith when they visited the ranch, had failed during the economic upheaval or had died, broken in mind and body. Business was ruined, fortunes disappeared, and conse-quently credit everywhere was destroyed even though assets trebled liabilities. The break-up of the ranch was inevitable, although Colonel Zack Miller fought bitterly to keep alive and keep together the famous Oklahoma institution.

From time to time creditors individually had brought fore-closure proceedings against portions of the ranch lands. On August 26, 1932, the Bar L part of the ranch, including 3,000 acres, was sold on the auction block at Perry, Oklahoma, to the Passumptic Savings Bank, of Maryland, to satisfy a mort-gage of $41,500 held on that land. Another tract of 1,060 acres was sold, September 19, 1932, to the Federal Land Bank, Wichita, Kansas, to satisfy a mortgage of $28,859. At New-kirk, Oklahoma, the John Hancock Mutual Life Insurance Company of Boston brought foreclosure proceedings October 24, 1932 against 1,160 acres to satisfy a mortgage of $50,000. On January 15, 1933, an additional tract of 1,200 acres was placed on the auction block for a mortgage of $36,587 held by the Kansas City Joint Live Stock Bank of Kansas City.

As fast as the auction sales of the 101 Ranch lands were made under foreclosure proceedings and the sales themselves were confirmed by the district court, attorneys representing Colonel Zack Miller would take exceptions to confirmation, thus laying the foundation for an appeal to the higher courts. As a result, a series of legal battles have been waged by Colonel Miller in the state and federal courts since the appointment of the operating receiver, September 16, 1931, in order to maintain possession of the ranch.

Bit by bit, the 101 Ranch, which once stretched as far as the eye could see, has been thrown on the auction block. Colonel Zack Miller still clung to the ranch White House, which he claimed as his homestead—but even this remnant of the once proud ranch was contested by the creditors. To complete ownership, the John Hancock Mutual Life Insurance Company of Boston filed injunction proceedings in the federal court, Guthrie, Oklahoma, demanding Colonel Zack Miller vacate the White House. Through foreclosure proceedings the insurance company had already taken over the land surrounding the White House homestead, but Colonel Miller refused to vacate his home. The federal court granted the injunction, June 3, 1936. And here is the account of the order:

"Zack T. Miller, last of the brothers who acquired fame through operation of the 101 Wild West Show and ranch, was ordered to vacate his famous White House on the banks of the Salt Fork, Wednesday in an injunction issued by Edgar S. Vaught, federal district judge.

"The order brought nearer the end of the once proud empire which had shrunk to a one-acre tract which Miller has occupied despite orders from both state and federal courts since 1932. Judge Vaught's order came during hearing of a suit filed in Kay County by Miller, in which he attempted to vacate deeds held by the John Hancock Mutual Life Insurance Company and Lew H. Wentz.

"Miller, through his attorney, contended the deeds were given to aid in bankruptcy proceedings and were in reality only mortgages. Judge Vaught held otherwise.

"Vaught pointed out that he had stricken the ranch from a list of assets filed by Miller in a bankruptcy petition, and held then that the insurance company and Wentz are in rightful possession of the land, which they obtained through foreclosure of mortgages held against it, and through regular court procedure of sheriff's sale.

"The federal judge then over-ruled Miller's objections as to jurisdiction and held that he should be ordered to vacate the White House and the yard which surrounds it. No definite time for vacating the property was set, Vaught indicating that will be settled between attorneys before a formal order is signed."[3]

As a sequel to this order of the federal court, the household furnishings, Indian curios, paintings, and relics of the famous 101 Ranch White House were advertised for sale by Colonel Zack T. Miller, July 25, 1936. He received permission to appeal the federal court's ruling if he posted an appeal bond by August 2, 1936. And the auction of the contents of the White House was for the purpose of raising money for that bond. It was Colonel Zack Miller's last desperate effort in his legal opposition to foreclose on the 101 Ranch. The appeal denied, Colonel Miller left the White House with his few remaining possessions before sundown Monday, March 29, 1937—thus marking the end of the famous 101 Ranch.

The following postal card went out to friends far and near announcing the auction:

101 RANCH WHITE HOUSE AUCTION SALE
JULY 5, 1936, SATURDAY at 3:00 P. M.

Entire contents of 101 Ranch White House, including many valuable & interesting curios, antiques, & the famous collection of buffalo paintings and one picture of White Eagle by Lenders, (The greatest of all artists on Indians and buffalo.) Antique guns, buffalo overcoats, rugs, etc.

ZACK T. MILLER, SALES MGR.

Among the articles auctioned was a muzzle-loading buffalo gun used on hunts around the ranch in the early days. Included, also, were buffalo robes, some of them made long before the Civil War, buffalo hides, rugs, and the famous col-

---

[3] *Daily Oklahoman*, June 4, 1936.

lection of buffalo paintings by Lenders. Old timers and neighbors gathered early to watch the passing of what once was the show place of the Southwest. The occasion is described vividly in the following article:

"Grim, gray-haired Zack T. Miller stood in the shadows of the old White House Saturday and watched the last of his vast empire crumble under the hammer of an auctioneer.

"He stood without visible emotion, although his face set in hard lines as one by one his personal belongings went on the block, ending another epic of the Old West.

"Down to the last fruit jar, the great 22-room house was cleaned out with the exception of one bedroom. Old buffalo guns, paintings, hides and Indian relics were stacked high.

"In the one room left untouched, Miller was preparing to make a final stand, although Roy Harper, deputy United States marshal, was on hand in the morning to eject the 59-year-old ranchman under orders growing out of a mortgage foreclosure.

"In the room there were only three pieces of furniture, made by Indians on the ranch.

" 'I'm going to stay here and fight until the last dog is dead —or run out of court,' he said. 'This has been my home for 50 years.'

"Miller was saved from ejectment at the last minute Saturday when Edgar S. Vaught, federal judge, granted a five-day stay to permit an appeal to the circuit court of appeals.

"Although Sid White, attorney, said in federal court Saturday a wealthy benefactress may come to aid Miller regain his ranch, the latter denied this.

" 'I'll fight it out by myself,' he said. 'When I'm through, that'll be all.' His voice was bitter.

"Old timers and neighbors gathered early Saturday to watch the passing of what was once the show place of the southwest. The auction was late starting as Miller wandered over the wide yard, peering intently at his old collections.

"Conversation was strained as friends tried to say a word to him.

" 'I, uh, just thought I'd drop by and say howdy,' said one.

"Miller smiled wryly.

" 'Looks sorta different than when you used to come, don't it?'

"The crowd was called to attention.

" 'It'll start on the north side, folks,' Miller said, as he led the procession.

" 'I'm bid $1, who'll give $1.50,' droned G. R. Cowen, a Miller friend of thirty years.

"Outside in a car sat Alice Lee, gray, herself, now, who ten years ago thrilled the crowned heads of Europe with her sensational shooting and daring riding.

" 'This is like a funeral to me,' she said in a choked voice. 'I've been here since 1908. I traveled all over the world with the show. They ought to put me up there with the rest of the relics.'

"Leopold Radgowsky, who came over from Russia to lead a dashing Cossack circus band, stood in the background.

" 'It's too bad,' he said. 'Zack's taking it pretty hard.'

"Seven fire extinguishers purchased by Miller for $100 went for $2.50.

"The auctioneer held up a box of dishes, 'part of a $200 set,' Miller said.

" 'Pass it,' Miller cried, as bids dropped to $1. 'If I'm going to give it away, I'll give it to my old Indian friends. Some of them never have had any dishes.'

" 'He's given away too many things now,' said a voice in the background.

"An old buffalo gun went for 50 cents, with the highest bringing only $2.

" 'That's the first breach-loading gun ever brought into this country,' Miller mumbled under his breath.

"Famous buffalo paintings went for as low as $85.

" 'I once heard Colonel Joe refuse $1,200 for that one while it was on the mantel,' Miller said.

"The sale ended, and bargain hunters scattered. The last of three famous sons of a famous father stood on the steps of the big white mansion, and gazed over what once was a 110,-000-acre ranch.

"Perhaps he saw another time, when 50,000 persons gathered in 1905 to cheer the first annual round-up that later grew into the wild west circus.

"Miller looked at deserted, fallen farm buildings that once housed the state's finest blooded cattle and hogs. He looked over weeds and disorder where once were showplace orchids, wheat fields, packing houses and power plants.

"Miller walked slowly down the steps to the car of his sister, Mrs. Alma England, and drove toward Ponca City."[4]

There were, no doubt, many causes contributing to the break-up of the 101 Ranch, but there seem to be at least three major ones: death, debt, depression. There is no question but that the accidental death of Colonel Joe Miller, the general manager, October 21, 1927, started this downfall of the ranch. Of the famous trio of brothers, he was the one who was able to synthesize the many diversified activities of the ranch into one living whole. The 101 Ranch, as a result, vibrated with life, progress, and development. In his untimely death, the famous Oklahoma institution lost the "guiding hand" that had directed its destiny for a quarter of a century, and his place could not be filled and still retain the spirit of the West of yesterday that prevailed in every nook and cranny under his leadership.

The death of Colonel Joe Miller had a deep effect on the spirits and mentalities of the two surviving brothers. While they were struggling to carry on the ranch affairs without him, the accidental death of Colonel George L. Miller occurred. His death removed the "financial wizard" from the famous trio of brothers and, coupled with the death of the elder brother, was the major cause in the break-up of the famous ranch.

This cause stands out more significantly when it is considered no one could fill successfully the vacant places in the famous trio of brothers. While, as in all great organizations, each man has his own particular part to carry on and for which he is responsible, yet in the kind of organization in which Colonel George W. Miller had brought up his sons, there must be cooperation in thought and agreement in action, or else a chaotic condition would develop and bring ruin to the whole thing. It was this splendid cooperation of the Miller brothers, schooled in from boyhood by their famous father, that enabled them to develop the largest diversified ranch in the world. When death broke up this famous trio, no one could step in and fill the vacancies because of the requisite training in mutual toleration so necessary in the kind of organization behind the 101 Ranch.

[4] *Daily Oklahoman,* July 26, 1936.

There were, no doubt, many business managers as highly trained in finance as Colonel George L. Miller but it was seemingly impossible to secure one with all the requisite qualities possessed by George L. Miller. This fact was demonstrated, again and again, in Colonel Zack Miller's attempt to fill the place of his dead brother. Any such arrangements always ended disastrously to the ranch, largely because co-operation in thought and agreement in action was conspicuously absent. As a result, a chaotic condition finally developed in the ranch affairs and, in the end, brought ruin to the whole thing. If Colonel Zack Miller could have had the support of his dead brothers, there is no question but that the 101 Ranch would have weathered the world's economic upheaval as it did the panic of 1893.

The second major cause in the break-up of the 101 Ranch was the financial debts incurred during the years leading up to the economic depression. The table on page 213 indicates the profits and losses of the ranch for each year from 1925 to 1930, inclusive.

This tabulation reveals that the 101 Ranch suffered a net loss each year, with the exception of two, for the five year period leading up to the economic depression. In 1925, the net profit from operation was $283,103.27 and in 1929 it was $880.48. The net loss for 1926 was $124,499.99; 1927, $69,-424.48; 1928, $149,014.16; and 1930, $301,064.08.

These losses were due largely to the decline in the income from the oil rents and royalties. The table opposite shows the income from this source dropped from $556,290.55 in 1925 to $25,169.39 in 1930. In addition, the 101 Ranch wild west show contributed heavily, in some years, to these deficits. At the close of the 1926 season, the show suffered a loss of $119,870.-45. This loss continued in succeeding years in varying sums until the show was stranded in Washington, D.C., August, 1931. The show was operated successfully from the fall of 1908 until the fall of 1916, during which time it made a net profit, but after its elaborate reorganization in 1925, it was a constant drain on the resources of the 101 Ranch.

With the 101 Ranch suffering heavy losses from operation during most of the years immediately preceding the economic depression, the Miller brothers borrowed large sums of money

PROFITS AND LOSSES OF THE 101 RANCH FROM 1925 TO 1930, INCLUSIVE

Year	Sales	Gross Profits from Sales	Rents and Royalties	Miscellane-ous Income	Gross Income	Expenses	Net Profits	Net Loss
1925	$526,310.83	$149,188.81	$556,290.55	$10,897.77	$716,357.13	$433,253.86	$283,103.27	
1926	588,508.17	185,637.87	311,954.13	4,061.32	501,653.32	626,153.31		$124,499.99
1927	596,594.21	205,421.50	135,751.85	17,581.43	358,753.78	428,178.26		69,424.48
1928	614,153.78	264,793.36	53,487.83	5,709.74	323,990.93	405,491.16		149,014.61
1929	620,909.79	346,416.49	41,327.49	6,410.52	396,664.50	393,784.02	880.48	
1930	460,587.14	95,941.59	25,169.39	....	121,110.98	422,175.06		301,064.08

from time to time in order to keep the various ranch enterprises going on a productive basis. Judging the economic condition prevailing at that time to be only temporary, as was the consensus of opinion of most business men, they placed mortgages with large insurance companies and banks on various portions of the ranch lands as security for these loans. When the economic depression hit the country in full blast, these loans totaled more than a half-million dollars. With no cash reserve to meet such an emergency, the mortgages, notes, interest, and taxes became due in the regular course of time, and the 101 Ranch encountered serious financial difficulties.

And then this happened. The bottom dropped out of the oil business. Cattle sold at their lowest figure. Wheat became worthless. Corn and hogs brought practically nothing. Drought harried the lands. There were no markets, no sales, no net profits. Values sank to their lowest ebb. The ranch operations came to a standstill and the debts mounted. This economic depression was the third and final cause in the disintegration of the Miller brothers' 101 Ranch.

XIII

THE 101 Ranch has been referred to frequently as "the heart of hospitality for Oklahoma" in that more people of prominence came to the state because of the ranch, and more people actually visited the ranch than any other portion of the state. This was true for more than twenty-five years, which was of importance to all Oklahoma, since it resulted in good will for the state at large. The Miller brothers, because of these visits, and also because of their extensive activities at all times, were worldwide figures. They were nationwide, world travelers, and wherever they went their personal charm and friendly manner carried an impression of Oklahoma's manhood which erased the ideas gathered from newspaper and movie accounts of our wild west. They were the best advertisement for Oklahoma the state has ever had.

The Millers, besides actually being western pioneers, looked the part. They were the bronzed, sturdy, steel-eyed men, typical of the plainsmen. And they lived the part. As showmen, they had but few equals, for they realized the value of the traditions of the West. They wore big Stetson hats, gaily colored handkerchiefs knotted about their necks, chaps and high-heeled, decoratively tooled cowboy boots—all of which suggested the Old West, and which added to the fame of the 101 Ranch everywhere.

They worked hard and they played hard. A delightful hospitality was always extended to the humble and great of far and near, and the home life was pleasant. There were few places in the United States more interesting to visit. Men, women, and children from all walks of life came in ceaseless numbers to observe the ranch and to enjoy its charms.

It is an evening's entertainment to look through the guest register, which the Millers always kept on a library table in the "White House," and learn how many people of prominence have been guests at the ranch. The best known figures in business, industry, art, politics and practically all other endeavors in the world have been guests of the Miller brothers.

Jorg Gordon-Davis, former big ranch owner and at that time representing a packing house and cattle exporting company at Buenos Aires, Argentina, was at the ranch and spent a day observing ranching methods in the United States. Many writers came to the ranch for western atmosphere, which the 101 cowboys and Indians colorfully provided. Will Irwin and wife, Mrs. Inez Haynes Irwin; Frazier Hunt, the managing editor of *Hearst's Magazine*; Mrs. Mary Roberts Rinehart; and Isaac Marcosson were among the prominent writers who have been guests of the Millers. When Will Irwin was at the ranch, he declared: "This is the most interesting corner of the United States." Two prominent cartoonists visited the ranch: Sidney Smith, who created "Andy Gump," and Williams, who draws "Out Our Way."

Oil men came frequently. The list includes Walter Teagle, President of the Standard Oil Company; John W. Farish, president of the Humble Oil Company; Arthur Corwin, President of the Carter Oil Company; and Harry Sinclair, President of the Sinclair Oil Company. Great civic leaders listed are: Dr. Harry Fish of Sayre, Pennsylvania; Frank Mulholland of Toledo, Ohio; Hart Seely of Waverly, New York; and others of the national Rotary officials. Cabinet officers, and important government officials have shared the hospitality of the Millers: Secretary of the Interior Hubert Work, Indian Commissioner Burke, William Jennings Bryan, Vice-President Curtis, General Pershing, Senator James Watson, and Senator Arthur Capper.

Fistic honor carriers were also frequent guests at the ranch: Jess Willard, Jack Dempsey, Gene Tunney, Jack Johnson, and many of the lesser lights. Major McLaughlin came to the ranch many times to buy polo ponies. In addition to Will Rogers, there were Tom Mix and his wife, Bill Hart, Jack Mulhall, Neal Hart, Helen Ferguson, Mabel Normand, Hoot Gibson, Tom Ince and numerous other movie stars whose names appear on the guest register. And Ezra Meeker, the old Oregon trail blazer, was there, too.

The National Editorial Association, with several hundred members, has visited the ranch twice and has been entertained there—twenty years between visits. Ten thousand newspaper columns were devoted to the story of the first visit.[1] The Oklahoma Press Association members were the ranch guests in 1922; the National Realtors in 1926; and the American Association of Petroleum Geologists in 1927. Crippled children workers were there; when the members of the Oklahoma State Board visited Lew Wentz at Ponca City in 1927, George L. Miller entertained the entire membership at dinner. The state Sunday school convention, the state florists—in fact, everybody visited the 101 Ranch, and for every visitor calling on the Miller brothers there was a friendly word and a smiling greeting that at once made the visitor feel welcome. The kindly greeting of Colonel Joe Miller in his southern drawling voice, "Come on in, children," lingered long in the minds of the multitude of visitors. To him all who came were "children" and his big heart found room for kindly thoughts for each individual. The 101 became deeply embedded in the hearts of thousands of Americans as a result of this friendliness, hospitality, and cordial generosity of the Miller brothers.

And the people of every walk of life evidenced their appreciation of the Miller brothers and the 101 Ranch at every available opportunity. The home people expressed their gratitude on numerous occasions, particularly through Mr. Harry Cragin, former Mayor of Ponca City, in the following words:

"In every respect, the Miller brothers of the 101 Ranch are valuable assets, not only to Ponca City, but to the state and district at large, and they are accomplishing a great work, with remarkable results. We look upon the Miller brothers as among the dependable citizens of the community and they are so considered by the entire business element, including banks and all other lines. We are glad to have them associated with us and of every opportunity to co-operate with them, for they are square in their business dealings, the best fellows on earth to be with and always ready and willing to give a helping hand. I want to say, too, they are genuine friends of the Indians, and have done more for them than have all other agencies combined. The 101 Ranch is one of the greatest show places in America."[2]

[1] *Daily Picayune*, New Orleans, October 28, 1908.
[2] *Daily Oklahoman*, February 6, 1927.

Tom Mix spent ten years of his early life on the 101 Ranch. It was there he learned his cowboy stunts and it was there he did a part of his first motion picture. This is his story in which he expresses his appreciation of the Millers and the 101 Ranch.

"In the old days, with the blue sky above me, a good horse under me, the vast acreage of the old 101 Ranch rolling green about me and a bacon-filled atmosphere from the chuck wagon calling me, I was the richest of men. How rich, the recent years alone have told me.

"My fondest recollections are those of my early days on the 101 Ranch and I attribute my present standing in the great industry of which I am a part to the training I received and experienced when working under the 101 brand. I could name hundreds of incidents and scenes in my pictures that really had their origin and happened along the banks of the old Salt Fork River.

"To me there has always been an inspiration in the broad expanse of far-stretching prairie, the ranch houses and the low corrals of the 101. But above all of these, I remember with keenest interest and happy memory my association with the three wonderful Miller brothers—each so different in character and temperament—and yet each reflecting so important an understanding and part in the development of that great country.

"Just as I remember the vast acreage, I remember Colonel Joe, with his horse sense and his keen, kindly understanding of men. It was from him that I learned the bigger things of life, faith in humanity and squareness of purpose in dealing with my fellow man. From George, astute, careful and watchful business man, I learned the great, broad principles of economics and of business fairness.

"From Zack, I got the laughs and pranks that were always such an essential factor in that great and wonderful organization. Many were the good laughs that I had as I recalled the old 101 Ranch days. From the efforts of the Miller brothers, men of varied mental make-up, a great and lasting cattle and farming industry has been developed, to say nothing of the enormous mineral progress in that section, for which they are directly responsible."[3]

[3] *101 Magazine*, March, 1926.

Mrs. Mary Roberts Rinehart, accompanied by her husband, came to the 101 Ranch for atmosphere when she was ready to write her "Lost Ecstasy," and Dr. Rinehart, in the following letter, expressed their appreciation for the hospitality accorded them during their stay on the ranch.

"April 23, 1926.

"Mr. George L. Miller,
Miller Brothers' 101 Ranch,
Marland, Oklahoma.

"MY DEAR GEORGE:

"To be socially correct, this letter should be written by hand but I know you are going to be grateful to me for dictating it so that you can read it in as short time as possible and get back to your work.

"We have hardly gotten back to commonplace affairs since our return from the ranch. Everything was so wonderful there, so kaleidoscopic, and done on such a big scale that our ordinary humdrum existence seems very drab. We can think of nothing now except in units of 10,000 and upwards. Instead of asking for one pork chop at breakfast, I am constrained to ask for 10,000 hogs. And we don't think of land as measured in square feet but in square miles. You see what you've done to us.

"I am wondering what kind of a day you are going to have tomorrow, but I suppose I'll keep on wondering until your brother catches up with us when he comes to Washington. I certainly hope there will be a fine turn-out and no rain to spoil the beauty of the Cossacks and make gutters down the grease paint on the girls.

"Mrs. Rinehart and I have been trying to find time to have the girls who are at school here come in to see us but the days have been pretty hectic so far. I have just written them, asking them to come in to tea some afternoon next week. Naturally we want to meet as many of the family as we can.

"This letter really should have been written earlier and addressed to Colonel Miller as well as to you, but now it is too late and we shall have to wait until he arrives to tell him how much we appreciated the kindness and wonderful hospitality of

[219]

all of you. You must give us a chance to pay you back some time by coming to Washington. Not that we could repay you in kind, but we'd like to do it in our humble way and with enthusiasm.

"Yours sincerely,

"S. M. RINEHART."

While Colonel Joe Miller lived he counted among his friends men and women of every walk of life; men and women of numerous races and creeds, and at his funeral on the "White House" lawn, these various classes and races and creeds came to pay in what measure they might a tribute to the memory of their friend.

An audience estimated at five thousand filled the lawn, overflowed out across the expanse toward the ranch store and its accompanying buildings, and extended itself in cars up and down the paved highway while the last rites were held for Colonel Miller. Possibly it was the most colorful funeral ever held in Oklahoma, and it was unusual in the annals of the nation. Indians, particularly the Ponca tribe, forgetting for once their stoicism, wept at the departure of their friend. Negroes, employees of the 101 Ranch and the ranch show, sat in a little group to hear the master's eulogy. Cowboys and cowgirls, Russian Cossacks in their splendid uniforms, ranch employees and their families; all were present in addition to financiers, state officials, and business men who gathered from all parts of Oklahoma and other states. Ranch show employees placed a final "set-up" of circus chairs, as they had often done in the past, but the seats were under the trees Colonel Joe Miller himself had planted around the "White House" yard and the "set-up" this time was for Colonel Joe.

Faithful to the last to the memory of a friend he had known from the old border days in the Cherokee Strip country, Colonel Zack Mulhall was there to bow in grief over the death of Colonel Miller. They had ridden the plains together in the old days in the cattle roundups. And they had played the show game together under the "big top" of the 101 Ranch show.

The Reverend G. Frank Sanders, pastor of the Christian Church of Ponca City, delivered the funeral oration in which he eulogized Colonel Miller as the man "who made two blades of grass grow on the Oklahoma Prairies where but one grew before —a man who built that others might have happiness." The words he spoke were taken from a letter to Colonel Miller several years ago from a friend, who after visiting the 101 Ranch and noting the agricultural work carried on wrote him in the above language.

An unusual feature of the funeral service was the death song by old Ponca Indian chiefs headed by Crazy Bear and Horse Chief Eagle, son of old White Eagle who had been a friend of the father of the Miller brothers. The father had negotiated the removal of the Ponca tribe into the Cherokee Strip country and won the everlasting respect of the Poncas. That respect was inherited by Colonel Joe Miller and was the cause of the sincere mourning by the surviving chiefs of the tribe. The Indians dressed in their paint and feathers and bundled into their blankets, formed a mourning group in front of the funeral platform on the veranda of the White House. There were White Deer, Ed Smith, Horse Chief White Eagle, John Bull, Charles Ray, George King, Jesse Walters, Silas Primeaux, Crazy Bear, Jim Williams, and John Deloge, upon whose allotment the first headquarters of the 101 Ranch were established in 1891.

The outpouring of love and appreciation of that vast assemblage is described realistically in the *New York Sun* under date of October 25, 1927:

"Reminiscent of another age, the age when adherents of clan or feudal barony gathered to mourn a departed chieftain —was the funeral of Colonel Joseph C. Miller at the White House of 101 Ranch, near Ponca City, Oklahoma. It was fitting that this should be so. The ranch is about as near a thing as we have to the estate of a medieval lord, what with its vast acres, its host of cowboys, Indians, Mexicans and others dependent upon the success of the Miller enterprises. The homage paid to its ruler is feudal in character even if wholly voluntary on the part of those who yield it. So far as the Indians are concerned, there is much of the literal clan feeling about it, since Colonel Joe was an adopted member of the Ponca tribe and was regarded as kinsman by the other tribesmen.

"Probably nowhere else in the United States could this odd admixture of the modern and the barbaric be found at a funeral. The services themselves were a blend of Christian and pagan rites. A clergyman and choir saw to the one; Indians in paint and mourning robes saw to the other. The audience was as mixed as were the ceremonies. The Governor and Lieutenant-Governor of the State, business men, bankers, survivors of the pioneer days like "Pawnee Bill" Lillie and Colonel Zack Mulhall, ranchers, cowboys, peons, circus men, laborers, camp cooks, Indian Chiefs, women and children met and mingled on terms of perfect equality.

"The coffin was placed upon a spacious veranda. The whole place was banked with flowers. Some of the floral offerings displayed the personal tastes of the donors. Among others was one in which the head of a longhorn steer had been set in pink flowers, with blossoms for the eyes. Near the gallery was Colonel Joe's favorite horse, Pedro, with the Colonel's chaparajos attached to the empty saddle horn. The minister pronounced a eulogy in which he appropriately described Colonel Miller as belonging to the West and "as the concept of the West of tomorrow and a link with the West of the past." A choir sang. Then room was made for a delegation of blanket-clad Poncas, among them Chiefs Crazy Bear and Horse Chief Eagle. After these had chanted a weird dirge in unison there was a moment of silence; then Horse Chief Eagle pronounced a brief oration, which was interpreted as follows:

" 'Our brother, Joe, Mr. Joseph C. Miller, he is one of us. He is gone. When he went away it meant more than anything else to Indians. The Indians cry. Because our brother, Mr. Joe Miller, will not be good to us any more. He has raised us from boys, some of us. Mr. Joe Miller gave us encouragement. God is a right God, so the Indians says. He gives each man a time. We all have a time. You see the paint on our faces. We do this because our brother, Mr. Joe C. Miller, who lived with us all these years is dead. That is all. We are sad.'

"Strange and stilted are these words when thus rudely rendered into English. Noble and moving no doubt, in the original tongue. It is safe to say that if the Colonel's spirit was hovering around to hear what men said of him after he was dead it caught no other message which a departing soul would be happier to take with it to the Happy Hunting Grounds."

Reared on the frontier, Colonel Joe Miller was informed of

the possibilities of the West; he knew and understood its people quite as well as its climate. His insatiable ambition caused him constantly to seek to improve himself, his ranch, and his country, and thereby his state and the nation at large. The foundation of his character is strikingly revealed in these lines:

"Colonel Joe Miller, who spent most of his life building up one of the world's richest ranch properties, dies, and 5,000 people of every walk of life pay homage at his bier.

"It is because Colonel Miller has always been doing things, performing, that he has been in the public eye. It was no eccentricity, no unusual colorfulness, no extraordinary brilliancy, which attracted the world to this rancher.

"Of course he met and talked with royalty, but thousands have done that and been buried without attention; of course he led a 'big top' show from one end of the world to another, but many a big show man has had last rites pronounced with a funeral home large enough to house the mourners; of course he was head of one of the largest ranches now in existence, but many ranchers of equal acreage will die and have minor corteges.

"It was the dogged performance of Colonel Miller which marked him with the world. Others have visions equal or beyond that of the Oklahoma rancher, but few have the determination of performance.

"If Colonel Miller took on a halo of color, if he paraded as a man from the 'wild west,' a romancer of pioneering, it was only the means to an end. His vision lay not in the expanseless prairies behind him, where his father stretched the first barrier of barbs, but in the new Oklahoma, the one of homes, of culture, of national leadership. He brought from out the old west the spirit of performance which pioneers must have, and used it in developing the new west. His works will live forever for us Oklahomans to whom he has taught so many lessons and blazed so many trails of progress. His performances will outlive for ages any colorfulness which he might have possessed."[4]

Following is the story of the last stand of Colonel Joe Miller with his own 101 Ranch wild west show, as told by Louise

[4] *Guthrie Daily Leader,* October 29, 1927.

Beard, reporter for the *Oklahoma News,* and published in the *Hastings Nebraska Tribune* under date of October 24, 1927. Miss Beard was the last person to gain audience in a press interview with the inimitable cowman-showman. It reveals in his true setting how radiantly alive, how vital he always was, how interested in people and their welfare.

"The big gentleman who showed me over the show lot last Monday is dead. Colonel Joe Miller's booming laugh will never again echo in the 'big tops' he loved.

"It was on the last day of the circus season that the show played Oklahoma City. Someone directed me to the main ticket wagon. I went in. There was Big Joe Miller, shaking my hand and saying, 'bless your heart, child, I'll show you all over the place, you bet I will.'

"So began the last newspaper tour of the 101 Ranch wild west show with Colonel Joe.

" 'My wife's about your size and age, I reckon,' he told me. 'Did you know I had a four months old son? Yes ma'am and he and his mother will be home before long. They've been up north visitin' her folks.'

"His diamond studded Elk tooth badge sparkled in the sun. I commented on the diamonds and counted stones. 'I never stopped to count 'em,' he laughed. Then, boyishly, 'these big yeller ones'—showing the diamonds on his tie and in his ring— 'are supposed to be 10 karats apiece.'

"As we moved through the tents everyone had a glad greeting for the big colonel who owned the show, and I suspect, had a lease on their hearts as well. Every horse got a pat from him as we passed.

" 'Guess you never saw my saddle,' he ventured. 'It's got 246 diamonds in it besides some rubies and other stones.' A helper opened the strong box where the saddle was kept. He lifted it from flannel wrappings. I managed a gasp.

" 'How did you ever happen to have it made?'

" 'Well, I went to Paris and saw Napoleon's saddle in a museum. So I jes' decided to outdo him and I reckon I did,' Joe smiled.

"Proudly he showed me over the kitchen and eating tents.

" 'I'm invitin' you to come out and have dinner with us. I reckon we could squeeze in a little girl like you.' He waved his hand at the stretches of tables set for lunch. I had told him I knew his son, 'Little Joe' Miller, at the University of Oklahoma.

" 'Pshaw, Joe's with the show but he's not down this morning yet. Why, that kid's assistant manager of the show, did you know that?'

"Again the booming laugh made the diamond studded Elk tooth badge sparkle in the sun.

"Before I left we went back to the ticket stand. He handed me a little booklet. I had no desire to end my interview with such a rancher, globe trotter and circus manager.

" 'Oh, say, Colonel Joe, you didn't show me the monkeys.'

" 'Why, so I didn't.' And he climbed down the ticket wagon steps. 'You ought to see the little rascals.'

"On our way to the monkey cage a shabby, middle aged man stopped the colonel.

" 'Colonel Joe, ain't you?'

" 'Yeah, I reckon I am,' Miller drawled, smiling.

" 'Why, I was awondering if you had a piece of land up there I could rent. I shore need a place to do.'

" 'You have a family, I reckon,' Colonel Joe said. 'Well, sir, I'm afraid we're getting short on houses for tenants up there. You write or go up to the ranch and if there's anything they'll let you know right away.'

" 'Wish we had all the land in the country to fix up fellows like that,' the colonel remarked to me.

"And that's the memory I will keep of him."

Again the response of grief came from people of all walks of life at the time of the accidental death of Colonel George L. Miller. From far and near telegrams and cables poured into the "White House" the day of the funeral services. Messages of condolence came from persons whom George L. Miller had befriended, bank presidents he had known, national politicians, railroad and oil magnates, newspapermen, circus folks, motion picture stars, cowboys and rough-riders—all bespeaking a wide acquaintance among many classes of people. Unusually interesting among the telegrams received was the following one from a party of Arabs living in New York City who had been previously connected with the 101 Ranch show:

"When one of our people pass, we commend him to Allah and then go into the desert to mourn. There is no desert in

New York City or vicinity, so we have commended the spirit of Mr. Miller to Allah and are meeting tonight to mourn for him."[5]

Another unusual communication was from Henry Knows-His-Country, a Ponca Indian:

"It is too far for me to come to George's funeral. When my mother died, not many people came. But George was there. No preacher came, but George spoke for her better than any preacher could."[6]

Ponca City mourned him intimately—Oklahoma claimed him reverently. All places of business in Ponca City were closed. The city's flag was at half-mast. Every activity was stopped while long-time friends met with each other in recalling and extolling his many virtues. The body lay in state in the "White House." Hundreds of friends called to view it, including the several hundred employes of the ranch and show, and many of the Ponca and Otoe Indians. The funeral services were conducted in the municipal auditorium at Ponca City where thousands of people from all over Oklahoma passed by to view the body for the last time. Reverend Frank Sanders of the First Christian Church, the church of Mrs. Mollie Miller, the mother, gave a short address, and Felix Duval, local attorney and life-long friend of Mr. Miller, gave a eulogy, a splendid tribute. Mr. Duval said in part:

"Mr. Miller typifies those busiest of men who would always have time to do something else, something for you. And through all his vigorous and varied efforts, busy as he was, George Miller lived on the sunny side of the highway of life; and he loved to call his friends to that more companionable side, for he was there and he wanted his friends there with him.

"Although our friend's material achievements provoke our admiration, we always turn instinctively to the genial George Miller we all knew so intimately, and then we realize that we know the meaning of friendship, loyalty and hospitality, for of all these he was the personification. His friendship was compelling. It lasted.

[5] *Chronicles of Oklahoma,* Volume VII, Number 2, June, 1929.
[6] *Ibid.*

Upper, funeral of Colonel Joe Miller on the White House lawn; center, the In-dians mourn the loss of their friend, Joe Miller; lower, wagons and implements lined up for auction at the 101 Ranch

"The first Indian he met in the cow path, and for whom he later built a road, was his friend last Friday; and the last friend he met is sorry that their companionship began so late in life. His was that friendship which brought optimism and good cheer into your presence; made you love him as he tarried; left you sorry for his going; and made you instinctively know that whenever he came back, he would be your friend.

"His loyalty was as constant as his friendship was sincere, and that loyalty was not latent, he expressed it, he lived it. He loved to talk of his friends; and his defense was quick when winds bore ill rumor. The quality of his loyalty was in its democracy. His praise or defense went as quickly to the cowboy as to the financier, and the Indian felt it as securely as the merchant.

"Though the race of time be fast, men will long remember George L. Miller; his influence upon all civic progress; his contribution to our agricultural prosperity; his zeal for the advancement of our general welfare; his many and varied achievements—all of these concrete evidences of his leadership will long endure.

"But even after their luster has faded with the years, still then, all those characteristically intimate, kindly acts, and the friendly, loyal and hospitable manner of their doing, will linger forever among the sweetest flowers in the garden of our memory."

Major Gordon W. (Pawnee Bill) Lillie, life-long friend of the Millers, was stricken with grief at the death of George L. Miller, and the famed Indian scout expresses interestingly, in the following lines, his memories of the man whom he had known from boyhood.

"Jerked from my sleep by the insistent ringing of the telephone, I hurriedly picked up the receiver and an excited voice said George L. Miller had been killed in an auto accident at 2:30 on his way from Ponca City to the 101 Ranch.

"Silence, overpowering silence, followed the questions I wanted to ask.

"I hung up the receiver and groped through the murky cold gray dawn to a chair. Immediately a flood of memories rushed into my mind. I recalled the tow-headed boy who always greeted me cheerfully when I visited the 101 Ranch.

"I watched him grow into manhood, an honest statured man who invested everything he did with fine enthusiasm and direct, open manner which never failed to accomplish that which he set out to do. It was his marvelous energy, together with the wonderful spirit of his brothers, Zack and Joe, who also died in an auto accident only a year ago, that made them successful ranchmen, oil men and show men.

"I can still remember when I first met those boys in the spring of '82. The largest drive of cattle that ever came up the old Chisholm trail was in progress. They were Miller cattle. I had purchased some horses in the Chickasaw nation about a year before. These horses had strayed and I was hunting them.

"My camp was about a mile from the Miller camp. I awoke in the morning to find that the horse I was riding had pulled his picket pin during the night and had also strayed. My search took me to their camp. They had caught my horse and I was subjected to some goodnatured guying on account of my long hair and rough clothes.

"The tall, fine young men made a handsome picture in their cowboy outfits which were the best money could buy.

"From then on I met them often and always was impressed by the business-like manner in which they did things.

"Their present ranch is composed of 110,000 acres. It is perhaps the most diversified ranch in the world and a splendid monument to their success.

"Just the same as in the old days a stranger dropping in at the ranch is extended the warmest hospitality.

"To me the death of George Miller means that I have lost a dear old friend. The years have taken heavy toll of these friends of mine and I grieve for everyone of them. My deepest sympathy goes out to the family in their moment of grief. They are all dear to me. Their loss is also my loss."[7]

In an unusual way George L. Miller maintained the enthusiasm of youth throughout his life. He was able to devote himself intently to business or pleasure and at the same time to carry on the many routine duties that were his daily tasks. His untiring aim was that the 101 Ranch should be everything prominent that was claimed for it. To him it meant dignity and stability. It had been known for many years as one of Okla-

[7] *Ponca City News*, February 9, 1929.

[228]

homa's outstanding assets and he delighted in that fact. He was averse to criticism of the ranch, for to him it was his life work. Walter Ferguson characterized forcefully in the following lines this striking and picturesque Oklahoman:

"George Miller had a heart without malice and a soul without fear. He had a mind without deceit and being without smallness. He died as he lived—tempting chance. His smile has been a beacon light that has guided thousands to Ponca City—his industry and determination created a great national institution at the gates of his deeply beloved home town.

"George Miller was the foremost host in the history of Oklahoma. The famous White House of the 101 Ranch became celebrated throughout all America, through the charm and warmth of George Miller's welcome. Whether a distinguished guest with a name that resounded to the very borders of the nation or the casual and curious itinerist journeying in a second-hand Ford, they were equally welcome. The public had the right of eminent domain at the 101 Ranch, and the gracious host was never more happy, nor ever more himself than when proudly showing the wonders that had been wrought in the new land."[8]

There were three brothers, but Colonel Joe, the eldest, and Colonel George L., the youngest, had gone down the long, long trail leaving Colonel Zack, the middle of the trio in age, to fight the battles alone. The story of his struggle to keep intact Oklahoma's famous ranch—the ranch that was the connecting link between the West of yesterday and the West of today—is a tragic climax in the career of an empire builder. He stood alone between the 101 Ranch, born of his father and carried on by him and his brothers, and an army of creditors, fearful for their loans as a result of the devastating economic depression that was engulfing the whole country at that time. He has never wavered in his position and has fought bitterly any attempt to dislodge him in all his efforts to keep together and alive the 101 Ranch. Almost everyone throughout the country rejoiced in their hearts, and scores even sent telegrams, when they learned that Colonel Miller had been released from imprisonment in the Kay County Oklahoma, jail. Of the many published articles, the following expresses best, perhaps, the

[8] *Wichita Eagle,* February 7, 1929.

feeling of many people toward the freedom of this old cowman of the plains:

"Down here in Texas we don't know a thing about the merits of the legal difficulties of Colonel Zack Miller of 101 Ranch, Oklahoma; but we just know in our bones that Colonel Zack is not the sort of man who belongs in jail, even if he can't pay his debts in cash, with lawyers camping all over his property and eating up his substance in suits and fees and receiverships. They say Colonel Zack got so mad that he even took a shotgun and chased a lawyer clean off his ranch. Maybe he did, but that doesn't lower him any in the opinion of Texas.

"Most of Texas is in debt, itself, and has a fellow-feeling for Colonel Zack, right or wrong. These are no times to get a man when he is down and take away from him every means of his being able to get back on his feet. At least that is the way Texas looks at it. Of course, now, Texas could be as wrong about that as wrong can be, but when the booted and spurred and Sam-Browne-belted 'milish' of Governor Murray hove into view and rescued Colonel Zack, Texas took off its sombrero and hollered. No, it didn't halloo; it hollered.

"Of course Governor Murray is acting like a carpetbag Governor in the Reconstruction days when he sends his army around to upset the courts and bully the Sheriffs. But he is as safe as the Ten Commandments when he picks out a character like Colonel Zack to rescue in that fashion. Colonel Zack and the Missus, it seems, have had some kind of ruction, and Texas figures that is their business and theirs only, but keeping an old cowman in jail ought to be against the law. It's too much like caging an eagle."[9]

All these spontaneous expressions of the humble and the great of far and near connote only one thing. They are genuine evidences that the 101 is deeply embedded in the hearts of the American people. To them the 101 Ranch belonged to the West of yesterday—the West of uncharted prairie where buffalo roamed in freedom. But to them it belonged also to the new West, the West of cultivated beauty of fields and of beautiful homes. To them the Miller brothers were three striking characters of the plains—three empire builders—three dominant personalities, friendly, hospitable, and generous to

[9] *Dallas Morning News,* December 1, 1932.

[230]

the core. Each honored the name they bore; each served their community with distinction and fidelity; and together they loom large in the growth and development of their state.

Today the 101 Ranch has shifted from the grand inland empire nursed into existence by the Millers on the prairies of Oklahoma. Where once fine corn, alfalfa, and seasonal crops grew and registered stock basked in the sun, there is now abandoned ruin. Yonder was once a splendid peach orchard; there a hennery; still another tract, once spotted with fine registered hogs. Across from the former hog group stand the stables, once the envy of the land and now deserted. Near this spot was once a flourishing ice factory, which is now only a memory. One used to see two or three score of cowboys riding across the broad and rolling prairie, inspecting the horses and cattle, and repairing fences. And with these cowboys, one always observed the necessary quota of Indians that gave a picturesque setting to the entire ranch as well as a thrill and pleasing aspects to the hundreds of visitors who streamed into the broad acres.

The tourists are missing too, from this famed resort. Riverside camp is now deserted and the guest houses, once the pride of Bostonians, are falling into decay. The curio shop is there with plenty of curios, but the customers are gone. A wonderful grape vineyard stretched itself across the east from the main road. Little of the vineyard could be seen from a commanding point; tall weeds practically obscured the acres of vines. A vinegar factory nearby showed evidence of decay, and reminded one that the famous 101 Ranch has passed into history.

Around the vast rodeo grounds, one sees in fancy the ghosts of departed thousands, visitors each season to this stirring spot. Across the river southward, where once roamed herds of buffalo, longhorns, and fine show animals, only a few ponies and longhorns were seen, and the only vestige of what used to be the world's renowned 101 Ranch Wild West Show—a dozen show wagons that have rambled over miles of foreign streets, in their last parade, ghosts of days gone by.

The famous Oklahoma institution with its broad expanse of far-stretching prairie is fast dissolving into nothingness and in a short time the broad fields and wide ranges will be no longer sequestered vales, but small individual farms and truck patches. Verily, the curtain has rung down on the Miller brothers' 101 Ranch, and it will soon be only a pleasant memory to thousands upon thousands of Americans who knew it in its heyday.

In the passing of the 101 Ranch, Oklahoma has lost its most famous institution. What a loss to the Oklahoma of yesterday! What a loss to Oklahoma of tomorrow! What a monument the "White House" would have made to the early day settlers of this state. Surely, the memory of those grim faced pioneers, such as Colonel George W. Miller, who were so instrumental in the growth and development of Oklahoma should be preserved at all hazards for the youth of tomorrow. The rich knowledge of early Oklahoma, so much a part of the 101 Ranch, should have been preserved for posterity. Walter M. Harrison, writing in the *Oklahoma City Times* under date of July 27, 1936, expresses, no doubt, the wishes of a multitude of Oklahomans:

"The White House is symbolical of the 101 Ranch. It has just about reached the end of the trail. Lenders' buffalo pictures have been pulled off of the walls and sold for a song. The rifles over the mantels have been hauled from their pegs and peddled for pennies. The Indian rugs have been rolled up and will find sanctuary in bungalows scattered everywhere and old Colonel Zack, militant but with the law against him, is living out the last few days that the law has allowed him in the place the Miller family called home.

"So much of the life of early Oklahoma centered about that empire on the Salt Fork, so much gayety and prosperity focused there at the turn of the century, that those who remember the ranch when the Millers were on the make speed by quickly on their way to and from Ponca City now, refusing to look at the decayed and stumbling remnants of the vast estate.

"It is a pity that this thing has to disappear. The ranch house, or White House, as they called it, should be preserved, with a collection of historical interest of the entire Cherokee Strip. It should be a main point of interest on a national highway, but who is there with money to save this treasure for another generation?

"Probably it is another one of those things that everyone would like to see done but that no one can afford to do."

APPENDIX I

DEED OF TRUST
FROM
JOSEPH C. MILLER, ZACK T. MILLER, GEORGE L. MILLER
and MILLER BROTHERS
TO
MILLER BROTHERS 101 RANCH TRUST

W. A. Brooks and J. E. Carson, Trustees

Dated September 12, 1921

FILED

Noble County, Okla., Oct. 18, 1921; Pawnee County, Okla., Oct. 28, 1921
Osage County, Okla., Nov. 18, 1921; Kay County, Okla., Sept. 26, 1921

Know All Men by these Presents:

THAT, WHEREAS, Joseph C. Miller, Zack T. Miller and George L. Miller, as individuals, are now the owners of all of the real estate described and listed in the schedule hereinafter set out.

And, whereas, the firm of Miller Brothers, a partnership consisting of Joseph C. Miller, Zack T. Miller and George L. Miller, is the owner of all livestock and personal property of whatsoever kind or character located and used on said real estate, and in connection with the operation of what is known and designated as the "101 Ranch."

And, whereas, the following is a complete schedule showing all of the real estate owned by each of the said Joseph C. Miller, Zack T. Miller and George L. Miller, showing the description of each particular tract of said real estate and the name of the record owner thereof, to-wit:

SCHEDULE

In the descriptions of the lands set forth in this schedule the letters "NE" shall be understood to mean "Northeast," and the letters "NW" shall be understood to mean "Northwest," and the letters "SW" shall be understood to mean "Southwest" and the letters "SE" shall be understood to mean "Southeast"; and where the letter "S" appears it shall be understood to mean "South," and where the letter "N" appears it shall be understood to mean "North," and where the letter "E" appears it shall be understood to mean "East," and where the letter "W" appears it shall be understood to mean "West." And the following abbreviations at the top of each page, to-wit: "Sec" shall mean "Section," and the abbreviation "Twp" shall mean "Township" and the abbreviation "Rge" shall mean "Range."

NOBLE COUNTY

Description:	Sec.	Twp.	Rge.	Acres	Record Owner:*
SE¼ of NE¼	1	24N	1E	40.	Z.T.M.
SW¼ of NE¼	2	24N	1E	40.	Z.T.M.
SE¼ of NE¼	11	24N	1E	40.	G.L.M. and Z.T.M.
SW¼ of NW¼	12	24N	1E	40.	G.L.M.
SW¼	12	24N	1E	160.	Z.T.M.
SE¼ west of Railroad	12	24N	1E	80.	Z.T.M.
All of SE¼	14	24N	1E	160.	Z.T.M.

*The initials under "Record Owner" refer to George L. Miller (G.L.M.); Zack T. Miller (Z.T.M.); and Joseph C. Miller (J.C.M.).

[233]

W½ SW¼	22	24N	1E	80.	Z.T.M.
SW¼ of NW¼ and NW¼ of SW¼ west of Railroad	24	24N	1E	31.8	G.L.M.
W½ of NW¼ and NW¼ of SW¼	26	24N	1E	120.	G.L.M.
SE¼ of NW¼	26	24N	1E	40.	Z.T.M.
E½ of SW¼	27	24N	1E	80.	Z.T.M.
NW¼ of SE¼	31	24N	1E	40.	G.L.M.
NE¼	33	24N	1E	160.	G.L.M.
NW¼	33	24N	1E	160.	G.L.M.
NE¼ of SW¼ and NW¼ of SE¼ and NE¼ of SE¼	33	24N	1E	120.	G.L.M.
SW¼ of SE¼	33	24N	1E	40.	G.L.M.
W½ of NE¼	34	24N	1E	80.	Z.T.M.
W½ of SW¼ and SW¼ of NW¼	36	24N	1E	120.	G.L.M.
SE¼ of SW¼ and S½ of SE¼	36	24N	1E	120.	Z.T.M.
SW¼ of NE¼	26	24N	1E	40.	Z.T.M.
E½ of SE¼	15	24N	3E	80.	G.L.M.
E½ of NE¼	15	24N	3E	80.	G.L.M. and Z.T.M.
NE¼ of NE¼	22	24N	3E	40.	G.L.M. and Z.T.M.
Lot 4 and NE¼ of SE¼	22	24N	3E	57.	G.L.M.
Lot 2 and S½ of SE¼ of NW¼	23	24N	3E	39.20	G.L.M.
W½ of NW¼ and N½ of SE¼ of NW¼	23	24N	3E	100.	G.L.M. and Z.T.M.
Lots 1 and 4	23	24N	3E	69.80	G.L.M. and Z.T.M.
Lot 1, Sec. 24 and Lot 1 and SW¼ of SW¼ and NE¼ of SW¼	13	24N	3E	156.50	G.L.M.
Lots 5 and 6	36	25N	3E	52.45	G.L.M.
Lot 5	6	24N	2E	39.	G.L.M.
Lot 1 West of Railroad	7	24N	2E	3.	G.L.M.
SE¼ of SE¼	19	24N	2E	40.	J.C.M.
S½ of NE¼ of SW¼	19	24N	2E	20.	Z.T.M.
W½ of NE¼ and SE¼ of NE¼	19	24N	2E	120.	G.L.M.
Lot 2 and E½ of NW¼	19	24N	2E	118.	G.L.M.
Lots 3 and 4	19	24N	2E	70.14	G.L.M.
SW¼ of NE¼	20	24N	2E	40.	G.L.M.
S½ of SW¼	20	24N	2E	80.	J.C.M.
NW¼ of NE¼	21	24N	2E	40.	G.L.M.
NE¼ of NW¼	21	24N	2E	40.	Z.T.M.
W½ of SE¼	21	24N	2E	80.	G.L.M.
E½ of NE¼ and NW¼ of SE¼	22	24N	2E	120.	G.L.M.
NE¼	29	24N	2E	160.	J.C.M.
S½ of SE¼ and NE¼ of SE¼	27	24N	2E	120.	G.L.M.
E½ of NW¼	28	24N	2E	80.	Z.T.M.
N½ of NW¼	29	24N	2E	80.	J.C.M.
E½ of SW¼ and Lots 3 and 4	30	24N	2E	149.49	G.L.M.
Lots 1 and 2	30	24N	2E	69.49	G.L.M.
SE¼	30	24N	2E	160.	G.L.M.
S½ of NW¼ and SW¼ of NE¼	32	24N	2E	120.	J.C.M.

W½ of NE¼	36	24N	2E	80.	G.L.M.
Lot 6	6	24N	2E	40.	G.L.M.
SW¼ of SE¼	26	23N	2E	40.	Z.T.M.
S½ of NE¼	26	23N	2E	80.	G.L.M. and Z.T.M.
SW¼ of NW¼	25	23N	2E	40.	G.L.M. and Z.T.M.
SW¼ and SE¼ of NW¼	25	23N	2E	200.	G.L.M. and Z.T.M.
N½ of NE¼	26	23N	2E	80.	G.L.M. and Z.T.M.
SW¼ of SE¼	23	23N	2E	40.	G.L.M. and Z.T.M.
N½ of N½ of NW¼ of SE¼	26	23N	2E	10.	Z.T.M.
N½ of N½ of NE¼ of SE¼	26	23N	2E	10.	G.L.M. and Z.T.M.
S½ of S½ of NE¼ of SE¼	26	23N	2E	10.	G.L.M.
N½ of S½ of NW¼ of SE¼	26	23N	2E	10.	G.L.M.
W½ of SE¼ west of R.R. and	26	24N	1E	} 33½	G.L.M.
NW¼ of NE¼ west of R.R.	35	24N	1E		G.L.M.
NE¼ of SW¼	26	24N	1E	40.	Z.T.M.
Lots 1 and 2	2	24N	1E	80.	G.L.M.
Lots 9, 11 and 13 and Lot 10 and SW¼ of SW¼	5	24N	4E	116.30	G.L.M.
S½ of SE¼	6	24N	4E	80.	G.L.M.
Lots 1 and 5 and SW¼ of NE¼	6	24N	4E	111.87	Z.T.M. and G.L.M.
Lot 4 and SE¼ of SW¼	7	24N	4E	79.93	G.L.M.
Lots 2 and 3 and SE¼ of NW¼ and NE¼ of SW¼	7	24N	4E	160.	Z.T.M. and G.L.M.
Lots 2, 3, 4 and 5 and W½ of SE¼ and SW¼ of NE¼	8	24N	4E	237.35	G.L.M.
W½ of NW¼ of NW¼	8	24N	4E	20.	G.L.M. and Z.T.M.
S½ of SE¼ of NW¼	8	24N	4E	20.	G.L.M.
NE¼ of SW¼	8	24N	4E	40.	G.L.M.
W½ of SW¼ and SE¼ of SW¼	8	24N	4E	120.	G.L.M. and Z.T.M.
Lot 4 and SE¼ of NW¼	17	24N	4E	48.25	G.L.M.
W½ of NW¼ and NE¼ of NW¼	17	24N	4E	120.	G.L.M. and Z.T.M.
Lots 2 and 3	17	24N	4E	35.	G.L.M. and Z.T.M.
E½ of NW¼ and S½ of SE¼ of NE¼	18	24N	4E	100.	G.L.M. and Z.T.M.
SW¼ of NE¼ and NE¼ of NE¼ and N½ of SE¼ of NE¼	18	24N	4E	100.	G.L.M.
Lots 9 and 10	31	25N	4E	55.	G.L.M. and Z.T.M.
Lot 6	18	24N	4E	15.	G.L.M.
Lots 1, 3 and 4	1	24N	3E	87¼	Z.T.M. and G.L.M.
Lot 2	1	24N	3E	40.	G.L.M.
SE¼ of SE¼ and NW¼ of SE¼	1	24N	3E	80.	G.L.M.
NE¼ of SE¼ and SW¼ of SE¼ and SE¼ of NE¼	1	24N	3E	120.	G.L.M. and Z.T.M.
Lot 8 and NW¼ of SE¼	2	24N	3E	60.40	G.L.M. and Z.T.M.
Lot 7 and E½ of SE¼ and SW¼ of SE¼	2	24N	3E	124.	G.L.M.
SE¼ of SE¼	3	24N	3E	40.	G.L.M. and Z.T.M.
NW¼ of NW¼	11	24N	3E	40.	G.L.M. and Z.T.M.
S½ of SE¼	11	24N	3E	80.	G.L.M.

Description	Sec.	Twp.	Rge.	Acres	Initials
NE¼ of NW¼	12	24N	3E	40.	G.L.M. and Z.T.M.
SE¼ of NW¼	12	24N	3E	40.	G.L.M.
W½ of SE¼	12	24N	3E	80.	Z.T.M.
E½ of SE¼	12	24N	3E	80.	G.L.M. and Z.T.M.
E½ of NE¼ of SE¼ and S½ of NW¼ of SE¼ and Lot 2	13	24N	3E	79.80	Z.T.M. and G.L.M.
NE¼ and NW¼ of SW¼ and W½ of NE¼ of SE¼ (G.L.M. and Z.T.M.)	13	24N	3E	220.	G.L.M.
S½ of SE¼ and (G.L.M.)					(See initials)
NE¼ of SE¼ and S½ of NE¼	14	24N	3E	140.	G.L.M. and Z.T.M.
W½ of SW¼ and SE¼ of SW¼	14	24N	3E	120.	G.L.M. and Z.T.M.
N½ of NW¼	25	23N	2E	80.	Z.T.M. and G.L.M.
SE¼ of SW¼	24	23N	2E	40.	G.L.M. and Z.T.M.
Lot 1 and S½ of N½ of NE¼ of NW¼	31	23N	2E	50.	G.L.M. and Z.T.M.
S½ of SW¼ (Inc. Lot 4)	30	23N	2E	80.	G.L.M. and Z.T.M.
Lot 2, SE¼ of NW¼ and N½ of S½ of NE¼ of NW¼	31	23N	2E	90.	G.L.M.
Lot 3	31	23N	2E	40.	G.L.M.
E½ of SW¼ and Lot 4	31	23N	2E	119.47	G.L.M.
NE¼	31	23N	2E	160.	G.L.M. and Z.T.M.
NE¼ and NW¼ and SW¼ and SW¼ of SE¼	6	22N	2E	520.	G.L.M. and Z.T.M.
E½ of SE¼ and NW¼ of SE¼	6	22N	2E	120.	G.L.M.
N½ of S½ of SW¼ of SE¼	25	22N	2E	10.	G.L.M.
W½ of SW¼	9	23N	1E	80.	Z.T.M.
SE¼	30	23N	2E	160.	G.L.M.
S½ of N½ of NE¼ of NE¼	36	22N	2E	10.	G.L.M.
SE¼ of SW¼	26	24N	1E	40.	G.L.M.

PAWNEE COUNTY

Description	Sec.	Twp.	Rge.	Acres	Initials
Lot 2 and SW¼ of NE¼	6	23N	3E	80.62	G.L.M.
NW¼	33	23N	3E	160.	G.L.M.
W½ of NE¼ and NE¼ of NE¼	33	23N	3E	120.	G.L.M.
S½ of S½ of SE¼ of SE¼	29	23N	3E	10.	G.L.M.
N½ of SW¼ and SE¼ of SW¼	33	23N	3E	120.	G.L.M.
SW¼ of SW¼	33	23N	3E	40.	G.L.M.
W½ of SE¼	33	23N	3E	80.	G.L.M.
S½ of S½ of SE¼ of NE¼	26	23N	3E	10.	Z.T.M.
N½ of S½ of SE¼ of NE¼	26	23N	3E	10.	G.L.M.
Lots 3 and 4 and S½ of NW¼	4	22N	3E	158.66	G.L.M.
NW¼ of SE¼	4	22N	3E	40.	G.L.M.
Lots 5 and 6	6	22N	3E	75.80	G.L.M.

[236]

W½ of SW¼ (undivided ¼ interest)	24	22N	3E	20.	Z.T.M.
SE¼	27	22N	3E	160.	G.L.M.
S½ of N½ of SW¼ of NE¼	4	22N	3E	10.	G.L.M.

OSAGE COUNTY

S½ of NE¼ of NE¼ of NE¼	36	26N	10E	5.	G.L.M.
NW¼ of NE¼ of NE¼	36	26N	10E	10.	G.L.M.
S½ of S½ of N½ of NW¼ of NE¼	34	28N	9E	5.	G.L.M.
N½ of N½ of S½ of NW¼ of NE¼	34	28N	9E	5.	G.L.M.
NE¼ and N½ of NW¼ of SE¼ and N½ of SW¼ of NW¼ of SE¼	10	21N	11E	185.	G.L.M.
NE¼	36	24N	7E	160.	G.L.M.
E½ of SE¼	8	21N	11E	80.	Z.T.M. and G.L.M.
W½ of SW¼	9	21N	11E	80.	Z.T.M. and G.L.M.
SW¼ of SW¼ of NW¼ and S½ of SE¼ of SW¼ of NW¼ and W½ of W½ of NW¼ of NE¼ of SW¼	9	21N	11E	17½	Z.T.M. and G.L.M.
Lot 4 and SW¼ of NW¼ Undivided ½ interest	5	24N	5E	40.35	Z.T.M.
W½ of SW¼ Undivided ½ interest	32	25N	5E	40.	Z.T.M.

KAY COUNTY

NE¼ of SW¼	3	25N	1E	40.	G.L.M.
NW¼ of SE¼	12	25N	1E	40.	Z.T.M.
W½ of SW¼	24	25N	1E	80.	Z.T.M.
E½ of SW¼	24	25N	1E	80.	G.L.M. and Z.T.M.
S½ of SE¼	24	25N	1E	80.	G.L.M. and Z.T.M.
N½ of SE¼	24	25N	1E	80.	G.L.M.
Lots 3, 4, 5, and 6, and NE¼ of SE¼	25	25N	1E	160.78	G.L.M. and Z.T.M.
Lot 10	25	25N	1E	35.42	G.L.M.
SE¼ of SE¼	26	25N	1E	40.	Z.T.M.
Lots 1 and 2	26	25N	1E	40.	Z.T.M.
NE¼ of NE¼	35	25N	1E	40.	Z.T.M.
Lots 7 and 8 (½ interest)	33	25N	1E	20.	Z.T.M.
Lots 4 and 5 and SE¼ of NE¼	35	25N	1E	97.20	G.L.M.
SE¼ of SE¼ and NE¼ of SE¼ and Lot 6	35	25N	1E	119.	All in Z.T.M.
N½ of NE¼ and SE¼ of NE¼	25	25N	1E	120.	Z.T.M.
Lots 1 and 2 and N½ of NW¼	25	25N	1E	115.65	Z.T.M.
S½ of SW¼	25	25N	1E	80.	Z.T.M.
Lot 7	25	25N	1E	10.87	Z.T.M.
Lot 1	36	25N	1E	3.	G.L.M. and Z.T.M.
E½ of SE¼	36	25N	1E	80.	Z.T.M.
E½ of NW¼ of NW¼ and E½ of W½ of NW¼ of NW¼ (Undivided ½ interest)	8	25N	2E	15.	G.L.M.

Description	Sec.	Twp.	Rge.	Acres	Owner
W½ of E½ of NW¼	15	25N	2E	40.	G.L.M. and Z.T.M.
NW¼ of SW¼ (undivided ⅓ interest)	17	25N	2E	13.33	G.L.M.
NE¼ of SW¼ and N½ of SE¼ of SE¼ of SW¼ and N½ of SE¼ of SW¼ and SW¼ of SE¼ of SW¼	19	25N	2E	75.	Z.T.M.
SE¼ of NW¼	19	25N	2E	40.	G.L.M.
W½ of NE¼ and Lots 1, 2 and 3	19	25N	2E	197.91	Z.T.M.
Lot 4	19	25N	2E	39.83	G.L.M. and Z.T.M.
Lot 7	20	25N	2E	27½	Z.T.M.
Lots 3 and 4 and SE¼ of SE¼	20	25N	2E	100.33	J.C.M.
NW¼	20	25N	2E	160.	G.L.M. and Z.T.M.
W½ of SW¼ and Lot 8	20	25N	2E	114.32	G.L.M. and Z.T.M.
Lot 2 West of Railroad and Lots 3, 4 and 5 and SW¼ of NW¼, N½ of SW¼ and S½ of SW¼ and SW¼ of SE¼	21	25N	2E	343.93	Z.T.M.
Lots 5, 6, and 7	27	25N	2E	80.40	G.L.M.
NE¼ of SE¼	28	25N	2E	40.	G.L.M.
N½ of SW¼ of NW¼ and NW¼ of NW¼	28	25N	2E	60.	G.L.M.
SW¼	28	25N	2E	160.	G.L.M.
E½ of NE¼	28	25N	2E	80.	G.L.M.
SW¼ and NW¼ of NE¼	29	25N	2E	200.	Z.T.M.
W½ of NE¼ and NE¼ of NE¼ and Lot 7	30	25N	2E	145.38	Z.T.M.
Lot 8	30	25N	2E	24.	G.L.M.
Lot 1	29	25N	2E	21.82	Z.T.M.
NE¼ of NW¼ and Lot 1	30	25N	2E	79.88	Z.T.M.
Lot 6	30	25N	2E	36.35	Z.T.M.
SE¼ of SW¼ and W½ of SE¼ West of Railroad	31	25N	2E	96.	G.L.M. and Z.T.M.
NE¼ of SW¼ and Lot 8 West of Railroad	31	25N	2E	79.98	Z.T.M. and G.L.M.
S½ of NE¼ and S½ of S½ of S½ of NW¼ of NE¼	31	25N	2E	85.	G.L.M. and Z.T.M.
Lot 5 and 6	31	25N	2E	80.	G.L.M.
W½ of NE¼ and NE¼ of NE¼ and Lot 4	32	25N	2E	157.17	G.L.M.
E½ of NW¼ West of Railroad	32	25N	2E	36.	G.L.M. and Z.T.M.

And, whereas, further, the real estate above described together with the live-stock and personal property used and located on the "101 Ranch" has been managed and operated in part separately by the individuals above named and in part by the said Joseph C. Miller, Zack T. Miller and George L. Miller, together under the firm name of Miller Brothers; and now in order to centralize the management of said property, both real and personal, and in order to insure the more efficient, economical and satisfactory management, control, development, operation and conduct of the business of the parties above named and for the purposes hereinafter described, it is desired by these granting parties to grant, deed, sell, and set over all of said real estate and personal property to W. A. Brooks and J. E. Carson, Trustees, in trust, for the uses and purposes hereinafter set out.

NOW THEREFORE, We, Joseph C. Miller, a single man, Zack T. Miller, a single man, and George L. Miller, a single man, do by these presents, quit claim, grant, bargain, sell, convey, assign, and set over unto and invest in W. A. Brooks and J. E. Carson as Trustees, all of our right, title, interest and estate jointly and severally, both legal and equitable, in and to all of the real estate set out and described and listed hereinbefore in that portion of this Trust Deed designated as the "Schedule," subject to any and all oil and gas mining leases, mortgages and liens of record, together with all of the livestock and personal property of whatsoever kind or character owned by the firm of Miller Brothers, and all notes, accounts, claims, demands, choses in action, judgments, suits in action, funds and moneys now held or owned by the firm of Miller Brothers, in trust, to take, receive and hold the legal and equitable title to the aforesaid real estate, stock, personal property, notes, accounts, claims, demands, choses in action, judgments, suits in action, funds and moneys, for the following uses and purposes and with the following powers, duties and obligations, to-wit:

To receive the rents and profits accruing from said properties and from other property acquired by them as hereinafter provided during the life of said trust, and pay the same to the shareholders entitled thereto as hereinafter provided.

To manage, operate and control the said property during the life of said trust, and to operate and develop the lands and properties herein granted in trust, for the following purposes, to-wit:

To manage, operate and develop said properties and any other property acquired by the trustees, and to carry on and engage in a general agricultural and livestock business, and to do all things necessary and incidental to a general agricultural or livestock business. And to engage in and do a wholesale or retail marketing of the entire products of said ranch; to manage, operate and develop said properties and any other property acquired by the Trustees, for oil and gas purposes and all purposes incidental to the oil and gas business, including the manufacture and sale at wholesale or retail of the products of said business; to operate a general mercantile business, including the wholesaling or retailing of any merchandise of whatsoever kind and character; and to operate, manage and develop said properties for any other lawful and profitable purposes in relation to or incidental to the purposes above set out.

To use, in their discretion, the profits arising from the operation of said properties in the acquiring of other lands and properties and to purchase from any funds coming into their hands, such equipment, chattels and stock as may be ordinarily necessary in the management, operation and development of the properties above described; to market and sell any and all products from said business, to employ and pay agents, servants, laborers and employees deemed, by them, necessary in the business of the trust hereunder, and in the management, control, operation and conservation of the properties herein described, and such other properties as said Trustees may acquire under the powers and authorities hereunder conveyed; to invest trust funds in revenue bearing securities.

To take and receive all judgments, claims, demands, both legal and equitable, as well as all moneys, funds, notes and accounts belonging to these grantors or to Miller Brothers, and to collect and use the same in carrying out the purposes and uses of said Trust; and the execution of this Deed of Trust shall operate as an assignment of all of the said above described choses in action, judgments, claims, demands, moneys, funds, notes and accounts to the said Trustees.

And said Trustees are authorized to pay all lawful notes, claims, choses in action, final judgments and liens of record against either Joseph C. Miller, Zack T. Miller, George L. Miller or Miller Brothers, which may have been contracted prior to the date of the execution of this Trust Deed, out of any funds coming into their hands under this Trust; the said Trustees shall in no wise by accepting said Trust, and the duties herein imposed, be personally obligated and bound to pay any of said notes, accounts, indebtednesses, judgments, liens, or choses in action; and said Trustees are authorized and empowered, in their discretion, to sell and convey any of the property conveyed to them by this Deed of Trust or accumulated and acquired by them under the powers and duties herein imposed and use the proceeds in payment of said obligations above described and in the purchase or acquisition of any other real estate and personal property in such manner and for such purposes as they may deem wise and beneficial in carrying on the business of said Trust; and to pay to the shareholders from time to time, such part of the proceeds of said sales or of the net profits arising from the operation of said trust as said Trustees may deem advisable.

To borrow money for their use as Trustees in carrying on the objects and purposes of this Trust; to execute notes therefor, and to obligate by mortgage any or all of the real estate and other properties held by them in trust, as security therefor; provided said Trustees have no power to bind the shareholders personally, and each contract entered into by them shall contain a recitation to the effect that said contract shall not operate to bind personally any of the shareholders, and the person, partnership, stock company or corporation contracting with said Trustees will look alone to the funds and properties of the trust for the payment of such contract, indebtedness, mortgage, judgment or decree or any money that may otherwise become due by reason of the failure on the part of said Trustees to perform said contract in whole or in part, and neither the Trustees nor the shareholders, present or future shall be personally liable therefor; to prosecute and defend in their own name any suit in law or equity affecting any of the properties, contracts, rights and powers held by them under this Trust.

In selling and disposing of any of the real estate or other property held by said Trustees as herein provided and authorized, they are empowered and authorized to execute conveyances, assignments, deeds, or bills of sale in their own name as Trustees, and acknowledge the same, and every such assignment, conveyance, deed or bill of sale executed by said Trustees and duly acknowledged by them in accordance with the form required for an acknowledgement to a warranty deed, shall operate to vest in the grantee, assignee, or purchaser the full legal and equitable title in and to the property described in such instrument; and it shall at no time be necessary for the shareholders to authorize or to join in the execution of any such assignment, conveyance, deed or bill of sale, and in mortgaging any of the assets or properties in their hands, the said Trustee shall execute and acknowledge such mortgage in their own name as Trustees, in the form hereinafter given and it shall thereupon operate as a legal and valid mortgage of the property therein described.

The official legal name of the trusteeship created by this deed of Trust shall be "Miller Brothers' 101 Ranch Trust." All titles to property, both real and personal, of whatever kind and nature conveyed by this deed of trust or hereinafter acquired thereunder shall be held and taken in the following name: "W. A. Brooks and J. E. Carson, Trustees, Miller Brothers 101 Ranch Trust," and all conveyances or transfers of the property held in trust by said Trustees shall be executed by "W. A. Brooks and J. E. Carson, Trustees, Miller Brothers' 101 Ranch Trust"; provided, that at all times titles shall be taken and given in the name of the then existing trustees.

The Trustees are hereby authorized and empowered, in their discretion and judgment, to make reasonable donations of money or property for benevolent, charitable and religious uses and purposes.

Said Trustees are authorized and empowered to appoint agents, and attorneys in fact, and they may by proper power of attorney in writing, authorize such agents and attorneys to execute contracts and instruments in the name of said Trustees in the management and business of this trust, and to carry on for them as their agents and attorneys in fact, all of the business incidental to this trust estate.

The period of this trust shall not extend beyond the term of the Twenty (20) years from the date of this trust deed and within that period the said Trustees or their successors shall sell, either at private or public sale, on such terms as they deem proper, all of the property then held by them in trust as herein provided and after paying all outstanding obligations against the trust, distribute the proceeds therefrom and also funds from any source, to the shareholders as their interest appears.

The Trustees shall pay all taxes out of the proceeds of any funds coming into their hands as such trustees, and shall have power and authority to contest in the courts or other tribunals, in their own names, the amount or validity of any assessment for taxation made against them or any of the assets in their hands.

Either of said Trustees or his successor in trust, may resign by executing a written declaration or resignation setting forth a conveyance to the other trustee of all of his right, title and interest held as trustee in the property held by him and his associate trustee, in trust, as herein provided; such resignation and conveyance shall be duly executed and acknowledged and filed for record in the office of the Register of Deeds in the counties in which said trustees hold property in trust as herein provided.

Any vacancy in the number of trustees may be filled by the remaining trustee until the next annual meeting of the shareholders or special meeting called for the purpose of filling such vacancy; the other trustee from time to time shall have all the title and powers of the original trustees. Upon resignation, decease, incompetency or removal or vacancy for any cause, the title of the outgoing trustee shall vest in the remaining trustee, and upon the filling of any vacancy by the remaining trustee or the shareholders as aforesaid, the title of the whole trust property shall vest in the new Board of Trustees, jointly with all the powers herein mentioned. Neither of the trustees, nor successors shall be required to give bond except upon demand of shareholders owning as much as one-half of the shares, which demand may be made at any time during the life of this trust, the amount of such bond to be fixed by the shareholders owning a majority of the shares. The premium and cost of such bond or bonds shall be paid by the trustees out of the trust fund in their hands. Each trustee shall be liable only for his own acts, and then only for a willful breach of trust. Neither shall the shareholders at any time become liable for any debt, obligation or act of the Trustees.

If at any time, in the judgment of the two existing trustees, it is deemed advisable and for the best interest of the trust estate, that the trust herein created be managed and operated by a trust company engaged in the general business of acting as trustee, then the two existing trustees are empowered and authorized to convey to any reliable, established trust company, all of their right, title and interest in and to the property and estate described and created in this Trust Deed. Such conveyance by the existing trustees to a trust company shall not become absolute and effective until said trust company shall, by its written instrument properly executed and acknowledged, accept the title to all of the property and trust estate herein defined and described, and agree to act as the trustee thereof and in accordance with all of the powers, duties, conditions and terms of this Trust Deed, specific reference to which shall be made in the instrument conveying title to said trust company and in the instrument by said trust company agreeing to accept title as trustee, and act as trustee of this trust under the terms, conditions, obligations and powers set forth in this Trust deed. It shall not be necessary for the shareholders to authorize or join in the execution of such conveyance by the Trustees to a trust company as aforesaid. Should a conveyance be made by the Trustees to a trust company as above set out, the instrument conveying title to said trust company and the instrument of said trust company accepting title as trustee under this Trust Deed, shall be recorded in all counties wherein any property described in this Trust Deed or then held by said trustees, may be situated.

Regular meetings of the shareholders shall be held on the third Monday of January of each year in the office of the trustees in Ponca City, Oklahoma, at which regular meeting the trustees shall make a report showing the condition of the business in their hands under this trust. The trustees or the holders of the majority of the shares may, at any time, on giving five (5) days written notice to the shareholders and Trustees, call a special meeting of the shareholders to be held at the office of the Trustees in Ponca City, Oklahoma, and such notice may be given by mail or telegraph. Shareholders may at any regular or special meeting vote by proxy. At any annual or special meeting of the shareholders called for that purpose, the holders of a majority of the shares may fill any vacancy existing in the number of trustees. Each share shall represent one vote and a majority interest in the shares shall constitute a quorum at a regular or special meeting.

The Trustees shall keep, or cause to be kept books showing the financial condition of the property and affairs in their hands and the state of the trust and how it is being administered; and they shall also keep a book to be known as "Shareholders' Record Book," in which shall be transcribed the proceedings of any meeting of the shareholders, regular or special; and they shall also keep a separate book entitled "Shareholders' Certificates," which shall contain certificates and stubs, upon the latter of which shall be entered the number of the certificates, the name of the holder, the date of its issuance and the number of shares represented by the certificate issued.

There shall be issued by said Trustees, One Hundred Thousand (100,000) shares, no more or no less. The share certificate shall recite that the holder thereof is the owner of a certain number of shares in "Miller Brothers' 101 Ranch Trust"; and said trustees certificates shall be substantially in the following form:

CERTIFICATES OF SHARES
IN
"MILLER BROTHERS 101 RANCH TRUST"

Whereas, there has been conveyed to us in trust by Joseph C. Miller, Zack T. Miller, George L. Miller, and Miller Brothers, on the 12th day of September, 1921, certain real estate and personal property described in a certain deed of trust on record in the office of the County Clerk of Kay County, Oklahoma, in record book, Vol_____, Page_____, to which reference is here made:

NOW, THEREFORE, this is to certify that _____ is one of the shareholders under the provision of said deed of trust, and that the aforesaid shareholder is the owner of _____shares, there being in all One Hundred Thousand (100,000) shares.

WITNESS our hands and signatures this _____ day of _____, 192____.

_____
_____
Trustees.

The form for use in transferring shares shall be substantially as follows:

FORM OF TRANSFER

FOR VALUE RECEIVED, I, the within named shareholder, do hereby transfer to _____, _____ shares in the Miller Brothers 101 Ranch Trust, mentioned in the within certificate, and hereby irrevocably constitute and appoint_____ _____ my attorney in fact to transfer said shares on the books of the Trustees.

WITNESS my hand this_____day of_____, 192____.
WITNESS_____ _____

Certificates shall be executed and delivered by said Trustees showing the issuance and distribution of said One Hundred Thousand (100,000) shares provided for in the immediately preceding paragraph in exchange for all of the property acquired by this deed of trust to the following shareholders in the amount set opposite their names, to-wit:

Joseph C. Miller _____ 33,333 Shares
Zack T. Miller _____ 33,333 Shares
George L. Miller _____ 33,334 Shares

Said certificates shall be transferable only upon the books of the Trustees upon surrender thereof; and by the term "Shareholder" as used herein, is meant the holder of record of a share certificate, as hereinbefore described herein. Upon the proper transfer showing share certificate and the surrender thereof, the Trustees shall issue a new certificate to the assignee, but neither the legal shareholders nor their successors shall have any legal or equitable title in or to any of the property herein described or hereafter accumulated by said trustee under and by the authority hereby granted.

Said Trustees shall have and exercise all the powers herein expressly authorized and granted by this trust and such other additional powers necessary to the full and complete exercise of the rights, powers and authority expressly conveyed upon them, it being the intention of the parties signatory thereto to divest themselves of all right, title and interest, legal and equitable, and to any of said property herein described, and to vest the legal and equitable title in said Trustees and their successors for the uses and purposes herein set forth and with the powers and authorities herein granted.

Said Trustees shall have for their services the sum of Twenty-five Hundred Dollars ($2500.00) per annum, but the shareholders, at any annual or special meeting called for that purpose, may by vote of those owning a majority of the shares, consent to a change in the compensation of said Trustees or any of them.

Said Trustees shall signify their acceptance of the trust herein granted by endorsing on this Deed of Trust, their written acceptance and signing and acknowledging the same.

IN WITNESS WHEREOF, we have hereto set our hands and seals this 12th day of September, 1921.

JOSEPH C. MILLER,
ZACK T. MILLER,
GEORGE L. MILLER,
MILLER BROTHERS,
By GEORGE L. MILLER,
Member of Firm.

STATE OF OKLAHOMA } SS.
COUNTY OF KAY,   }

Before me, the undersigned, a Notary Public, in and for said County and State, on this 12th day of September, 1921, personally appeared Joseph C. Miller, a single man, Zack T. Miller, a single man, and George L. Miller, a single man, to me known to be the identical persons who executed the within and foregoing instrument and acknowledged to me they executed the same as their free and voluntary act and deed for the uses and purposes therein set forth.

(SEAL)   MARGARET M. TIERNEY,
My Commission Expires March 29, 1925.   Notary Public.

ACCEPTANCE OF TRUSTEES

We, W. A. Brooks, and J. E. Carson, hereby accept the trust hereinabove provided for and agree to faithfully discharge the duties thereof to the best of our ability.

W. A. BROOKS,
J. E. CARSON.

STATE OF OKLAHOMA, } SS.
COUNTY OF KAY,   }

Before me, the undersigned, a Notary Public, in and for said County and State, on this 12th day of September, 1921, personally appeared W. A. Brooks and J. E. Carson, to me known to be the identical persons who executed the within and foregoing instrument and acknowledged to me that they executed the same as their free and voluntary act and deed for the uses and purposes therein set forth.

(SEAL)   ETHEL POST,
My Commission Expires March 29, 1924.   Notary Public.

[243]

APPENDIX II

SCHEDULE OF LEASED LANDS OF THE 101 RANCH WITH PREFERENTIAL RIGHTS

Allotment Numbers	Lessors	Acres	Kind of Lease	Amt. Paid Per Year
104	Mary Buffalo Head	116.35	Farming Land	$ 289.92
452	Barbes, Roy G.	80	Grazing	40.08
470	Buffalo Chief	40	"	100.20
634	Eugene Big Goose	37.42	"	40.08
650	Ethel Burtt	40	"	30.00
239	Black Hair Horse	40	"	40.08
639	Napolian Buffalo Head	160	"	39.96
675	Martha Blue Back	160	"	120.00
643	John Buffalo Head	159.39	"	120.00
103	Julia Crazy Arrow	40	"	30.00
761	Julia Crazy Arrow	120.18	"	120.00
661	Anna P. Cry	120	"	90.00
118	Parchall Cerre	40.80	"	19.92
758	Evelyn R. O. Cerre	160	"	90.00
460	George Childs	160	"	13.84
659	Melvin Collins	80	Farming	129.96
642	Nellie B. Head Sure	80	Grazing	39.96
	Logan Cure	40	"	30.00
211	John DeRain	80	"	60.00
106	John and Mary DeLodge	110	"	219.96
12	Pouis DeLodge	24.68	Farming	39.96
101	John D. DeLodge	42	"	84.00
471	Frank DeRain	10	Grazing	7.56
81	Babbist DeRain	10	"	7.56
411	Pearl DeRain	10	"	7.56
110	Louis DeRain	161.80	"	120.00
211	Cleve DeRain	80	"	50.04
668	Eunice Eagle	80	"	60.00
116	Valentine Elwell	280	"	139.92
579	Emily Fire Shaker	40	"	30.00
	Jennie Fire Shaker	80	"	1040.04
678	Mollie Gayton	80	'	60.00
679	John Gayton	80	"	60.00
208	Emily Green	23.75	Farming-Grazing	28.64
341	Jennie Goodboy	35.76	Grazing	30.00
111	Margaret Himman	80	Farming	160.08
439	Horse Chief Eagle	98.40	Grazing	199.92
455	Sam Himman	36.11	"	25.08
681	Dewey Harry Back	120	"	89.40
686	Agnes Headman	160	"	120.00
450	Mammie H. C. Eagle	80	"	60.00
444	Headman	40	Farming	60.00
685	Nellie Headman	160	Grazing	60.00
684	Mattie Headman	80	"	60.00
682	Cordelia Headman	120		124.80
	Harterbowll, A. J.	10	"	15.00
687	Mary Iron Thunder	120	"	90.00
201	Irenen Jones	40	Farming	80.04

742	Funston King	120	Grazing	120.00
674	Nellie Kent	120	”	90.00
487	Gail Kent	280	”	210.00
644	Marion Knudson	80	”	32.28
716	Katherine Kemble	80	”	60.00
326	Dick Kemble	120	”	
691	Francis King	40	”	30.00
335	Willie Kimble	120	”	90.00
522	Francis King	36	”	27.96
188	Little Standing Buffalo	39.92	”	59.88
301	Marion L. Cook	40	”	20.04
708	Chas. L. Warrior	120	”	125.04
645	Dorthy L. S. Buffalo	40	”	30.00
510	Josephine Linns	42⅔	Farming-Grazing	63.96
507	Rain L. Snake	31.90	Grazing	24.00
452	Mary LeClair	80	”	40.08
645	Meiman and Northcutt	30	”	30.00
	Lutts, L. H.	50	Farming-Grazing	125.04
584	Little Hardman	20	”	20.04
707	Jas. L. Warrior	40	Grazing	30.00
109	Jennie Makes Noise	25	Farming	24.96
373	Appering Morgan	40	Grazing	30.00
107	Susie Makes Noise	80	Farming	147.60
201	Mean Bear	40	”	80.04
201	Mean Bear	40	Grazing	40.08
726	Beatrice Makes Cry	80	”	60.00
503	Clara M. Vonall	120	”	120.00
235	Alice Murry	10	”	4.92
718	Alford No Ear	120	”	79.92
219	Fannie No Ear	73½	Farming	110.04
386	Effie Others	35.82	”	79.92
565	Wm. Others	120	Farming-Grazing	120.00
567	Lillian Others	80	Grazing	60.00
496	George Pickering	280	”	210.00
735	Frank Pumeaux	120	”	79.80
733	Swezette Plumbly	97.94	Farming-Grazing	200.04
121	Ponca Tribal Land	367.30	Grazing	367.32
577	Weak Bone	40	”	40.08
142	Eliza Pumeaux	33.50	”	24.96
306	Louisa Poor Horse	40	”	30.00
747	Mary Roy	40	”	30.00
736	Mark Pumeaux	80	”	120.00
214	Jimmie R. O. Waters	40	”	30.00
737	Margaret Rhodes	80	”	39.96
147	Antonie Roy	280	”	208.96
739	Acy R. Leaf	60	”	53.96
739	Reginal Leaf	60	”	53.96
477	Winona Roubedonx	10	”	7.56
499	Sarah P. Face	80	Farming	100.08
757	Clarence R. O. Arrow	160	Grazing	80.04
731	Helena P. Roy	20	Farming-Grazing	9.96
530	Mable B. Back	80	Grazing	60.00
676	Lucy F. Smith	80	Farming-Grazing	60.00
763	Steele Stands Back	120	Grazing	60.00
774	Lucy Steele	120	”	90.00
405	Sits On Hill	40	”	30.00
576	Ed. L. Smith	120	”	120.00
764	Henry Snake	120	”	90.00
502	Teresa Shadlow	160	”	120.00

270	Lizzie Stabler	80	"	60.00
12	Wentz, L. H.	40	"	30.00
47	Wentz, L. H.	40	"	30.00
Personal	Wentz, L. H.	120	"	120.00
30	Wentz, L. H.	20	"	15.00
32	Wentz, L. H.	32.4	"	24.24
35	Wentz, L. H.	40	"	30.00
5	Wentz, L. H.	120	"	90.00
	Freeman, W. R.	130	"	130.08
762	Gertrude T. Nail	120	"	90.00
760	Josiah T. Nail	80	"	60.00
516	White Buffalo Bull	40	"	30.00
539	White Deer	40	"	40.08
462	Edith W. Sky	40	"	30.00
775	Jessie W. Sky	120	"	60.00
374	Geo. Washington	86.70	Farming	120.00
779	Adriana W. Tail	80	Grazing	60.00
218	Anna Waters	60	Farming	225.00
	Eugene Wentz	40	Grazing	30.00

TOTAL LEASES WITH			TOTAL	
PREFERENTIAL RIGHTS			AMOUNT	
DECEMBER 31st, 1930		10509.28	PAID	$10,200.44

APPENDIX III

TOTAL ACREAGE OF DEEDED LANDS OWNED BY THE 101 RANCH*

BAR L LAND

Description	Sec.	Twp.	Rge.	Acres
NE¼ NE¼ and Lot 4 and NE ¼ SE¼	22	24N	3E	97
W½ NW¼ and SE¼ NW¼ and Lots 1, 2 and 4	23	24N	3E	169
Lot 1	24	24N	3E	38.25
E½ NE¼ and E½ SE¼	15	24N	3E	160
SE¼ NW¼ SW¼ and SW¼ SE¼ and N½ NW¼ SW¼ and S½ NE¼ SW¼ and S½ SW¼ and E½ SE¼	14	24N	3E	245
W½ NE¼ SE¼ and Lots 1 and 2 and SW¼ SW¼ and N½ SW¼ and S½ NW¼ SE¼ and E½ NE¼ SE¼ and NE¼	13	24N	3E	356
E½ NW¼ and NE¼ and Lots 6 and 7	18	24N	4E	272
Lot 1 and 2, 3 and 4, and NW¼ and NW¼ NE¼	17	24N	4E	265.45
W½ NW¼ NW¼ and S½ SE¼ NW¼ and SW¼ NE¼ and W½ SE¼ and Lots 2, 3, 4, and 5, and W½ SW¼ NW¼	8	24N	4E	357.35
Lots 9, 10, 11 and 13 and SW¼ SW¼	5	24N	4E	116.30
Lots 2, 3, and 4 and SE¼ NW¼ and E½ SW¼	7	24N	4E	239.93
NW¼ and SE¼	12	24N	3E	320.00
NW¼ NW¼ and S½ SE¼	11	24N	3E	120
Lot 8 and SE¼ SE¼	3	24N	3E	79.20
Lots 7 and 8 and SE¼	2	24N	3E	184.40
Lots 1, 2, 3 and 4 and SE¼ NE¼ and SE¼	1	24N	3E	318.25
Lots 1, 2, 5 and 6, E½ of Lot 3 and SW¼ NE¼ and SE¼ NW¼ and S½ SE¼	6	24N	4E	294.59
Lots 5 and 6	36	25N	3E	52.45
Lots 7, 8, 9 and E½ of Lot 10	31	25N	4E	170.64

LAND ABOUT THE 101 HEADQUARTERS
NORTH OF SALT FORK

Description	Sec.	Twp.	Rge.	Acres
E½ SW¼	3	25N	1E	80
NW¼ SE¼	12	25N	1E	40
E½ E½ E½ NE¼ and E½ W½ W½ E½ NE¼ (except Tracts 1 and 5)	13	25N	1E	20.
Lots 3 and 4 and SE¼ SW¼ and NE¼ SW¼	31	25N	1E	160
S½ and NW¼ NW¼ and SE¼ NW¼	24	25N	1E	400
Lots 1, 2, 3, 4, 5, 6, 7 and 10 NW¼ SE¼ and S½ SW¼ and N½ N½ and SE¼ SW¼	25	25N	1E	522.
W½ E½ NW¼	15	25N	2E	38.36
Lots 1, 2, 3, and 4 and SE¼ NW¼ and W½ NE¼ and NE¼ SW¼ and N½ SE¼ SW¼ and SW¼ SE¼ SW¼ and N½ SE¼ SE¼ SW¼ and S½ SE¼ SE¼ SW¼	19	25N	2E	353.74
NW¼ and W½ SW¼ and SE¼ SE¼ and Lots 3, 4, 7 and 8	20	25N	2E	401.70
Lot 1	29	25N	2E	21.82

*101 Ranch Records, May 11, 1932.

[247]

Lots 1, 6, 7, 8, 9 and NE¼ NW¼ and N½ NE¼ and SW¼ NE¼ and SE¼ NW¼ and NE¼ SW¼	30	25N	2E	547.35

SOUTH OF SALT FORK

Lots 1 and 2 and SE¼ SE¼	26	25N	1E	81.5
Lots 4, 5, 6, and E½ NE¼ and E½ SE¼	35	25N	1E	257.18
Lots 1 and 2 and E½ SE¼ and NW¼ SE¼ and N½ N½ N½ SE¼ SE¼ and N½ S½ N½ N½ SE¼ NE¼	36	25N	1E	171.04
Lots 2, 3, 4, 5 and SW¼ and SW¼ NW¼ and W¼ SE¼	21	25N	2E	331.93
Lots 5, 6, 7	27	25N	2E	80.40
NW¼ and SW¼ and E½ NE¼ and NE¼ SE¼ and W½ SE¼	28	25N	2E	520.00
SW¼ and W½ SE¼ and NW¼ NE¼ and N½ NE¼ NE¼ and N½ S½ NE¼ NE¼ and N½ S½ S½ NE¼ NE¼	29	25N	2E	315.00
Lots 1, 5, 6 and E½ SW¼ and SE¼ (west of RR) and S½ NE¼ and S½ S½ NW¼ NE¼ and NE¼ NE¼ and NE¼ NW¼ NE¼ and N½ S½ NW¼ NE¼	31	25N	2E	373.18
SE¼ NW¼ and NE¼ NW¼	32	25N	2E	76
Lots 2 and 3	33	25N	2E	80

HOLDINGS IN OSAGE COUNTY

S½ S½ N½ NE¼ NE¼ and N½ N½ S½ NW¼ NE¼	34	28N	9E	10
NW¼ NE¼ NE¼ and S½ NE¼ NE¼ NE¼	36	26N	10E	15
NE¼	36	24N	7E	160
E½ SE¼	8	21N	11E	
W½ SW¼ and SW¼ SW¼ NW¼ and S½ SE¼ SW¼ NW¼ and W½ W½ NW¼ NE¼ SW¼	9	21N	11E	177.50
NE¼ and N½ NW¼ SE¼ and N½ SW¼ NW¼ SE¼	10	21N	11E	185
NW¼ and S½ N½ SW¼ NE¼ and NW¼ SW¼	4	22N	3E	500
NW¼ and SW¼ and W½ NE¼ and NE¼ NE¼ and W½ SE¼	33	23N	3E	210

LAND AROUND MARLAND, OKLAHOMA

SE¼ NE¼ and SW¼ SW¼	1	24N	1E	80
E½ SE¼ and SW¼ NE¼ and Lots 1 and 2	2	24N	1E	200
N½ SE¼ and SE¼ NE¼	11	24N	1E	120
SW¼ and SE¼ (W of RR) and SW¼ NW¼				278.07
E½ NE¼ SE¼	13	24N	1E	240
SE¼	14	24N	1E	160
Lots 1 and 8 and SW¼ and NE¼ NW¼ and W½ and SE¼ SE¼ and NW¼ and E½ SW¼	6	24N	2E	304
Lot 1 (W of RR) E½ NE¼ and SW¼ SE¼	7	24N	2E	125

LAND SOUTH OF MARLAND, OKLAHOMA

N½ and N½ SW¼ and N½ SE¼ and SW¼ SE¼	33	24N	1E	520
E½ SW¼	27	24N	1E	80
W½ SW¼	22	24N	1E	80
W½ SE¼ (W of RR) and SE¼ NW¼ and NW¼ SW¼ and W½ NW¼ and E½ SW¼	26	24N	1E	270

NW¼ NE¼ (W of RR)	35	24N	1E	5
SW¼ NW¼ and NW¼ NW¼ (W of RR) and NE¼ NW¼	24	24N	1E	90
W½ NW¼ and NE¼ SW¼	25	24N	1E	120
NE¼ SW¼ and NW¼ SW¼ and S½ SW¼ and SE¼ and SW¼ NW¼				360
S½ and W½ NW¼	30	24N	2E	400
S½ N½ and NE¼ NW¼ and NW½ NE¼ and W½ SW¼ and S½ NE¼ SW¼ and SE¼ SE¼	19	24N	2E	390
SW¼ NE¼ and S½ SW¼	20	24N	2E	120
NE¼ and N½ NW¼	29	24N	2E	240
NE¼ NW¼ and NW¼ NE¼ and W½ SE¼	21	24N	2E	160
NE¼ and NW¼ SE¼ and NE¼ NW¼	22	24	2E	240
SE¼	27	24N	2E	160
SW¼ SE¼	23	23N	2E	
SE¼ SW¼	24	23N	2E	660
W½	25	23N	2E	
NE¼ and SW¼ SE½ and S½ N½ SE¼ and N½ N½ N½ SE¼	26	23N	2E	660
SE¼ NW¼	15	24N	2E	40

LAND SOUTH OF OTOE AGENCY

All of S	6	22N	2E	
SW¼ SE¼	32	23N	2E	
S½ SW¼	30	23N	2E	
E½ and SW¼ and W½ NW¼ and SE¼ NW¼ and S½ S½ NW¼ NW¼	31	23N	2E	1370

SCATTERED HOLDINGS SOUTH OF HEADQUARTERS

W½ SW¼	9	23N	2E	80
NW¼ SE¼	31	24N	1E	40
SE¼ and NW¼ NW¼	27	22N	3E	80
Lots 5, 6	6	22N	3E	75.81
S½ S½ SE¼ SE¼	29	23N	3E	10
N½ S½ SW¼ SE¼	25	22N	2E	10
W½ NE¼	6	23N	3E	80
S½ SE¼ NE¼	26	23N	3E	20
W½ NE¼	36	24N	2E	80

THE 101 RANCH, by Ellsworth Collings in collaboration with Alma Miller England, has been composed in Linotype Old Style No. 7. In essential details this face was modeled on a series originally cut by the Bruce Foundry during the decade following the Civil War. The Bruce cutting appears to have descended from a type cast by the famous Edinburgh founders, Messrs. Miller and Richard. Old Style No. 7 presents thought with exceptional candor and sincerity. It is unpretentious and unadorned with graces, but it possesses to an unusual degree the first requisite of type—ready legibility. A slight contrast between the heavy lines and hair lines relieves the printed page of what otherwise might be tiresome monotony

THE PRINTED PAGE IS  EVERYMAN'S UNIVERSITY

UNIVERSITY OF OKLAHOMA PRESS

PUBLISHING DIVISION OF THE UNIVERSITY

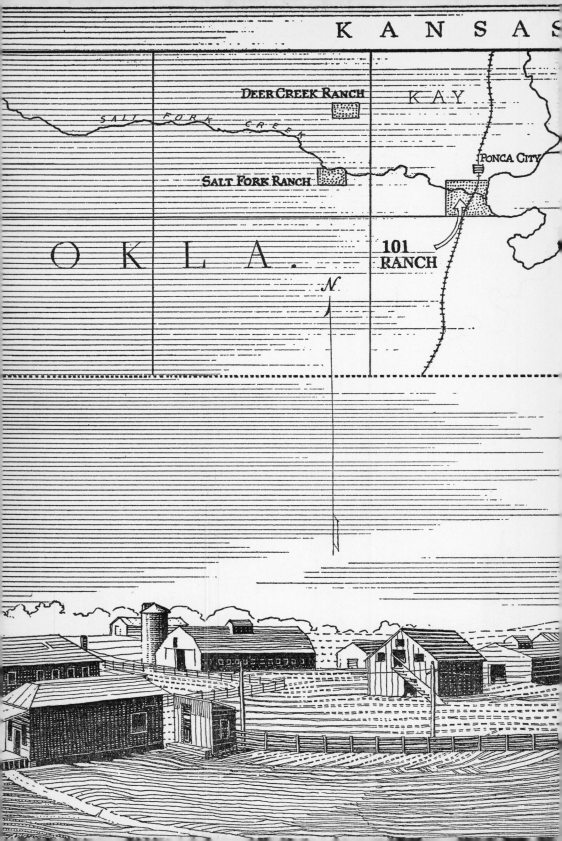